THE ARCHITECTONICS OF HOPE

THEOPOLITICAL VISIONS

SERIES EDITORS:

Thomas Heilke
D. Stephen Long
and C. C. Pecknold

Theopolitical Visions seeks to open up new vistas on public life, hosting fresh conversations between theology and political theory. This series assembles writers who wish to revive theopolitical imagination for the sake of our common good.

Theopolitical Visions hopes to re-source modern imaginations with those ancient traditions in which political theorists were often also theologians. Whether it was Jeremiah's prophetic vision of exiles "seeking the peace of the city," Plato's illuminations on piety and the civic virtues in the Republic, St. Paul's call to "a common life worthy of the Gospel," St. Augustine's beatific vision of the City of God, or the gothic heights of medieval political theology, much of Western thought has found it necessary to think theologically about politics, and to think politically about theology. This series is founded in the hope that the renewal of such mutual illumination might make a genuine contribution to the peace of our cities.

FORTHCOMING VOLUMES:

David Deane
The Matter of the Spirit: How Soteriology Shapes the Moral Life

The Architectonics of HOPE

Violence, Apocalyptic, and the Transformation of Political Theology

KYLE GINGERICH HIEBERT

FOREWORD BY CYRIL O'REGAN

CASCADE *Books* · Eugene, Oregon

THE ARCHITECTONICS OF HOPE
Violence, Apocalyptic, and the Transformation of Political Theology

Theopolitcal Visions 21

Copyright © 2017 Kyle Gingerich Hiebert. All rights reserved. Except for brief quotations in critical publications or reviews, no part of this book may be reproduced in any manner without prior written permission from the publisher. Write: Permissions, Wipf and Stock Publishers, 199 W. 8th Ave., Suite 3, Eugene, OR 97401.

Cascade Books
An Imprint of Wipf and Stock Publishers
199 W. 8th Ave., Suite 3
Eugene, OR 97401

www.wipfandstock.com

PAPERBACK ISBN: 978-1-4982-0941-0
HARDCOVER ISBN: 978-1-4982-0943-4
EBOOK ISBN: 978-1-4982-0942-7

Cataloguing-in-Publication data:

Names: Gingerich Hiebert, Kyle. | O'Regan, Cyril, foreword.

Title: The architectonics of hope : violence, apocalyptic, and the transformation of political theology / Kyle Gingerich Hiebert ; foreword by Cyril O'Regan.

Description: Eugene, OR : Cascade Books, 2017 | Series: Theopolitcal Visions 21 | Includes bibliographical references and index(es).

Identifiers: ISBN 978-1-4982-0941-0 (paperback) | ISBN 978-1-4982-0943-4 (hardcover) | ISBN 978-1-4982-0942-7 (ebook)

Subjects: LCSH: Christianity and politics. | History—Philosophy.

Classification: BR115.P7 G56 2017 (print) | BR115.P7 G56 (ebook)

Permission has been granted by the editors of *Telos* to reproduce a revised and expanded version of Kyle Gingerich Hiebert, "The Architectonics of Hope: Apocalyptic Convergences and Constellations of Violence in Carl Schmitt and Johann Baptist Metz," *Telos* 160 (2012) 53–76. The editors of *Political Theology* have also granted permission to reproduce a revised version of Kyle Gingerich Hiebert, "Beauty and Its Violences," *Political Theology* 17 (2016) 316–36.

Unless otherwise indicated, all quotations from the Bible are from the New Revised Standard Version Bible, copyright 1989, Division of Christian Education of the National Council of the Churches of Christ in the United States of America. Used by permission. All rights reserved.

Manufactured in the U.S.A.   09/18/17

For Tara, *sine qua non*

And I heard a great voice out of heaven saying, Behold, the tabernacle of God is with men, and he will dwell with them, and they shall be his people, and God himself shall be with them, and be their God. And God shall wipe away all tears from their eyes; and there shall be no more death, neither sorrow, nor crying, neither shall there be any more pain: for the former things are passed away. And he that sat upon the throne said, Behold, I make all things new.

—Revelation 21:3–5 (kjv)

In all faces the face of faces is seen veiled and in enigma. It is not seen unveiled so long as one does not enter into a certain secret and hidden silence beyond all faces where there is no knowledge or concept of a face. This cloud, mist, darkness, or ignorance into which whoever seeks your face enters when one leaps beyond every knowledge and concept is such that below it your face cannot be found except veiled. But this very cloud reveals your face to be there beyond all veils, just as when our eye seeks to view the light of the sun, which is the sun's face, it first sees it veiled in the stars and in the colors and in all the things which participate in its light. But when the eye strives to gaze at the light unveiled, it looks beyond all visible light, because all such light is less than what it seeks. But since the eye seeks to see the light which it cannot see, it knows that so long as it sees anything, what it sees is not what it is seeking. Therefore, it must leap beyond every visible light. Whoever, therefore, has to leap beyond every light must enter into that which lacks visible light and thus is darkness to the eye. And while one is in that darkness, which is a cloud, if one then knows one is in a cloud, one knows one has come near the face of the sun. For that cloud in one's eye originates from the exceeding brightness of the light of the sun. The denser, therefore, one knows the cloud to be the more one truly attains the invisible light in the cloud. I see, O Lord, that it is only in this way that the inaccessible light, the beauty, and the splendor of your face can be approached without veil.

—Nicholas of Cusa, *On the Vision of God*, 6.21

... it is not difficult to see that ours is a birth-time and a period of transition to a new era. Spirit has broken with the world it has hitherto inhabited and imagined, and is of a mind to submerge it in the past, and in the labour of its own transformation. Spirit is indeed never at rest but always engaged in moving forward. But just as the first breath drawn by a child after its long, quiet nourishment breaks the gradualness of merely quantitative growth—there is a qualitative leap, and the child is born—so likewise the Spirit in its formation matures slowly and quietly into its new shape, dissolving bit by bit the structure of its previous world, whose tottering state is only hinted at by isolated symptoms. The frivolity and boredom which unsettle the established order, the vague foreboding of something unknown, these are the heralds of approaching change. The gradual crumbling that left unaltered the face of the whole is cut short by a sunburst which, in one flash, illuminates the features of the new world.

—G. W. F. Hegel, *Phenomenology of Spirit*, Preface §11

Contents

Foreword by Cyril O'Regan | xi
Acknowledgments | xvii

1 Political Theology and the Task of Seeing | 1
2 The Founding and Re-founding of Political Theology | 12
3 Political Theology and the Persuasions of Beauty | 54
4 Political Theology and the Power of Nonviolence | 115
5 Retrospect and Prospect | 153

Bibliography | 183
Author Index | 205
Subject Index | 209

Foreword

IN THIS PASSIONATE AND lucidly written monograph on political theology, Kyle Gingerich Hiebert defends an original genealogical thesis, and provides, as stages in a cumulative argument, illuminating and fair-minded readings of a number of important contributors to political theology over the last hundred years, beginning with the notorious philosopher-jurist Carl Schmitt. The genealogical thesis is easy to state: in his articulation of political theology in the 1920s and its later iterations Schmitt set the terms for later efforts in political theology by J. B. Metz, John Milbank, and David Bentley Hart (more embryonically) among others, which seem to have very little in common with him, and who, if they mention Schmitt at all, reject him out of hand. Taking due account of the questionable reputation of the sometime Nazi apologist, the author argues persuasively that Schmitt's political theology is rendered in an apocalyptic key, indicated at both the rhetorical and substantive levels by recurring to binaries and exclusions, and animated by the perception of the urgency to contain violence. Thus the importance of the Pauline notion of the *katechon*, which licenses Schmitt to contain actual or potential chaotic violence within a state by violence directed outside against groups constructed as the "enemy." To use the author's felicitous phrase, Schmitt articulates "an apocalyptically inflected aesthetics of violence." If Schmitt's actual aesthetics is not worth repeating in principle, and is not repeated in fact in the Catholic or non-Catholic forms of political theology with which the monograph deals, this does not rule out repetition of what might be called a Schmittian pattern. Gingerich Hiebert suggests that the apocalyptically inflected forms of political theology represented by the likes of Metz, Milbank, and Hart repeat the violence of Schmitt's stance against violence (if largely in a rhetorical key), with the upshot that violence remains sovereign. At the very least this is an interesting and provocative thesis, and will likely garner attention from Catholic theologians who underscore the opposition of J. B. Metz to Schmitt's political theology, and admirers of Radical Orthodoxy who think of Christian political theology being defined by an ontology of peace and not by agonism as the ontological absolute. As it turns out, however, the genealogy is more comedic than tragic in structure in that *The Architectonics of Hope* argues that John Howard Yoder manages to escape the Schmittian aporetics and point the way forward to the construction and reconstruction of a viable political theology.

This is, indeed, a very ambitious book, and despite the provocative nature of its thesis, as well as the controversial nature of its reading of Metz and Radical Orthodoxy, one that scores a number of obvious successes. First, although the book does not entirely break new ground regarding the actual analysis of Schmitt's main works in political theology—the originality of the book lies more nearly in speaking to the "history of effects" of Schmitt's thought—even at the level of interpretation there are more than a few productive leads opened up. Arguably, first among equals is Gingerich Hiebert's insinuation that Schmitt depends as much—if not more—on Hegel than on Nietzsche. This is an intriguing suggestion that complicates our reading of Schmitt and makes more plausible the argument that he can promote successors in political theology that are anti-Nietzschean. Second, *The Architectonics of Hope* makes a highly plausible case for the relative adequacy of Yoder's apocalyptic modulation of political theology that both contests and complements Nathan Kerr's *Christ, History, and Apocalyptic*, which outlines a very different genealogy of Yoder's political thought that involves consideration of Troeltsch, Barth, and Hauerwas. Third, Gingerich Hiebert makes a real contribution in the area of political theology when in his discussion of Radical Orthodoxy he deconstructs the shibboleth that high aesthetic theological discourse and apocalyptic are mutually repelling, and with it the presumption that apocalyptic is solely or even mainly the discourse of the margins. Of the two forms of high aesthetic theology Milbank provides Gingerich Hiebert with the greater assistance, given the apocalyptic inflection he provides to his Augustinianism which highlights the refusal to negotiate with the secular.

Now, in my view, however, the value of *The Architectonics of Hope* lies at least as much in the questions it raises and the way it links to contemporary essays in political theology and apocalyptic as in the substantive theological positions it critiques and recommends. Gingerich Hiebert is best read not as proposing that the only way to understand the apocalyptically inflected theology of Radical Orthodoxy is through its success or failure to transcend the Schmittian paradigm, but rather that his is an illuminating—even if unexpected—reading of Radical Orthodoxy. Again we understand Gingerich Hiebert's claims about Yoder's apocalyptically inflected political theology better when we take him to be pointing out that Yoder enjoys a number of important advantages over the other forms of political theology under discussion rather than decisively trumping those forms of political theology, which, unwittingly, are in the Schmittian line because they are unable to escape the gravitational pull of counterviolence. This allows Gingerich Hiebert to claim without inconsistency that in each of the post-Schmittian figures he analyzes there are offsetting advantages. Indeed, one might suggest that Gingerich Hiebert's text presents an invitation to read Metz, Milbank, and Hart as providing apocalyptically inflected forms of political theology that complement and supplement Yoder's political theology in important ways. This would mean that even though on balance Yoder's apocalyptic political theology is more adequate than its rivals, it is not more adequate in all respects. In addition, given that the argued for primacy of Yoder's political theology rests largely on a particular reading of scripture, it might seem to follow that the crucial differential is between a biblically oriented political theology with apocalyptic inflection (Yoder) and a non-biblically oriented political theology with apocalyptic inflection (all others). But again this is hardly a good reading of Gingerich Hiebert's text. While it is definitely possible to regard both Milbank's and Hart's political theology as biblically underdetermined, this is definitely not true of the work of J. B. Metz, for whom the memory of the passion, death, and resurrection of Jesus is constitutive. Perhaps what differentiates in the end between forms of apocalyptic theology is, then, not so much the presence of scripture, but what texts of scripture are exercising determinative influence (implicitly or explicitly), how these texts are being interpreted, and the degree of filtration through the theological tradition.

All good books both initiate and contribute to ongoing conversations. Arguably, the one thing that will remain after reading this book is the possibly generative role of Schmitt in contemporary political theology. This is hardly old news, given not only Schmitt's reputation but also his general avoidance of substantive theological statement. One of the main achievements of *The Architectonics of Hope* is that it essentially defamiliarizes Schmitt, thereby enabling us to see him outside his relations to Nietzsche and Heidegger as well as the Third Reich. Gingerich Hiebert's monograph also contributes to a number of ongoing conversations that are foci of what we might call the "apocalyptic turn in theology." The first simply concerns a broadening of apocalyptic interlocutors. One can imagine a larger canvas of apocalyptically inclined theologies in which Yoder's systematic and biblical credentials would get tested. From within Catholicism Hans Urs von Balthasar and the increasingly theologically refined work of René Girard come to mind. From within Eastern Orthodox thought it is difficult to overlook the work of Sergei Bulgakov. Also worthy of mention is the more exploratory apocalyptic theological work of Thomas Altizer and Catherine Keller. The prospect in particular of engaging the Yoderian apocalyptic theology recommended by Gingerich Hiebert and the similarly self-consciously nonviolent apocalyptic of Girard seems especially appealing. Moreover, it is an engagement to which Gingerich Hiebert suggests that he is open. The second concerns the way in which different forms of apocalyptic seem to demand very different views of the church. If one thinks, for example, of the apocalyptic inflection of Milbank's theology as Augustinian and dependent on the book of Revelation as its main biblical base and Yoder's as more nearly deriving from the Synoptic Gospels, could one reliably project differences with respect to the construction of the church? The central focus on the connection between political theology and the church also raises the issue of the relevant differences between Oliver O'Donovan's parsing of the relation and Gingerich Hiebert's parsing and how that conversation yet to be had may help towards a more theologically satisfying account of the nature and role of the church. Third, given the importance of the Pauline notion of the *katechon* in Schmitt's political theology, it is obvious that Gingerich Hiebert's text can be inserted both into the ongoing conversations of the apocalyptic tendency in the Pauline writings, underscored not only by biblical exegetes such as Louis Martyn and Douglas Harink, but postmodern political philosophers such as Giorgio Agamben, Alain Badiou, and Slavoj Žižek. Fourth and lastly, Gingerich Hiebert's profoundly fertile ruminations on the apocalyptic theology of Yoder can be inserted into the ongoing general reception of Yoder with all its promises and tangles, but also into the more specific conversation as to what kind of apocalyptically philosophical discourse more nearly helps to give an orientation to Yoder. When that question has been allowed—and it is accepted, for example, by Kerr and Harink—Walter Benjamin is usually the preferred apocalypticist. Given Gingerich Hiebert's reading of Yoder's account of the church, is Benjamin the best choice? Is he even a good choice?

At once programmatic and substantive, this book offers a refreshing new look on both political theology, apocalyptic and their relation. It inserts itself into, contributes to, and refreshes ongoing conversations, while suggesting also that there might be new ways of looking at both and their relation. The book is marvelously suggestive and generative as well as being fundamentally complete given its clearly stated parameters. In addition, the tone throughout performs the shalom that it recommends in its readings of contributors to political theology that are as generous as they are provocative. One lays down *The Architectonics of Hope* with a clear sense of aesthetic closure and finality. It is nothing if not a well-wrought book. But throughout it gives a sense of an even larger genealogical frame when it comes to political theology. If Carl Schmitt turns out to be generative with regard to a good deal of contemporary political theology that either refuses to speak his name or speaks his name only to denounce, then which nineteenth-century thinkers are generative with respect to him? The stock answer, of course, has been Nietzsche. Throughout this accomplished text Gingerich Hiebert suggests that this is a dead end and recommends the political theology of Hegel as the ultimate origin and the one who generates the grammar of political theology. This is both counterintuitive and tantalizing, the latter because the former. But it connotes that evidences to the contrary *The Architectonics of Hope* is simply the first installment in an exciting ongoing project in political theology.

CYRIL O'REGAN

Huisking Professor of Theology
University of Notre Dame

Acknowledgments

THIS BOOK BEGAN ITS life as a doctoral thesis at the University of Manchester. Though the material has been reworked since then, the shape of the investigation undertaken in the pages that follow and the questions that prompted it have not significantly changed. Accordingly, I continue to owe a debt of gratitude to my supervisor, Graham Ward, who is the single soul that has had the most to do with the development of my thinking over the past number of years and with what actually follows. In Manchester I had the privilege of being the beneficiary of Graham's patient encouragement and of his carefully crafted ability to renew enthusiasm and productively shape curiosity, and for all of this I remain truly grateful. As a teaching colleague on a number of courses, Michael Hoelzl was also an important source of support throughout my time in Manchester and, with his assistance, I had the opportunity to spend some time at the Katholische Akademie in Berlin—and my sincere thanks also go to the staff there, and especially to Martin Knechtges. The initial process of thinking through how to transform a doctoral thesis into something more like a book began, to my surprise, at my *viva*, and I must record my sincere thanks to my examiners, Peter Scott and Cyril O'Regan, not least for the gift of their deep and generous engagement with my work. The book is undoubtedly better for having been subjected to their perceptive and probing questions, and in this respect I owe Professor O'Regan an extra measure of thanks for contributing an engaging Foreword. Travis Kroeker also read a draft of the entire manuscript and his comments, too, have been invaluable in my attempt to improve the argument. I am also grateful to the Toronto Mennonite Theological Centre for appointing me to a Postdoctoral Fellowship and, in particular, to John Rempel, whose energy and passion made this possible. I would also like to enter a note of thanks to Charlie Collier and the staff at Cascade as well as to Thomas Heilke, D. Stephen Long, and C. C. Pecknold for welcoming my book into the Theopolitical Visions series. I am particularly indebted to Professor Long, who not only read the manuscript but also offered an immensely helpful list of suggestions for improvement. I also owe a debt of gratitude to the various funding bodies that enabled the research for this book to be carried out: the Higher Education Funding Council for England, the University of Manchester, and the Canadian High Commission in London. Two of the chapters that follow contain material published elsewhere, and I am grateful to the editors of *Telos* and *Political Theology* for their permission to reprint modified versions of that work here.

The support of family and friends, many of whom are scattered in far-flung places around the globe, has been nothing short of instrumental. In this respect, I must mention my mom, oma & opa, and mother-in-law, all of whom have encouraged and invested themselves in my work in indispensable ways. In Manchester and beyond, the deep friendship of Brian and Jenny Haymes has been life-giving in a way that, I suspect, I may never be able to fully appreciate. Above all, to acknowledge here in a few words that the writing of this book would not have been possible without the unfailing love and support of my wife, Tara, is simply not enough. Although I am aware that this is by no means an adequate expression of the depth and breadth of my gratitude for all that she gives to me, I dedicate this book to her. Finally, all thanks and love to Hannah and Luke. Their arrival between the first incarnation of this book as a doctoral thesis and its present form has suffused my world with a new light, which with endless measures of awe and wonder illuminates parts of it that I had forgotten, misremembered, or failed to notice, and thereby grants me the extreme privilege of seeing anew.

CHAPTER 1

Political Theology and the Task of Seeing

Introduction

As the lonely pioneer of political theology, G. W. F. Hegel was vociferously denouncing the tendency to regard the modern state as an independent entity and to relegate religion to the domain of private belief as early as 1817:

> It has been the monstrous blunder of our times to try to look upon these inseparables as separable from one another, and even as mutually indifferent. The view taken of the relationship of religion and the state has been that, whereas the state had an independent existence of its own, springing from some source or power, religion was a later addition, something desirable perhaps for strengthening the political bulwarks, but purely subjective in individuals:—or it may be, religion is treated as something without effect on the moral life of the state, i.e. its reasonable law and constitution which are based on a ground of their own.[1]

In the immense wake of Hegel, there is perhaps no one else who so ardently strove to rectify this "monstrous blunder" than the German jurist and sometime Nazi apologist Carl Schmitt, who famously argued that "all significant concepts of the modern theory of the state are secularized

1. Hegel, *Philosophy of Mind*, 156–57 [*Enzyklopädie der philosophischen Wissenschaften im Grundrisse* §552].

theological concepts."[2] Indeed, Schmitt claims that his own vision of political theology "departs from the *ius reformandi* [right of reformation] of the sixteenth century, culminates in Hegel and is evident everywhere today" and cites this exact passage in Hegel to emphasize that the reciprocal relationship between religion and the modern state must be understood as a politico-theological problem.[3] Whereas there has been a deep and extensive engagement with Hegel within the theological disciplines, a similar kind of engagement with Schmitt has hitherto not been undertaken.[4] This fact is more remarkable given the extent to which there has been a veritable explosion of interest in the work of Schmitt in recent years, which is due in no small part to the work of the Italian philosopher Giorgio Agamben, who has used Schmitt's work to develop a powerful critique of our contemporary biopolitical situation.[5] However, despite his appropriation in philosophy and political theory, there is almost no theological work that rigorously engages in any significant way Schmitt's development of political theology.[6] To be fair, Schmitt does not self-identify as a theologian—in fact, there are places where he explicitly identifies himself as a "non-theologian"[7]—and his work is difficult and provokes notoriously different and even opposing interpretations, owing at least in some measure to his role as jurist for the Third Reich. Many interpreters understand Schmitt's involvement with the Nazi Party, of which he was officially a member from May 1933 to December 1936, to be the decisive locus around which his political theology is to be interpreted.[8] The rhetorical force of such accounts reach their crescendo in Schmitt's opening address from a 1934 conference on "Judaism and Jurisprudence": "But the most profound and ultimate meaning of this battle, and thus also of our work today, lies expressed in the Führer's sentence: 'In fending off the Jew, I fight for the work of the Lord.'"[9] Coupled with Schmitt's infamous

2. Schmitt, *Political Theology*, 36.

3. Schmitt, *Political Theology II*, 32–33. The Hegel citation occurs on 101 and is misidentified as §525 in the English translation. This should not be taken to imply that Schmitt straightforwardly follows Hegel. For a helpful account of their complex interrelationship, see Kervégan, *Hegel, Carl Schmitt*.

4. For an example of the theological engagements with Hegel that I have in mind, see Desmond, *Hegel's God*; O'Regan, *The Heterodox Hegel*; and Shanks, *Hegel's Political Theology*. For an exception that proves the rule with respect to Schmitt, see Northcott, *A Political Theology of Climate Change*.

5. See, for example, Agamben, *Homo Sacer*; and Agamben, *State of Exception*.

6. To cite but one example, Schmitt's place and continuing influence on political theology is mentioned and quickly set aside in Phillips, *Political Theology*, 4–5.

7. Schmitt, *Political Theology II*, 148n2.

8. See, for example, Arendt, *Origins of Totalitarianism*, 339.

9. Schmitt, "Eröffnung der wissenschaftlichen Vorträge," 14.

essay entitled "The Führer Protects the Law,"[10] which provided juridical support to the bloody purge of June 30, 1934, the so-called "night of the long knives," it is not unreasonable to argue that Schmitt's anti-Semitism was not an indirect result of his political theology but an intrinsic element.[11] Therefore, if Schmitt's work is mentioned in theological discourse at all it is invariably used as a negative foil against which a robustly Christian political theology must be boldly asserted. Anyone acquainted with the beginnings of political theology in Germany will undoubtedly be familiar with a plethora of rather vague assertions, such as that of Johann Baptist Metz, who claims that "the notion of political theology is ambiguous, hence exposed to misunderstanding, because it has been burdened with specific historical connotations."[12] Jürgen Moltmann makes similar claims, Dorothee Sölle eventually abandons the term "political theology" altogether, and Metz insists on using the qualifer *new* to describe his political theology— and all of them mention Schmitt's name only fleetingly. The underlying and largely unarticulated assumption within the discipline of theology seems to be, very simply, that Schmitt's political theology is little more than thinly veiled ideological legitimation of Nazi policy and, therefore, is not worthy of any sustained theological engagement beyond outright denunciation. Nevertheless, what I want to suggest in the pages that follow is that Schmitt's work deserves more sustained and charitable theological engagement than it has hitherto received and that the discipline of theology has prematurely bid *adieu* to Schmitt to its own detriment. Indeed, in what follows I will engage in a critical excavation and reconstruction of the Schmittian seductions that continue to bedevil contemporary political theology. By offering a genealogical reconstruction of the manner and extent to which recognizably Schmittian gestures are unwittingly repeated in subsequent debates that often only implicitly assume they have escaped the violent aporetics that characterize Schmitt's thought, the following chapters aim to illuminate hidden resonances between ostensibly opposed political theologies. Before turning to this task, however, it is necessary to say something about the method and shape of the argument, as well as its primary themes.

A Theopolitical Optics

On the twenty-ninth day of October, 1858, John Ruskin gave the inaugural address at the Cambridge School of Art in which he suggested that the

10. Schmitt, "Der Führer schützt das Recht."
11. Simon, "New Political Theology of Johann Baptist Metz," 239.
12. Metz, *Theology of the World*, 107.

most important thing to teach in the whole range of teaching was one thing, namely, Sight.

> To be taught to read—what is the use of that, if you know not whether what you read is false or true? To be taught to speak—but what is the use of speaking, if you have nothing to say? To be taught to think—nay, what is the use of being able to think, if you have nothing to think of? But to be taught to see is to gain word and thought at once, and both true . . . [w]e want, in this world of ours, very often to be able to see in the dark—that's the greatest gift of all;—but at any rate to see no matter by what light, so only we can see things as they are.[13]

While the reflections of a Victorian art critic may seem a strange way to elucidate the shape of a book on political theology, Ruskin's suggestion that to see rightly requires a certain kind of training opens out onto a host of suggestive possibilities for reading the signs of our times. Despite the fact that there are those who wish to argue that violence has actually declined in the modern era—though, it must be said, only on the basis of some rather creative accounting—it seems clear that the world in which we live is nevertheless racked with violence.[14] Indeed, it can often appear as though violence has saturated our everyday lives such that there is no escape from its panoptic-like gaze. For our purposes, the black smoke billowing from the chimneys at Auschwitz is perhaps the most potent symbol of the horrors of violence. While this overt physical violence continues in various forms, it is also important to recognize and expose the brutality of the marketplace, the commodification of knowledge and the pathos of modern politics and economics as also a kind of distributed violence that, while often disguised, is no less terrifying. All this is nothing new. The shattering of Enlightenment dreams of perpetual peace has been described by Nietzsche as nothing less than the advent of nihilism: "For some time now, our whole European culture has been moving as toward a catastrophe, with a tortured tension that is growing from decade to decade: restlessly, violently, headlong, like a river that wants to reach the end."[15] Nietzsche is particularly instructive here for our purposes because he sees violence itself as a discourse of the end, culminating in apocalyptic visions of catastrophe. Alongside violence, this apocalyptic tone has infiltrated our imaginations such that any crisis whatsoever can be given new urgency by describing it as

---

13. Ruskin, *Works*, 16:180.
14. I am referring in particular here to Pinker, *Better Angels*.
15. Nietzsche, *Will to Power*, preface, §2, as quoted in Kaufmann, *Portable Nietzsche*, 483.

"apocalyptic." In the midst of this situation, then, what might it mean to say, with John Howard Yoder and the author of the letter to the Hebrews, "As it is, we do not see everything in subjection to him. *But we do see Jesus*, revealing the grace of God by tasting death for everyone"?[16] Or, put differently, what might an account of the hope that is within us (1 Pet 3:15) look like in a world racked by violence? The following chapters are one attempt to answer these questions through a reading, which is, to be sure, also a kind of seeing, of the complex relationship between violence and apocalyptic as they are appropriated in political theology.

To set up the debate as a question of seeing immediately raises certain problems that must be confronted. Indeed, if much of recent French philosophy is to be believed, what was once celebrated as the most excellent of the senses must now be viewed as something of a disaster.[17] Perhaps the best-known example is Michel Foucault's influential reading of Jeremy Bentham's treatise on a model prison.[18] For our purposes we need not entertain the details of Foucault's argument but may simply note that his analysis implicates vision itself in the maintenance of disciplinary and repressive power. That Foucault's insights here cannot be dismissed is, however, no reason to despair that sight must always participate in such a manipulative scopic regime. Another possibility has been suggested by the Russian philologist Mikhail Bakhtin, who argues that meaning is constructed only through a mutuality of gazes that do not destroy but supplement the other's vision. Referring to what he calls the "excess of seeing," Bakhtin argues that "in order that this bud should really unfold into the blossom of consummating form, the excess of my seeing must 'fill in' the horizon of the other human being who is being contemplated, must render his horizon complete, without at the same time forfeiting his distinctiveness."[19] For Bakhtin, then, there is a certain fragile architectonics of seeing in which the possibility of the other's gaze is not a violent subjugation but one that "descends upon me from others like a gift, a grace, which is incapable of being understood and founded from within myself."[20]

To illustrate more clearly what I have in mind here it is worth lingering for a moment over Annie Dillard's discovery of a book by Marius von Senden that details the sometimes startling responses of blind patients who, after cataract surgery, were able to see for the first time:

16. Yoder, *Priestly Kingdom*, 61.
17. For a helpful treatment of this see Jay, *Downcast Eyes*.
18. See Foucault, *Discipline and Punish*, especially 195–228.
19. Bakhtin, *Art and Answerability*, 24–25.
20. Ibid., 49. Bakhtin elaborates on the notion of architectonics as an "aesthetic seeing" in Bakhtin, *Toward a Philosophy of the Act*, especially 56–75.

> For the newly sighted, vision is pure sensation unencumbered by meaning: "The girl went through the experience that we all go through and forget, the moment we are born. She saw, but it did not mean anything but a lot of different kinds of brightness." In general the newly sighted see the world as a dazzle of color-patches. In walking it also strikes them how—if they can pay attention—they are continually passing in between the colors and that when they can go past a visual object part of it then steadily disappears from view; and that in spite of this they always have a visual space in front of them. The mental effort involved in these reasonings proves overwhelming for many patients. It oppresses them to realize the tremendous size of the world, which they had previously conceived of as something touchingly manageable. A disheartening number of them refuse to use their new vision, continuing to go over objects with their tongues, and lapsing into apathy and despair. Some do learn to see, especially the young ones. A twenty-two-year-old girl was dazzled by the world's brightness and kept her eyes shut for two weeks. When at the end of that time she opened her eyes again, she did not recognize any objects, but, "the more she now directed her gaze upon everything about her, the more it could be seen how an expression of gratification and astonishment overspread her features; she repeatedly exclaimed: 'Oh God! How beautiful!'"[21]

I can think of no better way of describing the mysterious apocalyptic interplay of veiling and unveiling that is necessarily bound up with what it means to learn to see. As a distinctly theological metaphorics of vision, then, the architectonics of hope is my way of trying to understand what it might mean to give an account of the hope that is within us in the context of a world racked by violence.

Typology of the Argument

What follows, then, takes the form of a constructive genealogical engagement that argues, most broadly, that the five figures at the center of the book give voice to their respective understandings of political theology by articulating it, in some fashion, as inextricably bound up with the complex relationship between violence and apocalyptic. That I employ a genealogical method is not arbitrary. As Michel Foucault has argued, genealogy should not be understood in opposition to history but rather as

---

21. Dillard, *Pilgrim at Tinker Creek*, 27–31. The internal quotes refer to von Senden, *Space and Sight*.

that patient, laboring enquiry that seeks to recover a counter-memory that breaks through the crust of hermeneutical interpretations that have become torpid by repetition.[22] In my use of it, then, the genealogical method itself takes on something of an apocalyptic hue just to the extent that it seeks out sites of productive disagreement and willingly enters these in an attempt to disrupt any monotonous finality.[23] The argument itself proceeds through an examination of five central voices, each of whose differing intonations of the architectonics of hope are brought to the fore.

The first of these, then, begins with an analysis of the re-emergence of political theology in late modernity in the work of the German jurist and onetime member of the Nazi party, Carl Schmitt. While the understanding of Schmitt as "crown jurist for the Third Reich" has undoubtedly left an indelible mark on the entirety of his work that cannot be underappreciated, the prescience of Schmitt's vision with respect to our contemporary biopolitical situation is increasingly being critically appropriated, particularly in political theory and continental philosophy.[24] Such a critical appropriation of Schmitt in the theological disciplines, however, still seems some way off and thus my account attempts to fill this gap. Schmitt's own understanding of political theology is difficult to fully appreciate, not least because he initially articulated it in the midst of the decline of the Weimar Republic in 1922 and explicitly returned to it only much later, in 1970. Moreover, at least part of the problem is also that Schmitt's vocabulary—the state of exception, the friend/enemy distinction, decisionism, the concept of the political—has seeped into contemporary usage and becomes, perhaps unintentionally, decontextualized. Thus, in order to combat this, I will argue that Schmitt's political theology needs to be understood not simply in the context of his two books by that name nor primarily with reference to his involvement with Hitler but much more broadly. Accordingly, I proceed by suggesting that Schmitt's political theology must be understood with reference to what I argue is the companion volume to *Political Theology*, namely, his *Roman Catholicism and Political Form*, as well as with respect to his use of the figures of the counterrevolution, notably the Catholic political philosophers Donoso Cortés and Joseph de Maistre, and with Thomas Hobbes. Thus situated, I argue that, in the end, Schmitt's political theology is mobilized by an apocalyptically inflected aesthetics of violence concerned primarily with

22. For a helpful account of Foucault's understanding of genealogy see especially his analysis of Nietzsche in Foucault, "Nietzsche, Genealogy, History," 76–100.

23. It is important to note, even at this early stage, that this is *not* the "apocalyptic objectivity" of which Foucault speaks in ibid., 87.

24. For a broad account of Schmitt's reception, see Teschke, "Decisions and Indecisions," 63–95.

the maintenance of order, which is for Schmitt defined primarily in negative terms as the avoidance of civil war. Animated by a thoroughly negative theological anthropology, the best Schmitt's political theology can hope for is a structured geographical displacement of the inherent violence between human beings on to a public enemy that is essentially alien and different.

Schmitt's explicit return to political theology, and his positive endorsement of Metz, coincides with the development of the *new* political theology in Germany as developed not only by Metz but also notably by Jürgen Moltmann and Dorothee Sölle, among others. This political theology had to be called *new*, as Moltmann argues, precisely because of Schmitt's development of the term and his use of it to articulate a "political religion" capable of buttressing the policies of the Third Reich.[25] In Metz's development, which must be understood as a critical dialogue with the advances and limitations of Karl Rahner's work, the *new* political theology can be read as an attempt to confront the "explosive problematic" generated on a hitherto unprecedented scale in the treatment of the culture of modernity by the Second Vatican Council and, more specifically, in the Conciliar document *Gaudium et spes*. That said, I argue that the significance of the Frankfurt School is decisive in setting the tone for Metz's development of the *new* political theology and that this influence can be seen in three related encounters that, in turn, illuminate three significant signposts of the *new* political theology. Thus, through an analysis of Metz's interactions with Theodor Adorno and Max Horkheimer, Walter Benjamin, and Ernst Bloch, I argue that in the end Metz's *new* political theology is set within the larger context of a *theologia negativa* that strains with all its might against any affirmative ontology and thereby keeps Christ in reserve as a kind of grand ideological dismantler that attempts to safeguard the future from meaningless suffering and, in so doing, acquiesces to the ongoing necessity of violence.

My investigation of Schmitt and Metz does not simply end there, however. Indeed, I pose the disquieting suggestion that although their respective political theologies may be understood as instantiations of right- and left-wing Hegelianism, respectively, their complex interrelationship cannot thereby simply be understood to be diametrically opposed because there are far too many similarities between them. My argument here is not that there is, conversely, a straightforward symmetry at work but rather that their interrelationship is more complex and cannot be accurately captured by the conservative/critical dichotomy. In the end, I suggest that both of their reconfigurations of political theology, although still different, overlap

---

25. For a helpful account that sets up what is still the entrenched dichotomy between Schmitt and the *new* political theology, see Moltmann, "Christian Theology and Political Religion," 41–58.

in three significant ways, namely, that they are both structural in nature, animated by a negative theological anthropology and acquiesce to the ongoing necessity of violence. Thus I provocatively argue that when Schmitt and Metz are read in the light of the apocalyptic element that infuses and haunts their respective accounts of political theology, convergences emerge that otherwise remain hidden.

Understood against the background of the re-emergence of political theology in late modernity in the work of Schmitt and Metz, I turn in the second main section to the work of John Milbank and David Bentley Hart. If the interrelationship between Schmitt and Metz cannot be understood antithetically, as I argue in chapter 2, how can we understand Milbank's outright denunciation of the kind of *aggiornamento* Metz recommends alongside his frank acknowledgment that some of the most incisive thinkers of modernity belonged to the political right and were at least semi-complicit with Nazism? While Milbank and Hart do not articulate their political theologies primarily with reference to Schmitt or Metz, I suggest that it is immensely helpful to read them as heirs of the reconfigurations of political theology begun by these two German Catholics precisely because they continue to grapple with the relationship between violence and apocalyptic. Indeed, I argue that the narratives both Milbank and Hart unfold are audibly haunted by an attempt to reconfigure the Schmittian decision and by framing their discussions in apocalyptic terms that echo a kind of Metzian interruption. Their aesthetic reconfiguration of political theology represents a major shift from the primarily structural configurations seen in Schmitt and Metz that is immensely theologically significant, especially with respect to the question of violence.

Beginning with Milbank, then, I argue that his political theology develops by way of a double movement that simultaneously creates enemies that, in turn, serve as the backdrop against which a positive theological program is constructed, and interpretively reifies friends by foreclosing on possible alternative readings. This double movement illuminates what I call the Schmittian character of Milbank's theo-logic. I illustrate this by drawing attention to the way Milbank neatly parses arguments that arise in post-conciliar Catholicism, which has the fortuitous effect of also showing why his political theology is helpfully read as a reconfiguration of the debates that re-emerged in late modernity with Schmitt and Metz. In the end, I argue that Milbank's political theology takes on a mystagogical form that owes a great deal both to his theopolitical deployment of paradox and to his account of *poiesis*. In this way it becomes clear that Milbank's aesthetic reconfiguration of political theology proceeds decisively beyond Metz; however, it is precisely here that Milbank's account of beauty throws up a host of problems with respect to the question of violence. Particularly at issue here is the extent to which Milbank's linkage between beauty and reason seeks to control the operations of beauty itself and thereby has a distorting effect. By exploring Milbank's phenomenology of violence, whose descriptive power cannot be gainsaid, I argue that the subsequent formative prescriptions he claims naturally follow rest on a fundamental misapprehension of beauty and, concomitantly, that the vision Milbank leaves us with, then, is not the beauty of violence, which glories in endless spectacles of horror, but the violence of beauty.

It is at this point that Hart's theological aesthetics become particularly helpful. In distinction to those that understand Hart's telling of the story of the postmodern city and its wastes along the lines proposed by Milbank, I suggest that by decoupling Hart's narrative from Milbank's we will be in a better position to see more clearly the radical nature of his provocations and how they sharpen and inflect the question of violence and its relation to apocalyptic. I argue that we can see this in at least three ways. First, Hart's rhetorical ontology attempts to perform a delicate act of subversion by entering ever more deeply into the quagmires of the Western metaphysical tradition and pointing toward the decisive Christian interruption of that tradition, and it is here that we can see that Hart displays a significant counterpoint to the Schmittian theo-logic that infects Milbank's political theology. Second, Hart offers his rhetorical ontology as a reorientation of vision that takes the form of martyrdom and, in this way, Hart's theological aesthetics helpfully push beyond Milbank and highlight a lacuna in his aesthetic reconfiguration of political theology. Third, despite Hart's very persuasive account of Christian peace there remain, nevertheless, discernable vestiges of the logic of Hegel's "beautiful soul," which itself seems to play a role in inhibiting a robust account of the practices conformed to the peace of Christ. In this way, I will argue that Hart obliquely mirrors Milbank's critique of the pacifist gaze and suggest that an investigation of the unnamed pacifist that comes under Hart's interdiction is the most helpful way forward.

Hart's scathing criticism of John Howard Yoder prompts my investigation in chapter 4 of the generative capacities of nonviolence that Hart seems finally unable to countenance. Indeed, I argue that Yoder's work is indispensable for the genealogy of political theology I am attempting to construct precisely because he wrestles with the relationship between violence and apocalyptic in a way that embodies a nonviolent way of seeing that opens out onto possibilities of reconciliation by creatively orchestrating conflict. Continuing with a minor thread that is woven throughout the book, my suggestion here is that Yoder's work can helpfully be read as another of Hans Urs von Balthasar's "theological styles," as yet another "reflected ray of glory" that illuminates the transformation of political theology in immensely helpful ways. I argue that this can be seen in Yoder's "biblical philosophy of history," which is a logical unfolding of the meaning of the work of Jesus Christ himself, whose choice of suffering servanthood rather than violent lordship is paradigmatic. Key to Yoder's apocalyptic politics of Jesus is his understanding of doxology and patience, which together operate to strike down whatever immanent strategic calculus might promise desirable effects and thereby break open the future as a horizon of hope freed from such limiting possibilities. In this way, I argue that doxology, nonviolence, and patience are inextricably bound together and become something of a poetic art anchored in the apocalyptic politics of Jesus. In order to illuminate some of the less visible workings of the generative capacities of nonviolence constitutive of Yoder's apocalyptic politics of Jesus I turn to the work of the Russian philologist Mikhail Bakhtin, whose reading of Dostoyevsky's novels bears a striking resemblance to Yoder's understanding of the dialogic form of Anabaptism that emerged in the early sixteenth century. Yoder's particular reconfiguration of political theology, then, enables us to see more clearly that the power of nonviolence opens out onto creative possibilities for orchestrating conflict that are prematurely foreclosed upon when the possibility of violence, of silencing the other, remains as a viable option. By way of an examination of Nathan Kerr's recent reading of Yoder's apocalyptic politics of Jesus I also argue, *contra* Kerr, that Yoder's commitment to nonviolence is rooted in a particular understanding of what Yoder refers to as "the grain of the universe" and thereby also implies a theological metaphysics that makes no pretensions of being more determinative than the life, death, and resurrection of Jesus Christ.

Finally, chapter 5 attempts to bring the foregoing reconfigurations of political theology to bear upon one another such that they are not only able to critique but also to supplement each other. While this process of mutual critique and supplementation could proceed down a number of productive lines, I return to the discussion of politics and metaphysics that occupied the concluding section of chapter 4 because it helpfully pushes the analysis into the realm of ecclesiology and thereby also opens up possibilities for concrete engagement that serve to illuminate some of the relative strengths and weaknesses of each of the reconfigurations of political theology that have populated the foregoing genealogy. In so doing, I also seek to highlight the non-demonstrative character of the argument itself that recognizes the sense in which even though Yoder's reconfiguration of political theology holds crucial advantages for subverting the fundamentally violent aporetics of Schmitt's theopolitical vision, it does not, in the end, hold all of the advantages.

CHAPTER 2

The Founding and Re-founding of Political Theology

Introduction

REFLECTING ON THE FACT of pluralism and the extent to which Christianity appeared to be fragmenting in the wake of the Second Vatican Council (1962–65), the French Jesuit Michel de Certeau wrote that "in the past, everything that was not in agreement with the teaching of the *magisterium* was classed as 'ignorance,' 'superstition' or even as 'heresy.' This state of absolute certainty is now wavering. An unknown world stands before us, which calls itself Christian and yet is quite unlike our picture of what Christian is: 'another country,' one that is huge and many-sided beneath the forms of expression (whether missionary or theological) which concealed it."[1] Revealing not only the lasting impression of Hegel on modern theology, de Certeau's attempt "to grasp the situation of Christianity in modernity and to rethink Christian theology in the light of that situation" provides a helpful point of departure for thinking about the founding and re-founding of the term "political theology," which re-emerges within the same complex constellation of events.[2] Indeed, if the argument that Hegel was the lonely pioneer of what we have come to know today as political theology sounds questionable, especially

---

1. Certeau, "Is There a Language of Unity?," 91.
2. Bauerschmidt, "Michel de Certeau," 137.

given the extent to which his reception has been heavily influenced by the Marxist philosopher Alexandre Kojève, then the suggestion that Johann Baptist Metz must be read alongside Carl Schmitt for a full understanding of the emergence and enduring significance of contemporary political theology will seem more doubtful still.[3] However, that Metz plays an important role for Schmitt and vice versa comes into sharp relief upon a close examination of their work, despite the fact that these contemporaries did not engage each other in any substantive way.[4] Moreover, once this interrelationship is brought to life it helpfully illuminates not only the origins of the re-emergence of political theology in late modernity but also the subsequent trajectories that, I will argue, have their roots, in various ways, in the Schmitt/Metz debate.

To begin, then, it is instructive to note that almost none of the recent scholarly work that engages the work of Schmitt or Metz attempts to excavate the complex interrelationship between them with respect to their unique developments of political theology.[5] This is especially the case with the resurgent interest in Schmitt in philosophy and political theory and extends even to those who attend to the theological element in Schmitt's work.[6] This seems especially curious given the fact that Schmitt cites Metz

3. Andrew Shanks makes this point persuasively and with helpful comparisons to Metz, who, he argues, shares an original affinity with the basic Hegelian approach of building theology as a criticism of the privatization of religion in Shanks, *Hegel's Political Theology*, especially 149–55. See also Paul Lakeland, who makes a similar point in Lakeland, *Politics of Salvation*, especially 155–71.

4. Indeed, Schmitt mentions Metz only very briefly in Schmitt, *Political Theology II*, 49–50 and 53–54. Likewise, Metz is reluctant to acknowledge Schmitt in his work but does mention him on a few occasions. See, for example, Metz, "Politische Theologie," 1261.

5. There are precious few who even attempt to consider the relationship between Schmitt and Metz. For one such attempt, however, see Simon, "The New Political Theology of Johann Baptist Metz," 227–54. Simon focuses his attention solely on the extent to which Metz's *new* political theology is an attempt to undermine and delegitimize Schmitt's political theology and does not address the intriguing positive reception Metz receives in Schmitt, which should at least raise the question of whether Simon's reading is too straightforwardly dualistic an account of the interrelationship between Schmitt and Metz. For readings that complicate such a straightforward dualism, see Gingerich Hiebert, "The Architectonics of Hope," 53–76; and Losonczi, "Humanization, Eschatology, Theodicy," 116–29.

6. There has been a recent explosion of interest in Schmitt, due in part to the work of the Italian philosopher Giorgio Agamben. See Agamben, *Homo Sacer* and *State of Exception*. Other significant treatments of Schmitt in contemporary philosophy are Derrida, *The Politics of Friendship*; and Mouffe, *The Challenge of Carl Schmitt*. Even Heinrich Meier, whose work attends more than others to the theological element in Schmitt's thought, doesn't mention Metz even in a footnote. See Meier, *Carl Schmitt and Leo Strauss* and *The Lesson of Carl Schmitt*.

approvingly in *Political Theology II* and uses Metz's theological critique of society as a point of departure to reinstate his own political theology against the "Parthian attack" inflicted upon him by his onetime friend Erik Peterson.[7] Likewise, most of the recent work on Metz pays insufficient attention to the role that Schmitt plays in shaping the *new* political theology, at best acknowledging Schmitt in footnotes.[8] To be fair, Metz himself remains reluctant to explicitly mention Schmitt but he is almost certainly at work in the background for Metz as early as 1968 in his claim that "the notion of political theology is ambiguous, hence exposed to misunderstanding, because it has been burdened with specific historical connotations."[9] This at least suggests that the qualifier "new" that Metz insists on using in his articulation of political theology can be read as a direct response to Schmitt's development of political theology, which was subsequently implicated in offering constitutional justification and ideological legitimacy to buttress the policies of the Third Reich.[10] Indeed, it is difficult *not* to make this connection since much of Metz's work can be read as an attempt to do theology "after Auschwitz," taking seriously that everything cannot simply go on as usual but must rather attend to the "wreckage of history," as Walter Benjamin suggests.[11] Given this state of affairs, it will be the task of this chapter

---

7. See Schmitt, *Political Theology II*, 49–54. For Peterson's famous essay, see Peterson, "Monotheism as a Political Problem," 68–105.

8. See, for example, Ashley, *Interruptions*, 223n91.

9. Metz, *Theology of the World*, 107. See also Downey, *Love's Strategy*, 26. At times it is possible to detect, though difficult to conclusively substantiate, the covert presence of Schmitt in Metz's work. One such place is in Metz's brief encyclopedia article on miracles that concludes with what could be considered a veiled rebuttal of Schmitt's thesis that the exception in jurisprudence is analogous to the miracle in theology. See Metz, "Miracle," 962–64.

10. For helpful biographical accounts of Schmitt, see Bendersky, *Carl Schmitt*, and especially Mehring, *Carl Schmitt*, which takes into account Schmitt's extensive diaries and unpublished papers and thereby sheds further light on the question of the relationship between Schmitt's Weimar period and his subsequent involvement in the Nazi Party, which itself continues to be a matter of intense disagreement. For a helpful account—albeit a partisan one—of this debate, see Wolin, "Carl Schmitt, Political Existentialism, and the Total State," 389–416. This tension must be kept at the forefront of any interpretation of Schmitt if we are not to let his Nazi involvement set the terms of the debate and operate as the *decisive factor* in understanding his articulation of political theology.

11. See Benjamin, "Theses on the Philosophy of History," especially 249. Indeed, Metz cites the "catastrophe of Auschwitz" as one of the three fundamental concerns of the new political theology in Metz, *Passion for God*, 24. Also particularly relevant is his article in the same volume entitled "The Church after Auschwitz." Helpfully elucidating why this connection is not more readily made, Jürgen Manemann argues that there is a kind of local amnesia in German theology in Manemann, "Abandoned by God?," especially 20–23.

to spell out the interrelationship between Schmitt and Metz, paying special attention to the apocalyptic tone that infuses and haunts their respective accounts of political theology. In the end, I will argue that it is precisely around this apocalyptic element that their interrelationship is most helpfully understood. This reading of the interrelationship between Schmitt and Metz is offered not only to fill a gap in contemporary scholarship but also, and perhaps more importantly, as an attempt to face up to and articulate the unintended theological consequences of failing to directly confront the legacy of Schmitt's theopolitical vision by tracing the history of effects of this legacy in and on the development of Metz's *new* political theology, which is ostensibly diametrically opposed to it. Just to the extent that this chapter is able to provide such an account, it will also function to elucidate subsequent accounts of political theology that, like Metz, fail to seriously reckon with Schmitt's legacy and, in various ways, bear the hallmarks of some form of nonidentical repetition of Schmitt's theopolitical vision.

Schmitt's Political Theology

It seems prudent that any engagement with Schmitt's thought begin with the frank acknowledgment that the endeavor is, as Chantal Mouffe notes, "to think both *with* and *against* Schmitt."[12] This is not to say that we are obliged to agree with Mouffe's argument that the answer to Schmitt's challenge is to devise ways of transforming *antagonism* into *agonism* in order to ask how to improve liberal democracy.[13] Rather, it is to point out the sense in which Schmitt's questions and political diagnoses continue to be highly prescient today, perhaps especially so when read alongside the renditions, executions, and economic sanctions indicative of the so-called "war on terror," and to suggest that it would be a great mistake to dismiss him simply because of his inextricable involvement with the Nazi Party, which he joined in May 1933. Moreover, it is also necessary at the outset to acknowledge that there is no reigning scholarly consensus on the interpretation of Schmitt's political theology, so much so that scholars are even able to come to opposite conclusions in their interpretations.[14] Schmitt is notoriously difficult to pin

12. Mouffe, "Introduction," 6.
13. Ibid., especially 5–6.
14. One particularly salient example of this problem are the conflicting interpretations of Renato Cristi and Heinrich Meier on the question of rationality in Schmitt's use of the Roman Catholic Church in his explication of the exception. Cristi argues that, for Schmitt, the Church embodies a form of rationality, while Meier argues that Schmitt's political theology emerges within a fundamental aporia that demands a leap of faith that is not rational. See Cristi, *Carl Schmitt and Authoritarian Liberalism*, especially

down, especially when it comes to the theological element in his work, so the analysis that follows will endeavor to let these tensions stand in an effort to bring to the fore and disentangle some of the strands in his development of political theology. This stated aim already restricts the scope of inquiry to a more narrow slice of Schmitt's thought and, as such, the analysis that follows makes no claim to comprehensiveness, which could hardly be sought in a book of this nature in any case because of the variety and range of Schmitt's work itself that continues to be drawn upon in an arguably ever wider array of disciplines. Despite this broadening reception of Schmitt, which shows no signs of abating anytime soon, there remains a curious lack of engagement with this pivotal and troubling figure in the theological disciplines, despite the explicit recognition of the deep and continuing influence of Schmitt's work on the (re)birth of the discipline of political theology in the twentieth century.[15] The following analysis is offered as a modest attempt to redress this state of affairs with the conviction that a failure to charitably wrestle with Schmitt represents, at least, a significant blind spot and, at worst, a form of willful blindness to the effects of his legacy, which continues to bedevil political theology. Particularly important for such an attempt is Schmitt's articulation of the exceptional nature of sovereignty, his sustained virulent attack on liberalism, and his famous friend/enemy distinction, all of which are articulated in connection with his fascination with and reliance on the Catholic philosophers of the counterrevolution—particularly Donoso Cortés and Joseph de Maistre—and Thomas Hobbes. In the end, I will argue that what Schmitt leaves us with is an apocalyptically inflected aesthetics of violence, a powerful vision that, as we will see in subsequent chapters, continues to haunt the contemporary theopolitical imagination, even and perhaps especially those who claim to have decisively broken free of the aporetics defined by Schmitt.

To begin, then, undoubtedly the most oft-cited passages in Schmitt's entire oeuvre come from *Political Theology* (1922) and *The Concept of the Political* (1927). Schmitt coined the term "political theology" in 1922 and famously argued that "all significant concepts of the modern theory of the state are secularized theological concepts not only because of their historical development but also because of their systematic structure, the recognition of which is necessary for a sociological consideration of these concepts."[16]

75; and Meier, *Lesson of Carl Schmitt*, especially 122–23. For Schmitt's most sustained reflections on the Church, see Schmitt, *Roman Catholicism and Political Form*.

15. To cite one example of this tendency, Schmitt merits only an obligatory mention and is quickly set aside in Phillips, *Political Theology*, 5. For an exception to this see Northcott, *Political Theology of Climate Change*, especially 201–67.

16. Schmitt, *Political Theology*, 36.

It is important to note that Schmitt wrote *Political Theology* in an effort to counter the legal positivism of Hans Kelsen, a prominent Austrian jurist and legal scholar, who sought to develop a pure theory of law, devoid of any subjective elements and based on norms that could be universally valid. Against this strong neo-Kantian tendency in German legal theory, Schmitt claims that "all law is situational law" and that Kelsen merely "solved the problem of sovereignty by negating it."[17] The problem for Schmitt is that this kind of legal positivism is, quite simply, tautological. More specifically, the problem lies in the fact that the state has been reduced to nothing other than the legal order itself and when this happens it is incapable of addressing those emergencies that lie outside the law and thereby also incapable of thinking about the source of its own political legitimacy. Simply put, for Schmitt, positivism cannot think the ground of its own rationality. This brings to the fore perhaps the most significant concept that is taken up from Schmitt's work, namely, his argument that "sovereign is he who decides on the exception."[18] With reference to the Danish philosopher and theologian Søren Kierkegaard, Schmitt claims that "the exception is more interesting than the rule. The rule proves nothing; the exception proves everything. In the exception the power of real life breaks through the crust of a mechanism that has become torpid by repetition."[19] It is easy to make too much of this bold assertion by claiming, as Jürgen Habermas does, that this focus on the exception and the need for a genuine decision "results in the violent destruction of the normative as such," thereby making political discourse unintelligible.[20] Schmitt's own rhetoric may go some of the way in understanding Habermas's critique—after all, he does claim that "the norm is destroyed in the exception"[21]—however, Habermas misses the sense in which Schmitt's political theology is precisely a sustained struggle to think through the paradox of sovereignty in a manner that maintains rational order.

In what may be read as the companion volume to *Political Theology*, Schmitt writes in *Roman Catholicism and Political Form* (1923) of the kind

17. Ibid., 13 and 21.

18. Ibid., 5. This is due in large part to the work of Giorgio Agamben, who goes beyond Schmitt's view by claiming that there is a zone of indistinguishability that remains especially important since the exception cannot simply lie within the law as an emergency power authorized by the law as Schmitt seems to think. Agamben argues that an appeal to the exception paradoxically stands both inside and outside the law and, therefore, haunts all positive law as such. See Agamben, *State of Exception*, 38–39; and Agamben, *Homo Sacer*, 120–23.

19. Schmitt, *Political Theology*, 15. See also Kierkegaard, *Fear and Trembling*, especially 225–28.

20. Habermas, *New Conservatism*, especially 133–37.

21. Schmitt, *Political Theology*, 12.

of thinking that belongs intrinsically to the Roman Catholic tradition, differentiating it from the kind of instrumental rationality and "economic-technical thinking that prevails today."[22] At work in the background here is Schmitt's worry that his onetime teacher, Max Weber, was right that the modern state had actually become a huge industrial plant in which the political is eclipsed by the economic and technical-organizational, thereby paralyzing the decision in endless discussion. Opposed to this, Schmitt appeals to the rationalism of the Roman Church, whose "argumentation is based on a particular mode of thinking whose method of proof is a specific juridical logic and whose focus of interest is the normative guidance of human social life."[23] Schmitt is very clear that "the Church has its own rationality" that exists as a *complexio oppositorum*, a complex of opposites, which is able to hold together opposing forms of life without reducing one to the other or synthesizing them in a kind of Hegelian fashion to some "higher third."[24] Indeed, Schmitt claims of the Roman Church that "there appears to be no antithesis it does not embrace. It has long and proudly claimed to have united within itself all forms of state and government; to be an autocratic monarchy whose head is elected by the aristocracy of cardinals but in which there is nevertheless so much democracy that . . . even the least shepherd of Abruzzi, regardless of birth and station, has the possibility to become this autocratic sovereign."[25]

Noting the sense in which "it is not easily understandable that a rigorous philosopher of authoritarian dictatorship, like Spanish diplomat Donoso Cortés, and a 'good Samaritan' of the poor with syndicalist connections, like the Irish rebel Padraic Pearse, were both staunch Catholics,"[26] Schmitt's fascination with the so-called counterrevolutionaries comes to the fore and helpfully illuminates his discussion of the exceptional nature of sovereignty, which stands at the very core of his initial articulation of political theology. For Schmitt, the significance of the conservative authors of the counterrevolution, specifically the Catholic political philosopers Louis de Bonald, Joseph de Maistre, and Donoso Cortés, is rooted in their attempts to think sovereignty with the aid of analogies from Christian theology. Perhaps not surprisingly, given his distaste for varieties of neo-Kantianism, Schmitt points toward the German philosopher and mathematician Gottfried Wilhelm von Leibniz as "the clearest philosophical expression of that

---

22. Ibid., 65.
23. Schmitt, *Roman Catholicism and Political Form*, 12.
24. Ibid., 8–9, 13.
25. Ibid., 7.
26. Ibid.

analogy."[27] The critical link here is between sovereignty and the decision, that is, the recognition that the very idea of the decision had been thrust into the center of the political philosophy of the counterrevolution. From de Maistre, Schmitt gleans the nearly equivocal link between sovereignty and the decision. Indeed, he goes so far as to claim that "infallibility was for him [de Maistre] the essence of the decision that cannot be appealed, and the infallibility of the spiritual order was of the same nature as the sovereignty of the state order."[28] This affinity between sovereignty and decisionism is linked with a thoroughly negative theological anthropology that sets itself in explicit opposition to the kind of Enlightenment rationalism embodied in Jean-Jacques Rousseau's *Social Contract*, for example, which merely attempts an unsuccessful pedagogic runaround that obfuscates the enduring violent nature of humanity.[29] Schmitt's discussion of Donoso Cortés brings these connections into view even more sharply and begins to shed light on his virulent attack against liberalism.

> Donoso Cortés considered continuous discussion a method of circumventing responsibility and of ascribing to freedom of speech and of the press an excessive importance that in the final analysis permits the decision to be evaded. Just as liberalism discusses and negotiates every political detail, so it also wants to dissolve metaphysical truth in a discussion. The essence of liberalism is negotiation, a cautious half measure, in the hope that the definitive dispute, the decisive bloody battle, can be transformed into parliamentary debate and permit the decision to be suspended forever in an everlasting discussion.[30]

What is important to note here is that in the development of the nineteenth-century theory of the state there are two intertwined processes at work that Schmitt sees as decisive for thinking about the metaphysical kernel of the political, namely, "the elimination of all theistic and transcendental

---

27. Schmitt, *Political Theology*, 37. In his discussion of the division of the sciences, Leibniz makes the argument that theology "is a sort of jurisprudence," an argument that Schmitt sees reflected in the counterrevolutionaries and relevant for his own articulation of the political. See Leibniz, *New Essays on Human Understanding*, especially 526.

28. Schmitt, *Political Theology*, 55.

29. See ibid., 58–59. For Rousseau's arguments, see Rousseau, *Basic Political Writings*, especially 141–53. See also Schmitt, *Concept of the Political*, 63–65. Wolfgang Palaver also argues that this negative theological anthropology is one of the main elements of Schmitt's political theology in Palaver, "Girardian Reading of Schmitt's Political Theology," 43–68.

30. Schmitt, *Political Theology*, 63.

conceptions and the formation of a new concept of legitimacy."[31] The significance of the counterrevolutionaries for Schmitt lies precisely in their recognition that the historical unfolding of these two principles paralyzed the political "in a paradisiacal worldliness of immediate natural life and unproblematic concreteness," a heightened moment that could only be met with an "absolute decision created out of nothingness."[32] For Schmitt, the modern age is nothing but an outworking of the consequences of this historical unfolding, a veritable "onslaught against the political" that can only be met with one solution: dictatorship.

Here, as everywhere, Schmitt has something far more specific in mind than the imprecise understanding of dictatorship as simply a form of arbitrary despotism. Indeed, in what he himself considered one of his own major works, Schmitt gives us an historical analysis of the legal concept of dictatorship and argues for a transformation from what was a *commissary* dictatorship—one that suspends the constitution in order to protect it—to a *sovereign* dictatorship—one that suspends the constitution in order to create the possibility for another that is yet to come.[33] For our purposes, the distinction between commissary and sovereign dictatorship Schmitt draws here is less important than the fact that, in whatever form, dictatorship is understood as a nonarbitrary exception to a norm. As Schmitt puts it in his preliminary remarks, "Paradoxically, dictatorship becomes an exception to the state of law by doing what it needs to justify; because dictatorship means a form of government that is genuinely designed to resolve a very particular problem."[34] This understanding of dictatorship as the exception or suspension of law prefigures and anticipates much of Schmitt's later work and even here is not without theological overtones.[35]

Making the theological connection more explicitly, Schmitt claims that "the exception in jurisprudence is analogous to the miracle in theology."[36] Here we can begin to see the structural analogy that Schmitt

31. Ibid., 51.

32. Ibid., 65 and 66, respectively. Schmitt's endorsement of the political philosophy of the counterrevolutionaries stands in marked contrast to what he calls political romanticism, embodied for Schmitt in the figure of Adam Müller, whose theory of the state embodied the liberal indecisiveness of the bourgeoisie and was primarily a matter of aesthetics. See Schmitt, *Political Romanticism*, 115–43.

33. See Schmitt, *Dictatorship*, especially 112–31.

34. Ibid., xlii.

35. See ibid., 120–21, where Schmitt alludes to what he will later seize upon: namely, that dictatorship as the suspension of the law is a miracle. Though, it must be said, Schmitt is much more ambivalent about this structural analogy here, which he argues does not really hold for the concept of sovereign dictatorship.

36. Schmitt, *Political Theology*, 36.

draws between theology and jurisprudence and the importance of what he calls the sociology of juristic concepts emerging in his initial articulation of political theology. As we have seen, Schmitt is concerned to investigate the historical development of the philosophical idea of the modern state, a story that he sees as inextricably linked with the rise of a rationalist metaphysics that rejects the exception in all its forms. Schmitt explains that the sociology of juristic concepts "aims to discover the basic, radically systematic structure and to compare this conceptual structure with the conceptually represented social structure of a certain epoch."[37] Thus defined, we should not be surprised that his thinking is thereby pushed into the theological realm (where else could it have gone?) since the metaphysical image a particular epoch has of itself is structurally analogous to the shape of its political formation. Going back, then, to Schmitt's reliance on the Roman Catholic Church as an exemplary form of political representation, the question is not how to apply Roman Catholic theology to juridical problems but rather how to think through modern jurisprudence to find the root of its own metaphysical assumptions. Schmitt comes back to this again in the postscript to *Political Theology II* (1970) and helpfully articulates exactly what is at stake, namely, "the classical case of a transposition of distinct concepts which has occurred within the systematic thought of the two—historically and discursively—most developed constellations of 'western rationalism': the Catholic *church* with its entire juridical rationality and *the state of the ius publicum Europaeum*."[38]

In addition to his reliance on the conservative Catholic political philosophy of the counterrevolution, Schmitt turned to the English political philosopher Thomas Hobbes (1588–1679), who was for him the "true teacher of a great political experience; lonely as every pioneer; misunderstood as is everyone whose political thought does not gain acceptance among his own people; unrewarded, as one who opened a gate through which others marched on; and yet in the immortal community of the great scholars of the ages, a sole retriever of an ancient prudence."[39] Reflecting the enduring influence of Hobbes on his thinking, Schmitt articulates the importance of the *Leviathan* for his own political theology by explaining that "even during the Reformation of the Christian church in the sixteenth and seventeenth

37. Ibid., 45.

38. Schmitt, *Political Theology II*, 117. See also 109 where Schmitt makes the point more positively, pointing to the fact that "the scientific conceptual structure of both these faculties [theology and jurisprudence] has systematically produced areas in which concepts can be transposed, among which harmonious exchanges are permitted and meaningful."

39. Schmitt, *State Theory of Thomas Hobbes*, 86.

22 The Architectonics of Hope

centuries, what had begun as Christologo-political conflict over the *ius reformandi* [the right to reform] became a politico-theological revolution. Thomas Hobbes *brought the Reformation to a conclusion* by recognizing the state as a clear alternative to the Roman Catholic Church's monopoly on decision-making."[40] What Hobbes managed to do in the seventeenth century was precisely what Schmitt was attempting to do in the twentieth century, and in the immense wake of Hobbes, Schmitt's thinking can be read as a political theology of the mortal god. Summarizing Hobbes, Schmitt claims that "the terror of the state of nature drives anguished individuals to come together; their fear rises to an extreme; a spark of reason (*ratio*) flashes; and suddenly there stands in front of them a new god."[41] As Hobbes himself states, "This is the generation of that great *Leviathan*, or rather (to speak more reverently) of that *Mortall God*, to which wee owe under the *Immortal God*, our peace and defence."[42] What is clear from this reading is that the ontological primacy of violence borne out of the fear of death is at work in the background and feeds the thoroughly negative theological anthropology that drives much of Schmitt's thinking.[43] Moreover, despite the fact that Hobbes's project was a model for Schmitt, it was a project that ultimately failed insofar as it set the stage for the development of liberalism. Hobbes's introduction of a distinction between public and private reason in his discussion of belief in miracles opened up a crack in *Leviathan* that ultimately became "a sickness unto death" that destroyed the mortal god from within by transforming the administration of state power into a technical instrument. Indeed, Schmitt claims that "the *legislator humanus* became a *machina legislatoria*."[44] By allowing for private beliefs, Hobbes unwittingly paved the way for the introduction of a radical individualism and the positivist hostility to all metaphysics indicative of modern liberalism, the very historical processes that have led to the modern eclipse of the political.[45]

40. Schmitt, *Political Theology II*, 125–26.

41. Schmitt, *State Theory of Thomas Hobbes*, 31.

42. Hobbes, *Leviathan*, 120.

43. See ibid., especially 75–85 and 117–20. Further supporting Schmitt's argument that theories of the state are secularized theological concepts, Pierre Manent helpfully notes the sense in which Hobbes's definition of Leviathan's power is structurally analogous to Anselm's famous ontological argument for the existence of God in Manent, *Intellectual History of Liberalism*, especially 20–38.

44. Schmitt, *State Theory of Thomas Hobbes*, 65. It is also intriguing to note the sense in which Schmitt's argument that "the great machine now runs by itself" in some ways prefigures Michel Foucault's argument for the automatic functioning of power in societies of control. Compare, for example, Schmitt, *Political Theology*, 48; and Foucault, *Discipline and Punish*, 201.

45. It is interesting to note at this point that Schmitt lays the ultimate blame for

The Founding and Re-founding of Political Theology

We are now in a position to explore what is perhaps the most exploited aspect of Schmitt's entire oeuvre, namely, his contention that "the specific political distinction to which political actions and motives can be reduced is that between friend and enemy."[46] It is particularly interesting to note the sense in which Schmitt's reasoning here is not immune to the dualistic sickness he accuses Hobbes of instantiating. Indeed, Schmitt's articulation of the political can be read as an entirely modern and liberal construction insofar as he too relies on the public/private distinction to deal with what is, for him, the most formidable challenge to his definition of the political, namely, Jesus's injunction to "love your enemies" (Matt 5:44). In the space of one short paragraph, Schmitt points to a distinction in Plato's *Republic* between *hostis* and *inimicus*, that is, between a public enemy and a private foe, as sufficient evidence that Jesus's words are to be interpreted as private, spiritual and not politically relevant.[47] Alongside other forms of human activity that depend on fundamental distinctions, namely, beautiful/ugly in art, good/evil in morality, and profitable/unprofitable in economics, what is most important for Schmitt is the sense in which the political antithesis between friend and enemy remains decisive because it denotes the ultimate degree of intensity. The ever-present possibility of extreme conflict, that is, the real potential for war—notably not civil war, which Schmitt describes as a mere self-laceration—where life itself is at stake lurks behind every political decision. It is precisely in this situation of enmity that the friend/enemy distinction receives its real meaning since it refers to the real possibility of physical killing. Despite the stark nature of these reflections, Schmitt is careful to qualify them.

> It is by no means as though the political signifies nothing but devastating war and every political deed a military action, by no means as though every nation would be uninterruptedly faced with the friend-enemy alternative vis-à-vis every other nation. And, after all, could not the politically reasonable course reside in avoiding war? The definition of the political suggested

---

this catastrophic failure not with Hobbes but rather with the Jewish philosopher Benedict de Spinoza, who opens up this crack in the theoretical justification of the state in Spinoza, *Theological-Political Treatise*, especially 238–59. The complex issue of Schmitt's anti-Judaism foregrounded here is treated in Meier, *Lesson of Carl Schmitt*, especially 151–56.

46. Schmitt, *Concept of the Political*, 26.

47. Ibid., 28–29. In this regard we are also right to wonder whether the public/private distinction Schmitt attributes initially to Hobbes does not, in fact, have its roots much earlier in ancient Greek philosophy and is thereby not simply indicative of the introduction of liberalism but has, in some form, rather haunted Western thought from its very origins.

here neither favors war nor militarism, neither imperialism nor pacifism.[48]

This qualifier notwithstanding, it is clear that what fascinates Schmitt most in all of this are the antagonistic moments where the political becomes a meeting place for lethal violence. Indeed, this is why Schmitt claims that every genuinely political thinker—including Machiavelli, Hobbes, de Maistre, Donoso Cortés, and Hegel—presupposes humanity to be essentially evil.[49] In this respect, Hegel is arguably the archetype because, as Schmitt claims, Hegel remains political in the decisive sense everywhere from his polemically political definition of the bourgeois to his definition of the enemy as negated otherness.[50] So while Schmitt is careful to say that the political enemy "need not be morally evil," he is concerned, above all, with what Jürgen Habermas has called "the aesthetics of violence."[51]

This interpretation of Schmitt's *Concept of the Political* (1932) is quite consistent with the general thrust of his thought. In an earlier article written in 1930, Schmitt makes it clear that his articulation of the political is precisely designed to overcome civil war.

> The political, correctly understood, is only the degree of intensity of a unity. Political unity can contain and comprehend different contents. But it always designates the most intensive degree of a unity, from which, consequently, the most intensive distinction—the grouping of friend and enemy—is determined. Political unity is the highest unity—not because it is an omnipotent dictator, or because it levels out all other unities, but because it decides, and has the potential to prevent all other opposing groups from dissociating into a state of extreme enmity—that is, into civil war.[52]

As we have seen, his description of civil war as a mere "self-laceration" in *The Concept of the Political* continues this focus and his claim that "according to Hobbes, the quintessential nature of any state of nature . . . is none other than civil war, which can only be prevented by the overarching

---

48. Ibid., 33.

49. See ibid., especially 58–68.

50. See ibid., especially 62–63. For Hegel's definition of the enemy, which Schmitt claims has generally been avoided by modern political philosophers, see Hegel, *Political Writings*, 112.

51. See Schmitt, *Concept of the Political*, 27; and Habermas, *New Conservatism*, 137, respectively.

52. Schmitt, "Ethic of State and Pluralistic State," 203.

might of the state" underscores this again in 1938.[53] As Wolfgang Palaver helpfully notes, "War is for him an instrument to contain a more primordial form of violence *between* human beings."[54] Thus the key to Schmitt's development of the political is, as he puts it, "an anthropological profession of faith" that concurs with an interpretation of Genesis 3:15 in which, from the beginning, enmity is sown between humanity.[55] Everywhere that this fundamental distinction between friend and enemy is not made is, for Schmitt, a symptom of the eclipse of the political itself.

The interplay here is reminiscent of the way the exceptional nature of sovereignty functions as a kind of limit concept in which what emerges is an intense struggle to decide what belongs and what is excluded, a struggle in which the political enemy is "existentially something different and alien, so that in the extreme case conflicts with him are possible."[56] This reading of the structural nature of Schmitt's political theology is congruent with Slavoj Žižek's genealogy that sees Schmitt's political decisionism as being in agreement with the basic Hegelian position. In his argument that the Hegelian concrete universal is misunderstood when it is associated with "any kind of organic totality," Žižek claims that "the true politico-philosophical heirs of Hegel are . . . authors who fully endorse the political logic of excess constitutive of every established Order. The exemplary case, of course, is Carl Schmitt."[57] In this way it becomes clear that a thoroughly negative theological anthropology and a concomitant foundational act of violence must be understood as the fulcrum around which Schmitt's political metaphysics turns. That is, Žižek is right to claim that what seems like a very radical definition of the political in Schmitt "is *not radical enough*, in so far as it

---

53. See Schmitt, *Concept of the Political*, 32; and Schmitt, *State Theory of Thomas Hobbes*, 21, respectively.

54. Palaver, "Carl Schmitt's 'Apocalyptic' Resistance," 75 (emphasis added).

55. Schmitt, *Concept of the Political*, 58; and, for the Genesis reference, 68.

56. Ibid., 27.

57. Žižek, *Ticklish Subject*, 113. Interestingly, Žižek claims that Schmitt's political decisionism, which prioritizes the principle of order over its concrete content, amounts to an empty formalism that emanates from Hobbes. With regard to Hegel, there is certainly support for this reading in his claim that "sovereignty, which is initially on the *universal* thought of this ideality, can *exist* only as *subjectivity* which is certain of itself, and as the will's abstract—and to that extent ungrounded—*self-determination* in which the decision is vested. This absolutely decisive moment of the whole, therefore, is not individuality in general but *one* individual, the *monarch*." Nearly audible Schmittian inflections continue in Hegel's claim that sovereignty "attains its distinct actuality" not "in times of *peace*" but "in a *situation of crisis*" in Hegel, *Elements of the Philosophy of Right*, 316–17.

[simply] displaces the *inherent* antagonism constitutive of the political on to the *external* relationship between Us and Them."[58]

Turning back to Schmitt himself, it seems this displacement of violence is the best we can hope for. Indeed, Schmitt's later recommendation for what he saw as an impending global civil war (*Weltbürgerkreig*) is predicated on a division of the world into a plurality of *Großräume*.

> The denial of real enmity paves the way for the destructive work of absolute enmity. In 1914, the nations and governments of Europe stumbled into WWI without any real enmity. Real enmity arose only out of the war, which began as a conventional war among states on the basis of European international law, and ended as a global civil war of revolutionary class enmity. Who will be able to prevent the rise of unexpected new types of enmity in an analogous but much greater extent, whose fulfillment will produce unexpected new forms of a new partisan? The theory of the partisan flows into the concept of the political, into the question who is the real enemy and in a new *nomos* of the earth.[59]

Even in the absence of this continued division, that is to say, in the absence of a genuine political adversary, the inherent conflict constitutive of the political does not cease but is rather transformed: the juridical grounds upon which the state could legitimately declare war may be subverted, but in their place "executions, sanctions, punitive expeditions, pacifications, protection of treaties, international police, and measures to assure peace remain."[60]

This is also the point where the apocalyptic tone that has been implicitly at work throughout the development of Schmitt's political theology comes explicitly to the fore. In fact, it is not too much to claim that Schmitt's political theology is mobilized by an apocalyptically inflected aesthetics of violence or, more succinctly, that Schmitt is an "apocalyptician of counterrevolution."[61] Jacob Taubes describes Schmitt's thought as a "catechontic impulse," that is, as an attempt to "capture the chaos in forms, so that chaos doesn't take over."[62] Schmitt's emphasis on the exceptional need for decision, his reliance on Hobbes and the conservative Catholic authors

---

58. Žižek, "Carl Schmitt in the Age of Post-Politics," 27. In this way, Schmitt represents perhaps the most cunning and radical disavowal of the political and the invention of an *ultra-politics* that is little more than a direct militarization of politics itself.

59. Schmitt, "Theory of the Partisan," 78.

60. Schmitt, *Concept of the Political*, 79. In this respect, when read alongside the discourse of the "war on terror" Schmitt's analysis is all the more prescient.

61. Taubes, "Carl Schmitt—ein Apokalyptiker der Gegenrevolution," 7–30.

62. Taubes, *Political Theology of Paul*, 69.

of the counterrevolution, his friend/enemy distinction and his advocacy for a pluralism of *Großräume* to combat the real possibility of global civil war all reflect this underlying impulse.

In articulating this apocalyptic impulse the ambiguous figure of the *katechon* or "restrainer," to which Taubes alludes, makes its appearance.[63] Schmitt explains that "I do not believe that any historical concept other than *katechon* would have been possible for the original Christian faith. The belief that the restrainer holds back the end of the world provides the only bridge between the notion of an eschatological paralysis of all human events and a tremendous historical monolith like that of the Christian empire of the Germanic kings."[64] Schmitt borrows this term from 2 Thessalonians 2:6–7: "And you know what is now restraining him [the lawless one], so that he may be revealed when his time comes. For the mystery of lawlessness is already at work, but only until the one who now restrains it is removed." Heinrich Meier puts the matter succinctly: Schmitt "believes in the uninterrupted succession of the historical bearers of this force."[65] The ambiguous nature of this figure is exacerbated by the fact that while Schmitt is confident that there is a *katechon* for every epoch, this does not mean that we can actually name them. Moreover, Schmitt's own list of potential *katechons* includes individuals (Hegel) as well as institutions (Holy Roman Empire, Catholic Church). Again, Taubes is helpful in setting this figure within the larger context of Schmitt's thought.

> It's one thing to be a theologian, a second thing to be a philosopher, and it's a third thing to be a jurist. That—I've learned in life—is a completely different way of understanding the world. The jurist has to legitimate the world as it is. Schmitt's interest was only in one thing: that the party, that the chaos not rise to the top, *that the state remain*. No matter what the price. This is difficult for theologians and philosophers to follow, but as far as the jurist is concerned, as long as it is possible to find even one

---

63. Interestingly, Wolfgang Palaver suggests that the appearance of the figure of the *katechon* in Schmitt's work is evidence of an anti-apocalyptic impulse, though he seems to draw this conclusion on the basis of his argument that Schmitt's political theology is antithetical to the form of apocalyptic in evidence in the work of Réne Girard. See Palaver, "Carl Schmitt's 'Apocalyptic' Resistance," 85. Palaver's argument about the work Schmitt seems to assign to this ambiguous figure notwithstanding, Schmitt's political theology is only anti-apocalyptic in the very limited sense in which it (apocalyptically) works against other forms of apocalyptic such as those of Girard and, as Palaver also interestingly argues, Dietrich Bonhoeffer.

64. Schmitt, *Nomos of the Earth*, 60.

65. Meier, *Lesson of Carl Schmitt*, 160–61.

juridical form, by whatever hairsplitting ingenuity, this must absolutely be done, for otherwise chaos reigns.[66]

Despite the clear emphasis on the prevention of chaos and destruction, which is also the prevention of civil war, it is evident that as Schmitt narrates his own political theology it becomes an apocalyptically inflected aesthetics of violence concerned primarily with the maintenance of order from above. Put another way, Schmitt's political theology attempts to structurally capture the inherent violence between human beings and displace it on to an enemy that is essentially other and, in so doing, represents a form of apocalyptic preservation.

Significantly, this is also precisely the place where Metz makes an appearance in Schmitt's work. Indeed, Schmitt cites Metz's *Theology of the World* (1968) approvingly and claims that "he is right to reflect repeatedly, critically distancing the relation between Christian faith and society on the basis of the eschatological orientation of faith."[67] It is no coincidence that Schmitt turns to Metz for help here, despite the fact that Metz is at pains to distance himself from Schmitt. However, for a full appreciation of how Schmitt uses Metz as an ally to reinstate his own political theology, it is necessary to investigate Metz's *new* political theology. It is to that task that we now turn.

Metz's *New* Political Theology

As we have seen, Schmitt initially articulated his political theology in the early 1920s amid the demise of the Weimar Republic and subsequently returned to it much later, in 1970, just after the *new* political theology had begun to take shape in Germany. As one of the primary architects of the *new* political theology, Metz is at pains to articulate a practical fundamental theology that refuses to avert its gaze from the wreckage of history but paradoxically tries to accomplish this by only vaguely and with great reticence acknowledging Schmitt's political theology, which is inextricably linked with legitimating precisely the kind suffering that Metz's theology so desperately seeks to interrupt. Slightly more forthright than Metz, Jürgen Moltmann argues that the development of political theology had to be called *new* to differentiate it from the "pseudoreligiosity" of Schmitt's political theology that was, in the end, nothing more than a thinly veiled ideology constructed to legitimate the policies of the Third Reich and was therefore

---

66. Taubes, *Political Theology of Paul*, 103 (emphasis added).
67. Schmitt, *Political Theology II*, 53–54.

better understood as political religion.[68] It is a pity that Metz has not in any significant way engaged the development of Schmitt's political theology, especially since his own work attempts to face up to the "historical connotations" that continue to burden the discourse of political theology itself, and it is one of the aims, if not the primary aim, of this chapter to rectify this lack of engagement. However, before any such comparative endeavor can occur it is necessary to understand Metz's own development of the *new* political theology on his own terms.[69] There are, of course, numerous ways in which such an account may be given, and the analysis that follows proceeds on a similar basis to the investigation of Schmitt's political theology insofar as it attempts to take account of the self-professed theological and philosophical influences that drive the development of Metz's *new* political theology. Thus, the analysis that follows, like the analysis of Schmitt, can in no way be comprehensive in nature since it cannot possibly account for all of the influences Metz names and must therefore necessarily limit itself to a select formative group. Among these, Karl Rahner represents the background against which Metz launches his avowedly apocalyptic form of *new* political theology that is subsequently shaped by his interactions with the Frankfurt School—principally Theodor Adorno and Max Horkheimer—as well as with Walter Benjamin and Ernst Bloch.

It is clear that the most enduring influence on Metz is his onetime teacher and lifelong friend, Karl Rahner.[70] For Metz, Rahner's transcendental idealism represented a major shift from the then still dominant neoscholastic tradition, which bequeathed to the church the mandatory Thomism through the work of Spanish Jesuit Francisco Suárez. Metz identifies the significance of Rahner's work as "the attempt to appropriate the heritage of the classical patristic and scholastic traditions precisely by means of a productive and aggressive dialogue with the challenges of the modern European world."[71] Metz's development of the *new* political theology, or what he sometimes calls a post-idealist theology, must be understood against this background as a critical dialogue with the advances and limitations of Rahner's work.[72]

---

68. See Moltmann, "Christian Theology and Political Religion," especially 47.

69. For Metz's explicit avowal of the "historical connotations" to which I am referring here, see Metz, *Theology of the World*, 107.

70. Rahner's influence on Metz is well documented. Metz himself claims that "virtually everything in my theology has something to do with him [Rahner]" in *Hope Against Hope*, 18.

71. Metz, *Passion for God*, 32.

72. See, for example, Metz, "Political Theology: A New Paradigm of Theology?," 143–44, where Metz distinguishes between what he sees as the three main competing paradigms of theology, namely, the neoscholastic, transcendental-idealist, and

The Architectonics of Hope

Particularly important in this respect are the limitations that Metz locates in Rahner's work and, for our purposes, chief among these is his criticism of the distinction that Rahner opens up between eschatology and apocalyptic. In what is arguably his most important eschatological contribution, Rahner associates apocalyptic with a false form of eschatology that attempts to provide in advance a comprehensive view of the end of the world and thereby clearly exceeds the scope and limits that must be maintained for any genuinely Christian eschatology.[73] For Metz, Rahner's apparent disparagement of apocalyptic is highly problematic because although it rightly eschews overreaching claims about what shape the future will take, it nevertheless remains stuck in a transcendental-idealist version of Christianity that "takes the edge off the historical-apocalyptic struggle" for Christian identity.[74] As we will see below in connection with Metz's recourse to critical theory, his configuration of apocalyptic takes the form of interruption; however, before we can see how this works we must attend in particular to Metz's understanding of the vicissitudes of the modern world.

Metz's underlying conviction is that theology can and must survive the storms of secularization and, more positively, that a political theology articulated as a critical embrace of the Enlightenment represents the most significant political resource for modernity itself.[75] It would be difficult to

---

post-idealist traditions. The nature of the relationship between Rahner and Metz cannot be dealt with here; however, it remains a matter of contention. Compare, for example, Guenther, *Rahner and Metz*, who claims that Metz's political theology is a working out of Rahner's transcendental theology, and Martinez, *Confronting the Mystery of God*, who argues that Metz's political theology cannot be a simple development and that their relationship is better understood as a dialectical one. Complicating matters further is the fact that Rahner himself endorsed Metz's criticisms of his work and did not think there was a necessary contradiction between his theology and Metz's. For Rahner's comments in this respect, see, for example, Rahner, "Introduction," especially x.

73. See especially Rahner, "Hermeneutics of Eschatological Assertions," 323–46. Similar disparaging comments about "false apocalyptic" can also be found in Rahner, "Eschatology," 436–37.

74. See especially Metz, *Faith in History and Society*, 151–52. I refer to Rahner's "apparent" disparagement of apocalyptic here because although Metz seems to be convinced that the key component missing from Rahner's theology is this apocalyptic edge, Peter Joseph Fritz has provocatively argued that Rahner gives us a particular type of apocalyptic theology in Fritz, *Rahner's Theological Aesthetics*, especially 205–60.

75. See, for example, Metz, *Passion for God*, 149, where Metz claims that "the traditionally rooted a priori of suffering is still more promising—even and precisely for modernity's politics." The link Metz makes between his political theology and the memory of suffering will be investigated below. For a more theoretical confirmation of this claim, see Downey, *Love's Strategy*, especially 85 where Metz claims that the world in which we live "bears the deep impression of many systems and theories and which can therefore only be experienced and possibly changed in and through these systems and theories."

overestimate the extent to which this theme is woven into the very fabric of Metz's *new* political theology. In an article written in 1965 Metz acknowledges already that any fundamental theology must face the consequences of a world increasingly characterized by pluralism and secularization and claims that "unbelief is becoming a central question for theology itself."[76] In this way, Metz's initial articulation of the *new* political theology can be read as an attempt to confront the "explosive problematic" generated on a hitherto unprecedented scale in the treatment of the culture of modernity by the Second Vatican Council and, more specifically, in the Conciliar document *Gaudium et spes*. Characterized by a general enthusiasm for the culture of modernity, the Catholic church flung its doors open to the modern world. However, as Tracey Rowland argues, John XXIII's vision of *aggiornamento* lacked the specific theological hermeneutic of culture that would have made it intelligible and thereby initiated too uncritical an acceptance of the culture of modernity.[77] It is precisely within this post-conciliar theological climate that Metz began to construct what he often calls a practical fundamental theology. As we will see, despite his recourse to the revisionary Marxists of the Frankfurt School, Metz too suffers from a pervasive inability to adequately grapple with the consequences of founding his *new* political theology *on modernity's ground*.

With the publication of his *Theology of the World* in 1968 a striking and more explicitly positive endorsement of secularization sets the tone for the subsequent development of the *new* political theology:

> The secularity of the world, as it has emerged in the modern process of secularization and as we see it today in a globally heightened form, has fundamentally, though not in its individual historical forms, arisen not against Christianity but through it. *It is an originally Christian event* and hence testifies in our world situation to the power of the "hour of Christ" at work within history.[78]

For Metz, this claim has to be understood both incarnationally and eschatologically. Simply put, in the Christ event, God has accepted the world "in

---

76. Metz, "Unbelief as a Theological Problem," 59. Interestingly, this is an early point at which Metz points to inadequacies in Rahner's work, specifically with regard to his thesis of the "anonymous Christian," and addresses the question from the other direction, that is, from the position of the "unbelief of the believer." This phenomenological approach is undoubtedly a result of the influence of Martin Heidegger, who was the subject of Metz's doctoral dissertation in philosophy. For a condensed version of Metz's work on Heidegger, see Metz, "Heidegger und das Problem der Metaphysik," 1–22.

77. See Rowland, *Culture and the Thomist Tradition*, especially 11–34.

78. Metz, *Theology of the World*, 19–20 (emphasis added).

eschatological finality."[79] The crucial thing to note here, especially because this is the point at which Schmitt realizes the sense in which he can use Metz as an ally, is that the incarnation is read as a logical apparatus in which God's eschatological acceptance of the world is manifested not by means of Jesus's action within history but rather by the very operation of incarnation itself. What is most important for Metz is that the incarnation is the definitive historical action of God *for* the world, not *in* the world. Indeed, this insight is precisely what reveals the eschatological character of the world since "in an historical movement forward that it cannot itself know it has to attain an end that has already been promised to it. It [the world] must itself become what it already is through the deed of Jesus Christ: the new age, 'the new heaven and the new earth' (Rev. 21:1)."[80] Metz is careful to qualify this positive endorsement of secularization right from the beginning of his wanderings into political theology, and he makes a distinction between the eschatological acceptance of the world by God and the resistance of the world in acknowledging God through this process. In point of fact, Metz draws out the ambiguities he sees in the process of secularization, what he sometimes calls unconquered secularity, and makes them constitutive of the liberating dynamics involved in the unfolding of the Christian principle of history.[81] Again, this ambiguity is reflected in Christ, since suffering was a constitutive element of the incarnation—as Metz says, "the Glory of the Lord was plunged into the absurdity of death."[82] Already we can begin to see Metz's reluctance to resolve tensions and the sense in which he understands his *new* political theology to be a critical theory that holds history open to the liberating work of God.

This subjective posture, this thinking with and against, is woven throughout Metz's work. Indeed, this is helpfully illuminated in a later reflection on the enduring significance of the Frankfurt School in the articulation of the *new* political theology:

> Probably the theory of modernity to which [the *new* political theology] comes the closest is the one that became clear—certainly

79. Ibid., 25.
80. Ibid.
81. Ibid., 44–45.
82. Ibid., 30. There is some ambiguity in the early development of Metz's Christology with respect to the question of divine impassibility. However, in his later work he returns to this question and makes clear that to speak of suffering *in* God not only violates the doctrine of analogy, with its emphasis on the *maior dissimiltudo* that obtains between God and the world, but also smacks far too much of Hegel and ends in a secret aestheticization of suffering that is altogether different from a suffering-with. See Metz, "Suffering Unto God," especially 618–22.

as a corrective overexaggeration—in the "dialectic of enlightenment" (M. Horkheimer/Th. W. Adorno). In my opinion this theory allows one—even today—to get a better grasp of the problems at the limits of modernity than talk about "postmodernity" or even "second modernity." It can best enable one to learn how to think with modernity against modernity in order to rescue its achievements, especially its culture of freedom.[83]

Initiated in the early 1960s in dialogue with the so-called *Paulus-Gesellschaft*, which was dedicated to bringing Christians and Marxists into conversation, the influence of the work of Theodor Adorno and Max Horkheimer is decisive in setting the tone for the development of the *new* political theology.[84] Indicating the kind of shift in thinking that has imbued all his subsequent work, Metz says that his interaction with these revisionary Marxists "politicized me out of the existential and transcendental enchantment of theology."[85] The manner in which these interactions have effected this radical change can helpfully be seen, for our purposes, in three related encounters that, in turn, illuminate three significant signposts of the *new* political theology.

The first of these three, as alluded to above, is the powerful diagnosis of the failures of the Enlightenment articulated by Adorno and Horkheimer, on which Metz heavily relies. Significant for Metz is the sense in which Horkheimer and Adorno uncover a kind of short circuit in the "dialectic of enlightenment" whereby liberated human subjects are found not to be the "engineers of world history" but rather subject to a "corrosive rationality" that makes of them mere objects of power.[86] Understood in its widest sense as the "disenchantment of the world,"[87] that is, the attempt to "dispel myths, to overthrow fantasy with knowledge," Adorno and Horkheimer claim that the supposed emancipatory potential of the Enlightenment has fallen prey to a colonizing instrumental reason that dooms it to remain caught up in its mythical status.[88] Moreover, this kind of reason has itself become inherently

---

83. Metz, *Zum Begriff der neuen Politischen Theologie*, 182 (my translation).

84. The complex story of the history and development of the Frankfurt School is helpfully elucidated in Jay, *The Dialectical Imagination*.

85. Metz, *Passion for God*, 3.

86. See Horkheimer and Adorno, *Dialectic of Enlightenment*, especially 1–34.

87. See Weber, "Science as a Vocation," 129–58.

88. Horkheimer and Adorno, *Dialectic of Enlightenment*, 1 and 19–20, respectively. Although I am not aware of any explicit connection, this focus on the power of myth recalls Schmitt's reliance on the work of Georges Sorel in the development of his critique of parliamentary democracy in Schmitt, *Crisis of Parliamentary Democracy*, especially 65–76. See also Schmitt's discussion of Sorel in Schmitt, *Roman Catholicism and*

violent, exercising a kind of "mythic terror" that eviscerates particularities either by reducing them to what is familiar or by expelling them beyond the borders of intelligibility, thereby homogenizing its space of action.[89] This analysis pushed Metz beyond the existential-phenomenological (Heidegger) and transcendental (Rahner) enchantments of theology toward a more explicitly post-idealist, that is, practical theology based on the "primacy of praxis" or the "theory-praxis dialectic."[90] Indeed, for Metz, it is "impossible to justify the critical demands of reason in a purely theoretical way."[91] In this way the early primary task of the *new* political theology, which Metz identifies as a thoroughgoing deprivatization, is itself critically reoriented in the struggle for a theology of the subject with a more nuanced differentiation of praxis oriented not by some preconceived totality of meaning (Pannenberg) nor by being grounded in the doctrine of the Trinity (Moltmann) but rather in the narrative-practical *structure* of political discipleship itself.[92] In Metz's

---

Political Form, 12–15. For Sorel's own analysis of the historical, and often violent, force of myth see Sorel, *Reflections on Violence*.

89. Horkheimer and Adorno, *Dialectic of Enlightenment*, 22. Flowing from his analysis of commodity exchange, Adorno sees this kind of instrumental reason facilitating the growth of a new barbarism that is a form of "identity thinking," a kind of seamless totality that can only be interrupted with a "negative dialectics" that attempts, however precariously, to include within thought that which is heterogeneous to it. See Adorno, *Negative Dialectics*. Metz's formulation of a *theologia negativa* owes much to Adorno in this regard. For an enormously helpful introduction to the genealogy of "negative dialectics" and its relation to Benjamin, see Buck-Morss, *The Origin of Negative Dialectics*. It is also interesting to note at this point, especially since it eerily echoes Schmitt's analysis of the eclipse of the political, that Horkheimer and Adorno trace the source of the Enlightenment's mythic terror not to Hobbes but to Spinoza, whose notion of self-preservation "contains the true maxim of all Western civilization" in *Dialectic of Enlightenment*, 22. See also Spinoza, "Ethics," especially Part IV.

90. Metz, *Faith in History and Society*, 61. For a helpful overview of the theory-praxis dialectic that is sympathetic with Metz's position in many respects, see Lamb, "Theory-Praxis Relationship," 149–78.

91. Metz, *Zum Begriff der neuen Politischen Theologie*, 28 (my translation). This first signpost represents Metz's attempt to address a significant criticism of the initial development of the *new* political theology begun in *Theology of the World*. In particular, his student Marcel Xhauffaire had pointed out the dangers and limits of a purely theoretical political theology and criticized Metz's reliance on the Frankfurt School's dialectic of enlightenment. Metz himself cites Xhauffaire, *Feuerbach et la théologie de la sécularisation* as important in this regard, but see also Xhauffaire, *La "théologie politique."* Here again we can see Metz's subjective posture of thinking with and against at work and his reluctance to take up residence in what Georg Lukács has termed, in his criticism of the leading German intelligentsia, the "grand hotel abyss" in Lukács, *The Theory of the Novel*, 22.

92. There are two important debates at work in the background that are relevant here. First, in his initial discussion of the *new* political theology, Metz interestingly cites the work of Helmut Schelsky, an influential German sociologist and onetime

hands the dialectic of enlightenment becomes the dialectic of emancipation understood as the "*self*-liberation of human groups and classes in the modern history of revolution and enlightenment."[93] Important here is the sense in which emancipation is universal, that is, a kind of philosophy of history that illuminates the modern history of freedom.[94] There is an intense worry here for Metz that must be recognized since

> one would be fundamentally misunderstanding the negative-critical dimension of this dialectic of emancipation if one were to think that all that was necessary was to "complement it" with a Christian doctrine of redemption. A superficial reconciliation of this sort underestimates both the totalizing character (mediated negatively-critically) of the dialectical history of emancipation, and the indispensability of the Christian history of redemption. In my opinion, the noteworthy attempts "to introduce what Jesus is about into the emancipatory process" and to interpret the history of redemption as pushing the history of emancipation past its limits, of outdoing it or perfecting it, all break down at this point. It is simply not the case that emancipation is nothing but redemption's immanence, and redemption emancipation's transcendence.[95]

For Metz, it is of the utmost importance that the modern project, the dialectic of emancipation, be redeemed from its own self-destructive dynamic,

---

member of the Nazi Party, to bolster his argument against the privatizing tendencies of theology that "will tend more and more to be a 'rule without ruling power, a decision without deciding power'" in *Theology of the World*, 110–11. Resonances of Schmitt here are almost uncanny and should at least raise the question as to whether and to what extent, at least in Metz's early work, the task of deprivatization, devoted as it was to the prevention of delivering up faith to modern ideologies, involved the *power to decide* so central to Schmitt's political theology. Second, Metz's attempt here is to distinguish his *new* political theology from others that were developing at the same time, notably from Jürgen Moltmann's Trinitarian political theology as exemplified in Moltmann, *The Crucified God* and also, more indirectly, from Dietrich Bonhoeffer's articulation of a costly discipleship, which Metz claimed remained too exclusively a matter of individual ethical praxis, as exemplified in Bonhoeffer, *The Cost of Discipleship*. For Metz's comments, see Metz, *Faith in History and Society*, especially 65 and 259n12; and Metz, *Followers of Christ*, 38–39.

93. Metz, *Faith in History and Society*, 115–16.

94. Metz's insistence on the totalizing character of the dialectic of emancipation and its link to freedom can be seen much earlier in Metz, "Freedom as a Threshold Problem," 264–74. Moreover, it relies on Karl Marx's formulation that "*every* emancipation is a restoration of the human world and of human relationships to *man himself* [sic]," as cited in Metz, *Faith in History and Society*, 115. See also Marx, "On the Jewish Question," 46–70.

95. Metz, *Faith in History and Society*, 117.

and thus the *new* political theology must be understood not as a rejection of the Enlightenment *tout court* but rather as its very retrieval. The crisis here is, precisely, the "gradual disappearance of the Enlightenment" and the "atrophied remainders" that are left in its wake.[96] More specifically, this "is not a crisis of the contents of faith, but rather a crisis of the Christian subjects and institutions that reject the practical meaning of these contents (discipleship)."[97] This is why Metz refuses to complement the dialectic of emancipation with a Christian account of redemption because the liberating dynamics of the gospel would thereby be exposed to the risk of domestication and privatization characteristic of bourgeois religion. In this way, Metz establishes a kind of safeguard, which is the secret of the *new* political theology, that attempts to address "the total character of the dialectical history of emancipation, which sucks in even the transcendental roots of freedom" by positing a pure space from which a critique can be mounted.[98] This space, for Metz, is the church, which is nothing other than the institution of faith's critical freedom.[99] The negative-critical function of the church is of the utmost importance here insofar as it alone is what reveals the roots of totalitarian ideologies. This crisis of identity that the church is meant to confront culminates in an acknowledgment that the messianic future proper to Christianity is not one that stands alongside, complements, or even completes any preconceived bourgeois future but rather one that *disrupts* any such future.[100]

The emphasis on the theory-praxis dialectic coupled with the subsequent focus on the church as the social location for the practical exercise of the critical-liberating function of reason flows directly into the second interaction that is significant for setting the direction of the *new* political theology. The potency with which Metz claims the church can act to save those identities that are under threat of extinction is articulated with an account of memory that owes much of its theoretical formulation to the Jewish philosopher Walter Benjamin. Particularly relevant for Metz is Benjamin's critique of the reigning ideology of progress and the capacity of anamnesis to function as a "category of interruption."[101] Benjamin's sixth thesis on the philosophy of history is particularly illuminating in this regard:

96. Ibid., 48 and 58, respectively.
97. Ibid., 154.
98. Ibid., 117.
99. Metz, *Theology of the World*, 116.
100. See Metz, *Emergent Church*, 2.
101. Metz, *Faith in History and Society*, 170.

The Founding and Re-founding of Political Theology 37

> To articulate the past historically does not mean to recognize it "the way it really was" (Ranke). It means to seize hold of a memory as it flashes up at a moment of danger. Historical materialism wishes to retain that image of the past which unexpectedly appears to man [sic] singled out by history at a moment of danger. The danger affects both the content of the tradition and its receivers. The same threat hangs over both: that of becoming a tool of the ruling classes. In every era the attempt must be made anew to wrest tradition away from a conformism that is about to overpower it. The Messiah comes not only as the redeemer, he comes as the subduer of Antichrist. Only that historian will have the gift of fanning the spark of hope in the past who is firmly convinced that *even the dead* will not be safe from the enemy if he wins. And this enemy has not ceased to be victorious.[102]

For Metz, memory must be constructed as a resistance to an evolutionally interpreted flow of time and "becomes the medium for the actualization of reason and freedom which defends itself critically from an idea of the undialectical 'progress of reason' that is just as unreflective as it is banal."[103] With Benjamin, Metz insists that the real revolutions are not the locomotives of history, as Marx suggested, but rather occur when the human race, riding this runaway train, pulls the emergency brake.[104] Metz names this the anthropological revolution and articulates it with striking contradictions:

> This revolution is not, in fact, concerned with liberating us from our poverty and misery, but rather from our wealth and our totally excessive prosperity. It is not a liberation from what we lack, but from our consumerism in which we are ultimately consuming our very selves. It is not a liberation from our state of oppression, but from the untransformed praxis of our own wishes and desires. It is not a liberation from our powerlessness, but from our own form of predominance. It frees us, not from the state of being dominated but from that of dominating; not from our sufferings but from our apathy; not from guilt but from our innocence, or rather from that delusion of innocence which the life of domination has long since spread out through

---

102. Benjamin, "Theses on the Philosophy of History," 247. Resonances with Schmitt are again evident here, especially in his use of the concept of the Messiah as the one who restrains the Antichrist. For an account of the relationship between Benjamin and Schmitt that is relevant to the present discussion at several points, see Bredekamp, "From Walter Benjamin to Carl Schmitt," 247–66.

103. Metz, *Faith in History and Society*, 177.

104. See Marx, "German Ideology," 189; and Benjamin, "Paralipomena," 402.

our souls. This revolution seeks to bring to power precisely the nondominating virtues.[105]

Memory here functions in at least three significant ways. First, it acts to discipline reason such that it functions not only as a kind of remembering but also as a way of keeping track of the progressive amnesia that piles wreckage upon wreckage. It is this memory of the history of forgetting, the anamnestic structure of reason, that saves it both from being a piece of museum traditionalism and from dissolving in "the postmodern fictionalization of history" and, further, that enables "the recognition of the capacity for guilt as a dignity of freedom."[106] Second, it rewrites the history of redemption by looking backward toward solidarity with those silenced by death and thereby attempts to view the bloody theater of history from the standpoint of the victims. In doing so, "it does more than uncover the absurdity in history, against the brash optimism of the victors. For it [memory] the potentials of meaning in the history of freedom do not depend only on the survivors, the successful, those who made it."[107] Third, it is dangerous, fundamentally arresting to thought and goes "against the grain" of history, breaking through the crust of a mechanism that has become torpid by repetition.[108] Describing the dangerous power of memories, Metz says,

> They illuminate for a few moments and with a harsh steady light the questionable nature of things we have apparently come to terms with, and show up the banality of our supposed "realism." They break through the canon of all that is taken as self-evident, and unmask as deception the certainty of those "whose hour is always there" (John 7:6) . . . Such memories are like dangerous and incalculable visitants from the past.[109]

---

105. Metz, *Emergent Church*, 42.

106. Metz, "Anamnestic Reason," 191–92. Metz's early work on Heidegger is also relevant here.

107. Metz, *Faith in History and Society*, 124. Notably absent here is any account of redemption that would see the church function positively as a lived anticipation of the future community. Therefore the question of whether and to what extent the messianic virtues of hope and love, precisely those nondominating virtues Metz claims are actualized in the anthropological revolution, are themselves reduced to a merely negative-critical function. Two helpful examples that attempt to address this worry by pointing to the necessity of the practices of the faith, notably the performance of the Eucharist, can be seen in Lamb, *Solidarity with Victims*; and Morrill, *Anamnesis as Dangerous Memory*.

108. See Benjamin, "Theses on the Philosophy of History," 248. Metz builds on Benjamin's suggestion here in his notion of "productive noncontemporaneity," which he often explicates by means of a theological autobiography. See, for example, Metz, "Productive Noncontemporaneity," 169–77.

109. Metz, "Future in the Memory of Suffering," 15.

These dangerous memories are theologically grounded, for Metz, in the *memoria passionis*, but the horror of Auschwitz is the fulcrum around which they are most forcefully felt. Indeed, it would be difficult to overestimate the persuasive power Metz attributes to the memory of suffering in the development of the *new* political theology. It is perhaps this signpost that most strains toward a purely negative-critical structure since "it is suffering that stands in the way of any positive theory reconciling humankind and nature."[110]

The third and final encounter that is significant, for our purposes, in the development of the *new* political theology is Metz's friendship with Ernst Bloch. The influence of Bloch is perhaps best understood as an intensification of the apocalyptic themes that were already operative in Metz's work. However, the subjective posture that is woven into the very fabric of Metz's thought is again visible. In his *Untimely Theses on Apocalyptic*, an explicit tribute to Bloch that owes just as much to Benjamin, Metz recalls a letter written to him by Bloch about "how hard it is to live with a genuinely believed expectation of the imminence of the last things" and claims that "Christian theologians will be able to learn from him [Bloch] only by contradicting him."[111] His friendship with Bloch awoke in Metz an interest in the Jewish traditions that had largely been concealed in Christianity and in the revolutionary potential of Christian hope contained within the eschatological impulses of the biblical narrative. Bloch himself stands within the history of revisionary Marxism as an ambiguous figure, harshly criticized as a traitor for attempting, however precariously, to appropriate the mythical kernel of the biblical tradition in the creation of a new human Utopia.[112] The question, for Bloch, "is not of giving the death-blow to fantasy as such, but of destroying and saving the myth in a single dialectical process, by shedding light upon it."[113] Often referred to (disdainfully) as the "atheistic theologian" or, with allusion to the title of one of his own books, as the "theologian of the revolution," Bloch is concerned to "save the Bible's choked and buried 'plebeian' element" and sees his task as a kind of "detec-

---

110. Metz, *Faith in History and Society*, 104. This is reinforced in Metz's claim that "the slightest trace of meaningless suffering in the world as we experience it gives the lie to this whole affirmative ontology and the whole of teleology, and reveals them to be modernity's mythology" (ibid.).

111. Ibid., 156.

112. The magisterial series of essays by Francis Fiorenza provide a tremendously helpful historical background to the issues raised here. The second essay is particularly illuminating with regard to Bloch's influence on both Metz and Jürgen Moltmann. See Fiorenza, "Dialectical Theology and Hope, I," 143–63; "Dialectical Theology and Hope, II," 384–99; and "Dialectical Theology and Hope, III," 26–42.

113. Bloch, *Atheism in Christianity*, 37.

tive work" that aims to wrest this element from the clutches of the "upper classes and of deified despotism."[114] Helpfully situating Bloch within the tradition of revisionary Marxism, Francis Fiorenza notes that "for Bloch the myths and transcendence of the Judeo-Christian religion are *not opium, but protest.*"[115] This is precisely the sense in which Metz uses Bloch as a springboard for his own elaboration of an apocalyptic eschatology that is the very horizon for understanding how Christianity represents a dynamic way of becoming a subject before God in history. The way in which Metz accomplishes this can be helpfully seen, for our purposes, in the way he appropriates Bloch's interpretation of Exodus 3:14 for his own elaboration of the *new* political theology. In his *Atheism in Christianity* Bloch is concerned above all to make a distinction within the biblical text between the Creator God and the God of the Exodus.

> Religion is re-ligio, binding back. It binds its adherents back, first and foremost, to a mythical God of the Beginning, a Creator-God. So, rightly understood, adherence to the Exodus-figure called "I will be what I will be" and to the Christianity of the Son of Man and of the Eschaton, is no longer religion.[116]

There are at least two significant aspects that Metz picks up on here. The first is the way in which Bloch's Christ functions to radically hold history open. Indeed, for Bloch the Son of Man "does not play any part in the creation of the world, precisely because he is to be the active principle at the end of time—active in the creation of a new heaven and a new earth—and not before."[117] To be sure, Metz does not uncritically adopt Bloch's argument here, especially since Bloch makes the *homo absconditus* the subject of history rather than God.[118] Despite this, Metz affirms, in a Festschrift for Bloch, that the only way to understand history is within this context of a

---

114. Ibid., 62. Bloch's position here in relation to the biblical tradition is reminiscent of Schmitt's reflections on Hobbes's Leviathan and Fyodor Dostoevsky's Grand Inquisitor in which he claims that "a clever tactician gives up nothing as long as it is not completely useless" in Schmitt, *Glossarium*, May 23, 1949.

115. Fiorenza, "Dialectical Theology and Hope, II," 389 (emphasis added). See also Marx's own criticism of religion to which Fiorenza here alludes in Marx, "Towards a Critique of Hegel's Philosophy of Right," especially 72.

116. Bloch, *Atheism in Christianity*, epigraph. Jürgen Moltman takes up this theme even more explicitly than Metz in describing the social shape of Christianity in modernity as an "Exodus Church" in Moltmann, *Theology of Hope*, especially 288–322.

117. Bloch, *Atheism in Christianity*, 147.

118. At this point we are right to wonder whether Metz simply modifies Bloch's *homo absconditus* and makes of it a *Deus absconditus*. See also Chopp, *Praxis of Suffering*, 74–78.

radical suspension, in relation to that end that alone gives it meaning and with reference to the reality of a "God before us" in history that is the basis for Christian hope.[119] Thus, for Metz, "Christianity can only formulate the decisiveness ('absoluteness') and universality of its message without falling into an ideology when it formulates it as critical negation (of and in given situations)."[120] This echoes both his earlier claim that "Christian eschatology is a *theologia negativa*" and his later claim that "wherever a party, group, race, nation or class—even the class of technocrats—tries to define itself as this subject [of divine will], the Christian *memoria* must oppose that, and unmask this attempt as political idolatry, as political ideology with a totalitarian or—in apocalyptic terms—a 'bestial' tendency."[121] What distinguishes and preserves the *new* political theology from becoming yet another ideological construction is not that it knows *more* but that it knows *less* "about the sought-after future of humanity" and that it faces up to this "poverty of knowledge."[122] Second, Metz begins to think more explicitly about time and temporality, which returns him, in part, to his earlier work on Heidegger, whose reception in theology Metz claims is symptomatic of the forgetfulness of time. Indeed, Metz claims that Heidegger "is not received as the one who, with his *Being and Time*, began to analyze the premises of a time-less metaphysics; rather, he is recalled as the existential analyst of *Dasein*."[123] Guided by the insight from Bloch that the Exodus God is the God of liberation, the God of deliverance, Metz's reflections on time take on an explosive and perhaps even a militant character that is precisely designed to rupture the "present-day orgies of violence" that attain the "normative power of the real world."[124] Metz is worried that there is not only a certain kind of amnesia at work here but also a kind of dangerous apathy that somehow muffles the call to be subjects before God. Evidence of this for Metz is that we are more informed than ever before of the catastrophes that occur in our world but less moved to act in response to them. Citing Bertolt Brecht, Metz notes that "catastrophes are reported on the radio in between pieces of music. The music plays on, like the 'passage of time' rendered audible, rolling over everything mercilessly, impossible to interrupt. When atrocities happen it's like when

119. See Metz, "Gott vor uns," 227–41.
120. Metz, "Political Theology," 1241.
121. See Metz, *Theology of the World*, 97; Metz and Moltmann, *Faith and the Future*, 15.
122. Metz, *Theology of the World*, 97.
123. Metz, *Passion for God*, 87. See also his plea for the re-temporalization of metaphysics within the eschatological context of the Bible in Metz, "Die Rede von Gott," especially 319.
124. Metz, "God: Against the Myth of the Eternity of Time," 38.

the rain falls. No one shouts 'stop it!' anymore."[125] Against the backdrop of this diagnosis of the deadened sense of time and its concomitant paralysis of hope, which is also nothing more than the creeping evolutionary dissolution of history itself, Metz intensifies his eschatological proviso by shaping it as an "apocalyptically expectant praxis of discipleship."[126] There is a palpable urgency at work here.

> Imminent expectation will not let discipleship be postponed. It is not the apocalyptic feeling for life that makes us apathetic, but the evolutionistic! It is the time symbol of evolution that paralyzes discipleship; in contrast, what imminent expectation does is to offer a vantage point on time and on expectation to a consciousness that has been evolutionistically anaesthetized and seduced. It introduces the pressure of time and the pressure to act into Christian life; that is, it does not paralyze responsibility, but grounds it. It is not primarily the vantage point of threat and of paralyzing fear that apocalyptic consciousness adopts, but a perspective that challenges one to practical solidarity with "the least of one's brothers and sisters," as it goes in the little apocalypse of the Gospel of Matthew.[127]

Interestingly, these reflections increasingly lead Metz to focus on the role of the religious life in the church. No longer simply the institution of faith's critical freedom, the church itself now seems to be infected and in need of its own apocalyptic shock, a passionate protest that must be produced inside the church by those attentive to what is outside it.[128] This apocalyptically shaped eschatology must remain perpetually aware of the always threatened character of Christian hope and be formulated as a "hope against all hope," that is, as the "*explosive force* of lived hope."[129]

In no way can these three signposts of the *new* political theology be understood as separate developments with their own trajectories. On the contrary, they are inextricably intertwined and mutually reinforcing and my presentation of them here is merely heuristic. Taken together, they provide an illuminating picture of the direction of the *new* political theology. All

---

125. Metz, *Faith in History and Society*, 157.

126. Ibid., 81. It should also be noted here that, for Metz, this intensification stands in marked contrast to Rahner's distinction between eschatology and apocalyptic. For more on this compare Metz's discussion of the dangerous Jesus in Metz, "Communicating a Dangerous Memory," 46–53, with Rahner's distinction in Rahner, *Foundations of Christian Faith*, especially 432–33.

127. Metz, *Faith in History and Society*, 163.

128. See Metz, *Followers of Christ*, 78.

129. Ibid., 82 (emphasis added).

The Founding and Re-founding of Political Theology   43

three signposts reveal a tension that comes to the fore most explicitly in Metz's discussion of bounded time. At issue is whether and to what extent the imminent expectation that apocalyptically shapes Metz's eschatology can, in fact, precipitate the kinds of liberating activity that he claims are at the heart of the Gospel. Perhaps more to the point, how does bounded time function as an antidote to the sweet poison of evolutionary progress when it is set within the larger context of a *theologia negativa* that strains with all its might against any affirmative ontology lest it be enlisted, willingly or not, in the subjugation of others? Although Metz does not shy away from tarrying with this tension it seems that what we are left with in his narration of the *new* political theology ends up being decisively on the side of an ontology of the not-yet in which Christ is kept in reserve as a kind of grand ideological dismantler that attempts to safeguard the future from meaningless suffering. This is why Metz often interprets the *memoria passionis* in passive terms as a simple acceptance of suffering. Indeed, he claims that "discipleship in imminent expectation . . . does not cause suffering, but shoulders it."[130] Elsewhere he suggests that the religious orders in the church should develop something like an "*ars moriendi*, an art of dying" that could "produce a freedom and determination that in their turn would become a charismatic witness within and on behalf of the Church."[131] Metz is insistent that the *new* political theology counters both fatalistic apathy and desperate fanaticism with a politics of waiting that does not engender a violent praxis; however, we are left gazing squarely on the meaningless ongoing suffering of others with no account of the lived provocations that would render such suffering historically meaningful. Thus, despite his own best efforts, as Metz narrates his *new* political theology we are again met with an apocalyptically inflected aesthetics of violence, albeit one that is willing to die rather than have itself implicated in the never-ending cycle of violence. More damning still is the extent to which Metz's narration itself is not without its own form of violence. Indeed, Metz must necessarily acquiesce to the inevitability of violent interruption because he founds the *new* political theology on a critical rupture between the present and the future. Moreover, as we have seen, the character of the praxis of political discipleship toward which Metz points is articulated with striking power as an "explosive force," and the fi-

---

130. Metz, *Faith in History and Society*, 163.

131. Metz, *Followers of Christ*, 20. Again, the influence of Heidegger is evident. See Heidegger, *Being and Time*, especially 296–311. However, how this *ars moriendi* can produce freedom and what this freedom looks like is a question that goes unanswered. Metz does characterize this *ars moriendi* as a "preparation for death," something that should at least signal his awareness that it must involve some account of the lived provocations that would make such an act intelligible.

nal and decisive interruption for which Christ stands as the sign is itself a violent in-breaking of the "God before us" into history.[132] The consequences of this configuration of the *new* political theology are severe indeed, and there are points at which Metz seems to recognize this. At one point he claims that "the Christian memory of suffering is in its theological implications an *anticipatory* memory."[133] Elsewhere he seems almost to want to revisit his exclusive stress on the critical-disclosive power of the Christian *memoria* in his claim that "nothing is more urgently needed today than a moral and political imagination springing from a messianic Christianity and capable of being more than merely a copy of accepted political and economic strategies."[134] The question of whether and to what extent Metz's *new* political theology with its attendant apocalyptically inflected aesthetics of violence is able to contribute to this task remains open.

Apocalyptic Convergences and Constellations of Violence

We are now in a position not only to understand how Schmitt uses Metz to reinstate his own political theology after its postwar hibernation but also, more significantly, to understand the complex interrelationship between the founder and re-founder of political theology as it emerged, transfigured, in late modernity. On a very basic level the intellectual fault line between Schmitt and Metz can be provisionally drawn with reference to Hegel. As we have seen, on the one hand, Schmitt's lineage can be traced back through the conservative Catholic political philosophers of the counterrevolution (Bonald, de Maistre, and Donoso Cortés) to what amounts to, in very broad strokes, a political theology of the Hegelian Right.[135] On the other hand, Metz's sympathies in his development of the *new* political theology clearly lie with the revisionary Marxists of the Frankfurt School (Adorno, Benjamin, and Bloch), which binds his intellectual heritage,

---

132. It is noteworthy that, in a forum with then Cardinal Joseph Ratzinger, Metz set himself squarely against any interpretation that suggests, as Origen did, that God can suffer-with. See Ashley, *End of Time?*, especially 50–53.

133. Metz and Moltmann, *Faith and the Future*, 115 (emphasis added).

134. Ibid., 24.

135. Schmitt locates himself in relation to Hegel in Schmitt, *Political Theology II*, 32–33; and Schmitt, "Die andere Hegel-Linie" (July 25, 1957). As we have seen, Schmitt's historical lineage can be traced back even further through Spinoza to Hobbes and back even to Eusebius of Caesarea. For an illuminating comparison of Schmitt and Hegel that is relevant to the present discussion at several points, see Winfield, "Rethinking Politics," 209–25.

again in very broad strokes, to the Hegelian Left.[136] This way of putting the matter quite easily lends itself to interpretations that argue the relationship between Schmitt and Metz is straightforwardly oppositional: Schmitt is read as the conservative heir of the Hegelian Right, while Metz is read as the critical or revolutionary heir of the Hegelian Left.[137] Put this way, it is abundantly clear that Schmitt is indeed a significant interlocutor for Metz in his development of the *new* political theology. Citing Schmitt's *Concept of the Political*, Metz makes his own distinction between Schmitt's political theology and his own reconfiguration that seems to substantiate this basic oppositional framework.

> The universalizability of the memory of suffering safeguards theology in that the memory of suffering is not understood self-referentially but as the memory of the suffering of the other and the remembrance of the victims of the history of freedom. Such a remembrance of the suffering of the other belongs to the cultural reserves of liberated democracy. I emphasize this so explicitly because, if I am not mistaken, the other version of political theology, that of Carl Schmitt, is gaining ground in the contemporary scene (not only in Germany). While the New Political Theology proceeds from the universality of the experience of suffering without being misled by a utopian myth of escape from suffering, the political theology of Schmitt rests on the universality of original sin. This is the basis not only of Schmitt's skepticism towards the capacity of human beings for democratic self-governance, but also for his political premise of the friend-enemy constellation and his picture of a society that at all times is entangled in deep-rooted conflicts and which therefore, to check this constitutive danger, demands the decisionist state.[138]

---

136. Metz locates himself as an heir of the Hegelian Left in his claim that "this is the perspective in which political theology regards the new theory-practice relationship as propounded in the dialectical philosophies of history (with the history of revolutions in mind) in the 19th century, especially since Hegel, and in the tradition of the Hegelian Left" in Metz, "Political Theology," 1240. Although he does not explicitly claim that Metz can be situated among the Left Hegelians and notes that Metz's criticism of modern evolutionary ideology is explicitly anti-Hegelian, Shanks's discussion of Metz's debts and revisions to the basic Hegelian position are illuminating and fit within this general trajectory. See Shanks, *Hegel's Political Theology*, especially 149–55.

137. This is precisely the conceptual strategy adopted in Siebert, "From Conservative to Critical Political Theology," 147–219.

138. Metz, "Religion und Politik," 187–88 (my translation).

46   *The Architectonics of Hope*

This brief excursus is both helpful and revealing. Indeed, this juxtaposition is what leads Derek Simon, in what is one of the few sustained readings of Schmitt and Metz in English, to claim that "the New Political Theology clearly repudiates a Schmittian interaction between religion and politics whereby authoritarian religious traditions are used to legitimate decisionism in support of a violent identity politics of exclusion."[139] Throughout his reading, Simon is at pains to distance himself from Schmitt, but in so doing he implicitly understands Schmitt's involvement with the Nazi Party, of which he was officially a member from May 1933 to December 1936, to be the decisive locus around which his political theology is to be interpreted. Indeed, the rhetorical force of Simon's account reaches its crescendo in his discussion of Schmitt's anti-Judaism where he cites Schmitt's opening address from a 1934 conference on "Judaism and Jurisprudence": "But the most profound and ultimate meaning of this battle, and thus also of our work today, lies expressed in the Führer's sentence: 'In fending off the Jew, I fight for the work of the Lord.'"[140] Coupled with Schmitt's infamous essay entitled "The Führer Protects the Law," which provided juridical support to the bloody purge of June 30, 1934, the so-called "night of the long knives," Simon argues that Schmitt's "anti-Semitism was not an indirect result of his political theology but an intrinsic element."[141] On this basis Simon proceeds to give an account of Metz's *new* political theology as an embrace of a "decentralized identity-politics of difference, empowering responsibility for movements of justice and reconciliation in pluralistic societies through a deliberative social democracy committed to solidarity through the memory of the suffering of others."[142] Without a doubt, the most interesting and helpful aspect of Simon's reading is the attention he draws to a short es-

139. Simon, "New Political Theology of Johann Baptist Metz," 244.

140. Schmitt, "Eröffnung der wissenschaftlichen Vorträge," 14.

141. Simon, "New Political Theology of Johann Baptist Metz," 239. For Schmitt's article, see Schmitt, "Der Führer schützt das Recht," August 1, 1934. The issue of whether and to what extent Schmitt's work in the Weimar period can be directly linked to his subsequent involvement in the Nazi Party is one of the looming questions taken up in the resurgent interest in Schmitt. At its most basic, the fault line can be drawn between Hannah Arendt, who claims that Schmitt was a "convinced Nazi" and Jacob Taubes, who claims that Schmitt merely "flirted with the Nazis." See Arendt, *Origins of Totalitarianism*, 339; and Taubes, *Political Theology of Paul*, 100. Fortuitously, my argument does not require a choice between these two alternatives; rather, the point to be emphasized here is that the connection between Schmitt's political theology, which he formally explicated in 1922 and then again only in 1970, and his "Nazi period" is so strong for Simon that he interprets Schmitt's political theology *in the light of* his writings as "jurist for the Third Reich," a strategy that is by no means as straightforward as Simon assumes and that subsequently informs and impairs his reading of Metz.

142. Simon, "New Political Theology of Johann Baptist Metz," 251.

say that is essentially a reconfiguration of Schmitt's *Roman Catholicism and Political Form* in which Metz claims that "when the authority of suffering is 'represented' it is not an issue of the representation, the political power, but of *political powerlessness*."[143] Helpfully noting that Metz's reflections here are influenced by French political philosophy, especially Jacques Derrida's "weak messianism," Simon argues that Metz "counteracts the reduction of the apocalyptic messiah to the hegemony of the dictator by insisting that it is precisely the role of deliberative democracy to ensure that the empty seat of power remain vacated, so that power remains provisional and distributed throughout the political community, never totalized."[144] This way of putting the matter is quite consistent with the claim that Metz's *new* political theology, in its fundamental orientation, is a *theologia negativa*; however, this is precisely the point at which we are left again to wonder *how* the messianic powerlessness of anamnestic reason and the negative universality of suffering can keep the seat of power empty. By his own admission, Simon notes that "Metz offers no alternative reconstructive account of radical and pluralist democracy arising from the exercise of anamnestic reason."[145] Just as problematic for maintaining a straightforwardly oppositional account of the interrelationship between Schmitt and Metz is Simon's claim that "Metz's implicit social theory of identity politics functions *within* the parameters of the Schmittian logic of inclusion-exclusion."[146] Simon seems to think that Metz somehow escapes Schmitt's logic because the *new* political theology is constructed to "contest its rigidly fixed boundaries and hostile formations"; however, it is also not clear *how* the critical-disclosive power of Metz's negative political theology is able to accomplish this feat.[147] At least peripherally aware of these deficiencies, Simon hesitatingly asks, "Seeking primarily to delegitimate reactionary political theology, is it possible that the New Political Theology fails to move beyond the terms of debate and hermeneutical

---

143. Metz, "Zum 'katholischen Prinzip' der Repräsentation," 194 (emphasis added; my translation).

144. Simon, "New Political Theology of Johann Baptist Metz," 250. Simon does not note, however, that Derrida's work here is profoundly indebted to Schmitt (and Benjamin). See, for example, Derrida, *The Politics of Friendship*, especially 84–91 and 106–67; and *Rogues*, especially 78–107.

145. Simon, "New Political Theology of Johann Baptist Metz," 252.

146. Ibid. (emphasis added). It is also important to note here that Simon's argument that Metz has an implicit social theory of identity politics is contentious since one of the main critiques of Metz's *new* political theology is precisely that it lacks any such social theory. See Ashley, *Interruptions*, 191–99.

147. Simon, "New Political Theology of Johann Baptist Metz," 252.

circles originally defined by Schmitt, even while contradicting them and rendering them untenable?"[148]

The short answer to Simon's question must be an emphatic "Yes!" However, the question itself must be qualified and ultimately reformulated if we are to understand the complex interrelationship between Schmitt and Metz. Thus, while perhaps conceptually useful for thinking about the re-emergence of political theologies and their subsequent developments, the kind of diametrical opposition of the sort Simon provisionally offers conceals as much as it illuminates because it fosters too undifferentiated an account of the interrelationship between Schmitt and Metz. Drawing on the foregoing reflections of the development of both Schmitt's and Metz's respective configurations of political theology, I would like to make the somewhat audacious, disquieting suggestion that there are actually far too many similarities between them for their configurations of political theology to be understood as diametrically opposed. This is not to claim, however, that there is, conversely, a straightforward symmetry at work but rather to suggest that the interrelationship between them is more complex and cannot be accurately captured by the conservative/critical dichotomy. Furthermore, I suggest that the apocalyptic tone that infuses and haunts their respective accounts of political theology represents the most adequate key for understanding the visions of hope they offer. The apocalyptic convergences and constellations of violence in play here can be demonstrated in at least three related ways.

First, both Schmitt's and Metz's respective configurations of political theology are primarily *structural* in nature. Recall that for Schmitt, the link between jurisprudence and theology amounts to a structural analogy that illuminates the shape of the political formation of a particular epoch. Thus, Schmitt's political theology is misunderstood when it is read primarily as an attempt to plumb the depths of the Christian tradition in search of a way to legitimate decisionism. The question for Schmitt is *not* how to apply the rationality of the Roman Catholic Church to questions of modern jurisprudence but rather how to think through modern jurisprudence to locate its own metaphysical assumptions, which are often historically imbibed from one of the most developed constellations of Western rationalism, namely, the Catholic Church. Noting the same formal structure at work here, Derrida suggests that "a framework had to be given to the problematic of the theory of right, to order its 'entwined thematic,' and to discover 'a topology

148. Ibid., 253. Ironically, Simon ends his discussion by suggesting that Metz's *new* political theology might benefit from an engagement with the radical and plural democracy developed in Laclau and Mouffe, *Hegemony and Socialist Strategy*, which is profoundly indebted to Schmitt.

of its concepts."[149] This topological concern is precisely what motivates Schmitt's articulation of the exceptional nature of sovereignty as a kind of limit concept that prioritizes the principle of order over and above any concrete content. Thus, as Karl Löwith rightly notes, "what Schmitt defends is a politics of sovereign decision, but one in which content is merely a product of the accidental *occasio* of the political situation which happens to prevail at the moment."[150] Schmitt's political theology, then, is primarily concerned with creating the conditions under which a decision, *any* decision, can be made; what is essential is not "that a question be decided in one way or another but that it be decided without delay and without appeal."[151] Likewise, Metz's concept of dangerous memory places the utmost importance on the anamnestic *structure* of reason, which is what saves it from being implicated in the vicious dialectic of enlightenment. Indeed, throughout his narration of the *new* political theology Metz is at pains to emphasize its negative-critical structure since "the slightest trace of meaningless suffering in the world as we experience it gives the lie to this whole affirmative ontology and the whole of teleology, and reveals them to be modernity's mythology."[152] It is this negative-critical structure of the *new* political theology that Metz claims has the power to reveal the roots of totalitarian ideologies. This structural concern is by no means limited to Metz's reliance on the revisionary Marxists of the Frankfurt School. Indeed, recall that his Christology is often articulated in structural terms as a logical operation whereby the significance of the incarnation is read as God's definitive action *for* the world, not *in* the world. In fact, it is this earlier reading of the incarnation in *Theology of the World* that subsequently inflects his reading of Bloch. With Schmitt, then, Metz cannot escape the formalist trap and prioritizes function, specifically interruption, over any concrete content.

Second, both Schmitt's and Metz's respective configurations of political theology are animated by a thoroughly *negative theological anthropology*. For Schmitt this can be seen most explicitly in his reading of Hobbes. Indeed, Schmitt expresses his astonishment that Hobbes "appropriated as a characteristic of the condition of peace brought about by the police the formula of Francis Bacon by speaking of man becoming god to man, *homo homini deus*, whereas in the state of nature man was wolf to man, *homo homini lupus*."[153] The innate incapacity to contain the primordial violence between

149. Derrida, *Politics of Friendship*, 115.
150. Löwith, "Occasional Decisionism of Carl Schmitt," 144.
151. Schmitt, *Political Theology*, 56.
152. Metz, *Faith in History and Society*, 104.
153. Schmitt, *State Theory of Thomas Hobbes*, 31. It is noteworthy that Schmitt cites John Neville Figgis's *Divine Right of Kings* to make the point that Hobbes's Leviathan is a secularized version of John Calvin's concept of God.

human beings is what motivates Schmitt's link between sovereignty and the decision. On this point, Metz's assessment that Schmitt's political theology "rests on the universality of original sin" is entirely accurate.[154] However, it is curious that Metz draws our attention to this fact so polemically because his presentation of it in this way raises the question of his own views, which also seem to rest, at least implicitly, on a thoroughly negative theological anthropology. Indeed, Gaspar Martinez goes so far as to argue that an early and distinct feature of Metz's approach is his "radical understanding of human fallibility, of the human inescapable temptation to sin and evil. In this sense, Metz is an atypical Catholic theologian with powerful Protestant intuitions that make his anthropology close to that of Reinhold Niebuhr."[155] We need not quibble here about Metz's relationship to Niebuhr; however, what is important to note is that Metz wonders if "there are not rather forms of man's self-alienation which cannot be resolved by a release from economic-social situations, however successful, and from which man will always draw the 'sorrow of his finiteness'?"[156] While certainly not decisive for Metz in the same way that it is for Schmitt, their respective developments of political theology converge here too.

Third, both Schmitt's and Metz's respective configurations of political theology acquiesce to the *ongoing necessity of violence*. As we have seen above, Schmitt's reliance on the ambiguous figure of the *katechon* and its attendant emphasis on the prevention of chaos and destruction explicitly illuminates the apocalyptic nature of his political theology. However, Schmitt's vision of hope does not consist in the prevention of war as such, which for him is an unavoidable consequence of his theological anthropology, but rather the prevention of civil war. This hope can only be realized with a structured geographical displacement of the inherent violence between human beings, which represents the ever-present possibility of civil war itself, on to a public enemy that is essentially alien and different. It is clear that what fascinates Schmitt most are the borders between norm and exception, "peace" and violence where the real possibility of physical killing lurks behind the political decision. Despite his claims that his political theology is disinterested in either war or pacifism, Schmitt's gaze is most acutely attuned to diagnose the inevitable eruptions of violence. This apocalyptically inflected aesthetic of violence is also evident in Metz's *new* political theology in which we are left gazing squarely on the meaningless ongoing suffering of others with no positive account of the lived provocations that would render

---

154. Metz, "Religion und Politik," 188 (my translation).
155. Martinez, *Confronting the Mystery of God*, 43.
156. Metz, "Controversy about the Future of Man," 223–34.

The Founding and Re-founding of Political Theology   51

such suffering historically meaningful. The hope engendered by Metz's dangerous memory, while bigger than Schmitt's hope because it makes no differentiation between kinds of war, rests in the capacity of anamnestic reason to interrupt the vicious cycles of violence. Thus even while we must recognize a significant difference that emerges especially here, it is still the case that, like Schmitt, Metz gives priority to violence and articulates a political theology that is fundamentally reactionary and lives out of what it opposes. Indeed, Metz's narration is constructed to disrupt the "present-day orgies of violence" that attain the "normative power of the real world."[157]

Understood in the light of these apocalyptic convergences, then, it becomes clear that in no way can the interrelationship between Schmitt and Metz be understood as straightforwardly oppositional. On the contrary, when Schmitt and Metz are read in the light of the apocalyptic element that infuses and haunts their respective accounts of political theology dangerous convergences emerge that otherwise remain hidden. This reading also sheds light on why it is the case that Metz receives such a positive reception in Schmitt's *Political Theology II*, while other, no less "liberal" theologians—such as Ernst Feil, who defends a particular interpretation of Metz's *new* political theology—are routinely dismissed. If both Schmitt's and Metz's configurations of political theology do indeed converge in the ways I have suggested, then the most interesting and significant reason that Schmitt positively cites Metz is not simply that his own political theology can be rehabilitated and whitewashed in and through Metz or that Metz provides a way to "rip Peterson's arrow from its wound," so to speak.[158] Although both these claims have at least some validity, perhaps the programmatic reason Schmitt defends Metz's eschatological orientation is that he sees that the practical implications do not impinge on his own political metaphysics. Could it be that Schmitt, the clever tactician, has accurately diagnosed Metz's *new* political theology as creating, paradoxically, a vacuum of depoliticization in which it subsequently operates? On the one hand, it is difficult to imagine that an apocalyptically expectant praxis of discipleship of the kind Metz urgently attempts to narrate could be so characterized. However, on the other hand, Metz's insistent emphasis on the negative-critical structure of his *new* political theology and his concomitant stress on safeguarding the future from meaningless suffering makes it difficult to imagine that its practical political manifestations can get much further than support groups and organized public protests, all of which presents precisely the grounds

157. Metz, "God: Against the Myth of the Eternity of Time," 38.

158. The reference to Peterson is meant to call to mind his essay on the closure of political theology to which Schmitt's *Political Theology II* responds. See Peterson, "Monotheism as a Political Problem," 68–105.

upon which Schmitt can co-opt and, indeed, deform Metz's vision.[159] This is also the reason why it is, at least, an unfortunate blind spot and, at worst, a symptom of willful blindness that neither Metz himself nor the subsequent developments of political theology have significantly engaged Schmitt because, if these apocalyptic convergences are not simply the result of fanciful reconstruction, they may well continue to exert malign effects that will be all the more difficult to detect because they remain suppressed, hidden from view or, perhaps conveniently, forgotten. That is to say, if Metz's *new* political theology, which musters the power of anamnesis to do theology in the light of Auschwitz, exhibits disturbing convergences with Schmitt's political theology, which was used to justify the horrors of Auschwitz, it is incumbent upon us to reckon with the dangerous effects of this legacy.

By no means does tracing the effects of the legacy of Schmitt's development of political theology, which, as I have argued, infects even the development of the *new* political theology that is ostensibly diametrically opposed to it, mean that these two can be reduced to each other or can be understood as proffering the same vision. The apocalyptic convergences I have outlined do not imply any straightforward symmetry. Indeed, a further advantage of examining the convergences between Schmitt and Metz is that when we take account of these we will be in a position not only to understand their interrelationship in a more nuanced way but also to articulate the differences between the apocalyptic inflections that reverberate through both their accounts of political theology. This process of differentiation, which I suggest is best done in the light of the dangerous convergences that emerge between their positions in the first place, is arguably the more theologically significant move because it illuminates not simply the sites of resistance already operative in Metz's *new* political theology, which could be identified without recourse to the convergences between them, but also, more importantly, the lack of such sites. That is to say, if Schmitt's recourse to Metz effectively reveals dangerous apocalyptic convergences between them, then examining their divergences in the light of these former will, in turn, reveal potential sites of resistance to Schmitt's political theology that would otherwise remain hidden.

It is not unreasonable to think that one of the primary reasons why there has been so little engagement with Schmitt in the theological disciplines is that his theopolitical vision, if it can even properly be called such, is so obviously and manifestly of a different kind to that offered by

---

159. In support of the case for the practical impotence of Metz's *new* political theology, Slavoj Žižek argues that the paradoxical outcome of the massive public demonstrations in London and Washington against the war in Iraq was that the protests in no way prevented the war but, in fact, served to legitimate it in Žižek, "Resistance Is Surrender."

Metz or, indeed, any other self-avowed political theologian since. It is not difficult to see that Schmitt's vision of restraining chaos through the maintenance of the existing political order, which in extreme cases may require the suspension of the law, stands opposed to Metz's vision of a form of political discipleship that springs directly from a Christian messianism that is capable of being more than simply a (re)instantiation of the existing political order. These larger differences notwithstanding, I want to focus on the less visible ones that emerge only in the light of their apocalyptic convergences. I have suggested above that, in the end, both Schmitt and Metz narrate an apocalyptically inflected aesthetics of violence and, in the course of uncovering such a disturbing convergence, I have also hinted that the particular apocalyptic inflection Schmitt gives to his account of violence and suffering and that which Metz gives to his account differ in important ways. Indeed, whereas Schmitt's vision puts its hope in maintaining the political order by apocalyptically displacing the inherent violence between human beings onto an other that is essentially alien and different, Metz's vision is convinced that apocalyptic hope must take the form of a radical critique of the present political order in the name of an unanticipatable future to come. In this sense, Schmitt represents a kind of apocalyptic preservation, while Metz represents a kind of apocalyptic disruption. Despite this not insignificant difference, the question that emerges is whether Metz's disruptive apocalyptic inflection is finally able to subvert the violent theopolitical aporetics articulated by Schmitt or whether, even in its differences, Metz remains in a crucial respect too close to Schmitt's apocalyptic configuration.[160] It should be clear from the foregoing analysis of the convergences between them that I strongly suspect the latter to be the case. Put succinctly, while Metz's form of apocalyptic shows us the need to move beyond Schmitt, it cannot, in the end, show us the way.

---

160. In this sense, the reading of Metz that I have offered diverges from the one offered by Cyril O'Regan just to the extent that I read Metz's convergences with Schmitt—which, to be fair, O'Regan does not consider—to be a kind of doubling of the influence of what O'Regan calls the non-eidetic apocalyptic of Benjamin that, like Schmitt, has very little in it in terms of content. See O'Regan, *Anatomy of Misremembering*, 424–66 and especially 468–517. While I agree with O'Regan that Metz's form of apocalyptic does give us some kind of content, I worry that it veers too close to Schmitt's (and Benjamin's) more nearly exclusive focus on the structural nature of apocalyptic and thereby puts even the limited content it admits in danger of being instrumentalized or, at the very least, subjects the content of its vision to the interruptive function of his form of apocalyptic. There are a number of ways in which this plays out in Metz, perhaps most visibly in the functional nature of his Christology, and I shall return to this struggle between form and content in the final chapter.

CHAPTER 3

Political Theology and the Persuasions of Beauty

Introduction

IF, AS I HAVE argued in the previous chapter, the apocalyptic inflection of Schmitt's political theology is not only germane to the development of the *new* political theology of Metz but also, more importantly, that troubling convergences between these two ostensibly opposed political theologies culminate in what I have called an apocalyptically inflected aesthetics of violence, then a question arises about whether, how, and in what ways this theopolitical vision is modified in subsequent debates. If, as I have suggested, Metz shows us the need to move decisively beyond Schmitt but his form of apocalyptic disruption seems either unable or unwilling to muster much of a positive vision, then are there other subsequent developments in political theology that can show us the way? Again, while the lack of any serious theological engagement with Schmitt presents some difficulties in identifying potential candidates, any number could potentially be called upon on here, including thinkers as diverse as Jürgen Moltmann, Jon Sobrino, and Stanley Hauerwas. However, if the theopolitical vision that both Schmitt and Metz offer is articulated not only in an apocalyptic key but also in an aesthetic key, as I have argued, then it seems reasonable that this elective affinity should guide the choice of subsequent interlocutors, which also helpfully restricts the scope of potential candidates.

Chief among these candidates is undoubtedly the Swiss Catholic theologian Hans Urs von Balthasar, who not only began his career with a three-volume work on apocalyptic in German thought but also attempted to "develop a Christian theology in the light of the third transcendental, that is to say: to complement the vision of the true and the good with that of the beautiful."[1] Following Anselm's claim that theology is the most beautiful of the sciences, Balthasar makes several connections that helpfully bring together the various threads that are integral to the contemporary reconfigurations of political theology with which we shall be concerned in this chapter. Balthasar claims that

> the contemplation of the Trinity reveals that here Hegel's principles of truth and beauty are fulfilled and more than fulfilled as the identity of identity and non-identity, of movement and peace. Strictly speaking, it is this that makes God's power and sovereignty enlightening, convincing, and persuasive.[2]

The connections Balthasar makes here between sovereignty, beauty, persuasion, and peace culminate with the recognition that "if we seek Christ's beauty in a glory which is not that of the Crucified, we are doomed to seek in vain."[3] Given Balthasar's reception as a leading adversary—some may even say reactionary—of dominant trends in post-conciliar Catholicism, helpfully seen for our purposes in his attack on the transcendental Thomism of Karl Rahner, it would hardly seem that his supposed conservatism would hold out much hope for contemporary reconfigurations of political theology.[4] After all, the development of Johann Baptist Metz's *new* political theology is, as we have seen, constructed in the immense wake of Rahner as a critical dialogue with the advances and limitations of the revisionary Marxism of the Frankfurt School that attempted to liberate the political potential of the Gospel from the existential and transcendental enchantments of theology. However, Balthasar's invocation of Hegel should at least give us pause since, as I have argued, political theology re-emerged in late modernity in the work of Schmitt and Metz as reconfigurations of right- and left-wing

---

1. Balthasar, *Glory of the Lord I*, 9. For Balthasar's early three-volume work, see Balthasar, *Apokalypse der deutschen Seele*. For an insightful introduction to this early untranslated work, see Nichols, *Scattering the Seed*.

2. Balthasar, *Glory of the Lord I*, 55.

3. Ibid., 55–56.

4. See Balthasar, *Moment of Christian Witness*, especially 100–113. For a helpful account of the complexity of the tension between Balthasar and Rahner, see Williams, "Balthasar, Rahner and the Apprehension of Being," 86–105.

Hegelianism, respectively.[5] Moreover, these Hegelian reconfigurations take on a specific apocalyptic inflection that attempts to contain and account for the eruptions of violence that have powerfully scarred the very face of history, a form with which Balthasar was very familiar indeed.[6]

Among the most powerful and persuasive of the contemporary apocalyptic reconfigurations of political theology, John Milbank's "postmodern critical Augustinianism" stands out here since it proceeds in a kind of "kindred ambiance" with Balthasar and other members of the Catholic *ressourcement* movement, often pejoratively dubbed *la nouvelle théologie*, most notably Henri de Lubac, as well as with the more distant but no less relevant philosophical satellite Maurice Blondel.[7] Read this way, Milbank's narration of an apocalyptically inflected Trinitarian metaphysics is constructed precisely to "unthink the necessity of violence."[8] Helpfully following up on and extending some of Milbank's best insights with regard to the question of violence, the Eastern Orthodox theologian David Bentley Hart honestly and starkly articulates precisely what is at stake for the Christian tradition in its attempt to instantiate a truly peaceable political theology by asking the following:

5. Cyril O'Regan's magisterial account of Balthasar's apocalyptic resistance to Hegel, which simply cannot be dealt with here, is particularly instructive. See O'Regan, *Anatomy of Misremembering*. See also Quash, "'Between the Brutally Given, and the Brutally, Banally Free,'" 293–318, and his later, more comprehensive work *Theology and the Drama of History*.

6. That I do not pursue Balthasar himself as the primary interlocutor here is in no way an indication that he could not usefully serve this purpose. Indeed, in the wake of Cyril O'Regan's *Anatomy of Misremembering* I take it that Balthasar's credentials as an apocalyptic theologian are decisively established and believe that a Schmitt-Balthasar confrontation, which O'Regan does not offer, would be immensely illuminating. The decision not to pursue such a line is, therefore, made not because Balthsar does not fit but rather because the projects of Milbank and Hart are judged to be closer than Balthasar's to the central theme of violence and to the subdiscipline of political theology. That Balthasar's voice remains throughout the book as a minor thread, however, is evidence of the need for further engagement with him, especially in the light of O'Regan's excavation of Balthasar's resistance to Hegel.

7. See Milbank, "'Postmodern Critical Augustinianism,'" 225–37. The term *la nouvelle théologie* was originally intended as one of derision in Garrigou-Lagrange, "La nouvelle théologie où va-t-elle?," 126–45. While the shape of Milbank's particular apocalyptic inflection will gradually emerge throughout this chapter, it is worthwhile to note at this early stage that many of the figures that positively shape Milbank's vision are themselves being recognized as apocalyptic figures. This is the case not only for Balthasar but also for de Lubac and Nicholas of Cusa. In addition to O'Regan's work on Balthasar cited above, see also his *Theology and the Spaces of Apocalyptic* as well as Flipper, *Between Apocalypse and Eschaton*; and Hoff, *The Analogical Turn*, especially 168–89.

8. Milbank, *Theology and Social Theory*, 411.

> Amid a war of persuasions ... how does Christian rhetoric distinguish itself as a peaceful gesture ... without merely abjuring from persuasion as such, and how does it comport and unfold itself in the midst of this war as the practice of a peace more primordial than every war? ... Or to phrase the question differently, what name can be given to the rhetorical practice of the church that sets it apart from other styles of persuasion?[9]

Drawing out an Augustinian reorientation of vision that in many ways follows Milbank, Hart ostensibly offers up a theological aesthetics, which I will argue is articulated as an apocalyptic Trinitarianism, that is built upon a rhetorical ontology capable of enduring the illusory "peace" of neutrality and to persuade us that Christ brings the "fire of an infinite love."[10] The performance of Hart's narrative outstrips even Milbank's christological poetics in its orchestration but is, likewise, constructed as a theopolitical optics, a way of seeing that indicates a significant reconfiguration of political theology. In comparison with Schmitt and Metz, both Milbank and Hart offer an apocalyptic inflection that, while certainly not eschewing form, makes significant and productive, though not wholly unproblematic, use of the persuasions of beauty and thereby harnesses more than either Schmitt or Metz the aesthetic potentials of apocalyptic theology and its capacity to interrupt the present-day orgies of violence that, as Metz claims, "attain the normative power of the real world."[11]

Understood against the background of the re-emergence of political theology in late modernity in the work of Schmitt and Metz, the question that presses itself upon us, then, is not simply the facile one of *if* Milbank and Hart are able to somehow break out of the hermeneutical circles defined by Schmitt, which they themselves diagnose and consign to the wastebasket of nihilism. The question that begs to be asked is a more complicated and dangerous one, namely, that of *how* and *in what ways* the apocalyptic reconfigurations of political theology enacted and performed by Milbank and Hart seek to overcome the endless cycle of exhaustion and return of violence within which, they claim, all narratives but the Christian one, properly understood, are doomed to remain. Furthermore, if the interrelationship

---

9. Hart, *Beauty of the Infinite*, 414.

10. Ibid., 443. It is of the utmost importance that Hart's rhetorical ontology not be understood as arguing for a peaceful rhetoric, which throws up the question of how Christians can "assume the form of a ceaseless practice of peace" without a rhetoric that participates in such practices. Indeed, Hart's provocative suggestion lies in his embrace of a participatory metaphysics that undermines the assumption that rhetoric as such is *essentially* violent. This will be investigated in more detail below.

11. Metz, "God: Against the Myth of the Eternity of Time," 38.

between Schmitt and Metz cannot be understood antithetically, as I have argued, how can we understand Milbank's outright denunciation of the kind of *aggiornamento* Metz recommends alongside his increasing acknowledgment "that the most incisive thinkers of modernity belong to the political right and that some of them were at least semi-complicit with Nazism?"[12] While Milbank and Hart do not articulate their political theologies primarily with reference to Schmitt or Metz, I suggest that it is immensely helpful to read them as modifying the types of political theology begun by these two German Catholics precisely because they continue to grapple with the relationship between violence and apocalyptic. Indeed, as we will see, the narratives both Milbank and Hart unfold are audibly haunted by an attempt to reconfigure the Schmittian decision, for which they substitute a supposedly less violent notion of persuasion, and by framing their discussions in apocalyptic terms that echo a kind of Metzian interruption.[13]

This struggle, as I have hinted at above, represents a further reconfiguration of the apocalyptically inflected aesthetics of violence seen in Schmitt and Metz that is immensely theologically significant. In one sense, Milbank is more helpful than Hart here because, as is becoming increasingly clear in the development of his work—particularly in *Beyond Secular Order* and its proposed sequel, *On Divine Government*—he quite self-consciously understands himself as a political theologian of the very highest order, that is, as a systematic and philosophical theologian that is not beholden to the presuppositions that delimit the subdiscipline of political theology and is thereby capable of better illuminating the crucial strands of the tradition.[14] Con-

12. Milbank, "Preface to the Second Edition," xiv. For our purposes, it is noteworthy that Milbank names not only Carl Schmitt but also two important Catholic counterrevolutionaries on whom Schmitt relied, namely, Joseph de Maistre and Donoso Cortés.

13. In this way, my reading of Milbank and Hart as reconfiguring the debate between Schmitt and Metz can be understood as an attempt to follow up on and extend Gillian Rose's suggestion that a "strategic Messianism . . . has come to found political theologies based on a proleptic soteriology of the dead" in Rose, *Broken Middle*, 289. Rose explicitly suggests that Metz's notion of dangerous memory bears comparison with Milbank's claim that the city of God "provides a genuine peace by its *memory of all the victims.*" See Milbank, *Theology and Social Theory*, 392 (emphasis added); and Rose, *Broken Middle*, 292n186. Given Schmitt's proximity to both Metz and Milbank, it is instructive to include him in the discussion.

14. See Milbank, *Beyond Secular Order*, 1–18. The outlines of the proposed sequel also appear here, and further specific lines of inquiry to be pursued are also scattered in footnotes throughout the text. For our purposes, perhaps the most interesting among these further lines of inquiry are Milbank's acknowledgment that much of the work he is doing is also "the work of jurists" and his cryptic observation that even given Schmitt's "aberrant" understanding of the relationship between nature and grace he may well have had a clearer sense of their political importance than de Lubac. See *Beyond Secular Order*, 2 and 205n195, respectively.

comitantly, and perhaps even more importantly, while Milbank is certainly more ambivalent about the language of apocalyptic than Metz, whose form of apocalyptic negativity he critiques, he nevertheless self-consciously positions himself as a kind of seer whose work not only shakes the foundations of our understanding of the complex relationship between the religious and the secular but also illuminates what others are finally unable to clearly see.[15] Indeed, *Beyond Secular Order* opens with an explicit elaboration of these formal dimensions:

> human history but rarely comes to the light of day and we remain unable clearly to see ourselves. The task of the genealogist is therefore to penetrate these shadows, and to reach a level where we can regard actions in the light of their presuppositions and theories in the light of their practical tendencies. Yet precisely because this dimension of full daylight is hidden, to try to reach it can appear to be a further venture into the murk ... The assumption of my genealogy is that there can be perspectives from which one can see the homology between human theory and human action. Yet this truly illuminating light is hidden under a divided bushel, and can be glimpsed but fleetingly, because what history most disguises through division into thought and event is the deepest substance of its own occurring. Hence, in the name of truth, one must run the risk that any claim to illuminate human history at depth will present conclusions that can seem excessively abstruse or even implausible. Yet it may be this very abstruseness that is the mark of their authenticity.[16]

In this sense, then, Milbank's work is apocalyptically inflected through and through, and while what he variously refers to as a genealogical or archeological approach genuinely opens up new vistas it also problematically rings the death knell for others. It is in the light of these problems that emerge in Milbank's work that the theopolitical vision of Hart becomes especially important, not only because it points up a significant lacuna in Milbank's political theology but also because it obliquely suggests a way forward. So while this chapter will spend considerably more time excavating Milbank's work, which also seems justified on the basis of its sheer volume, Hart's theopolitical vision is nevertheless crucial for the genealogy I am attempting

---

15. In this sense Milbank's work seems to claim for itself the greatest gift that Ruskin identifies: the ability to see in the dark. See Ruskin, *Works*, 16:180.

16. Milbank, *Beyond Secular Order*, 1–2. The form Milbank's apocalyptic takes very often veers away from the weaker form that seeks to trace these hidden resonances and toward the much stronger form that such a homology necessarily *must* exist. As we shall see below, this tendency is not without significant theological consequences.

to narrate and is arguably, in the end, even more significant in terms of its philosophical and theological nuances than is Milbank's vision. To see why we must first turn to Milbank.

Milbank's Schmittian Theo-Logic I: On the Creation of Enemies

That Milbank belongs to the particular trajectory in which I am suggesting his political theology can be read has not been widely recognized. The mounting body of secondary literature is primarily focused on critically evaluating Milbank's readings of significant interlocutors, notably Augustine and Aquinas, and even those sympathetic to his broader vision take up a combative posture in an attempt "to avoid being steamrolled by John's energetically erudite polemic."[17] While this posture is certainly understandable because, as Stanley Hauerwas quips, "almost no one is free from having his or her ox gored," the extent to which these combative postures are genuinely able to contribute to advancing the debate is seriously hampered because they remain largely stuck in the labyrinth Milbank constructs.[18] In an attempt to avoid getting lost in the dark thickets into which Milbank beckons us to follow, I suggest we will be better served by observing the manner in which Milbank himself engages his interlocutors. To do so, I would like to begin by suggesting that Milbank's avowed "genealogical" or "archaeological" approach proceeds by way of a double movement that simultaneously creates enemies that, in turn, serve as the backdrop against which a positive theological program is constructed and interpretively reifies friends by foreclosing on possible alternative readings.[19] This double movement

---

17. Lash, "Where Does Holy Teaching Leave Philosophy?," 433. A representative sampling of the critical reception of *Theology and Social Theory* can be found in several journals that devoted special issues to Milbank's work. See *Modern Theology* 8, no. 4 (1992); *New Blackfriars* 73, no. 861 (1992); and *Arachne* 2, no. 1 (1995).

18. Hauerwas, "Creation, Contingency, and Truthful Nonviolence," 188.

19. See Milbank, *Theology and Social Theory*, 3; and Milbank, *Beyond Secular Order*, 2. This method, which can also be understood as a style or hermeneutic disposition, is by no means unique to either *Theology and Social Theory* or *Beyond Secular Order* and is reflected in much, if not all, of Milbank's work. Furthermore, this method is what allows Milbank in *Theology and Social Theory* to claim that "secular discourse does not just 'borrow' modes of expression from religion but is actually *constituted* in its secularity by 'heresy' in relation to orthodox Christianity," a refrain repeated in *Beyond Secular Order* in his claim that "what is apparently 'secular' . . . in reality derives from specific currents of theology, questionable from the point of view of the most authentic Christian tradition." See Milbank, *Theology and Social Theory*, 3; and Milbank, *Beyond Secular Order*, 3, respectively.

Political Theology and the Persuasions of Beauty 61

illuminates what I will call the Schmittian character of Milbank's theo-logic. The glaring example that stands out as representative of Milbank's entire *oeuvre* is undoubtedly the enormous millstone hung around the neck of John Duns Scotus, who is excoriated for establishing "a radical separation of philosophy from theology by declaring that it was possible to consider being in abstraction from the question of whether one is considering created or creating being" that eventually "generated the notion of an ontology and an epistemology unconstrained by, and transcendentally prior to, theology itself."[20] Despite the fact that Scotus is, perhaps, Milbank's enemy *par excellence*, I suggest that by drawing attention to the way Milbank neatly parses arguments that arise in post-conciliar Catholicism we will not only be able to see how his Schmittian theo-logic functions but will also thereby see why his political theology is helpfully read as a reconfiguration of the debates that re-emerged in late modernity with Schmitt and Metz.

To claim, as I have, that the indebtedness of Milbank's political theology to Schmitt and Metz has not been widely recognized is not to claim, conversely, that there are significant barriers inhibiting such a recognition.[21] Indeed, Milbank's proximity to and preference for certain strands of French Thomism, broadly associated with *la nouvelle théologie*, is evidence of important historical continuities and overlaps.[22] Even before the publication

20. Milbank, "Knowledge," 23. Milbank's denigration of late medieval nominalist philosophy, for which Scotus stands as the exemplar, punctuates his work, and I cite this example in particular because it shows that his interest in rehabilitating these two Lutheran thinkers consists precisely in the fact that, *contra* Luther, they called into question the entire post-Scotist legacy. Here again a Schmittian theo-logic is at work. For a fuller explanation of Scotus's significance that follows up on Milbank's arguments, see also Pickstock, *After Writing*, 121–40; and Pickstock, "Duns Scotus," 543–74. For an alternative account that aims to challenge this understanding of post-Heideggerian onto-theology and, importantly, of Scotus's central place in this narrative of decline, see in particular the work of Richard Cross: "'Where Angels Fear to Tread,'" 7–41; *Duns Scotus on God*; and "Duns Scotus and Suárez at the Origins of Modernity," 65–97. In broad strokes, the disputed question here, as Cross narrates it, is whether Scotus's theory of the univocity of being is to be understood semantically (as Cross would have it) or ontologically (as Milbank and Pickstock read it). Whether or not Cross's argument that reading Scotus through Heidegger amounts to a damaging distortion is ultimately convincing, or indeed if his own reading simply opts to read Scotus through Kant, what is most interesting for our purposes is that Cross too notes that Milbank's reading of Aquinas is just as suspect as his reading of Scotus since it is driven by an anxiety to find a hero.

21. The only article that I am aware of that explicitly treats Schmitt, Metz, and Milbank together, albeit in a much looser way, is Souletie, "Le statut contemporain du théologico-politique," 205–23.

22. For a historically nuanced account of the rise of *la nouvelle théologie*, see Nichols, "Thomism and the Nouvelle Théologie," 1–19. See also Boersma, *Nouvelle Théologie and Sacramental Ontology*. Although he makes no explicit connections between them,

of *Theology and Social Theory* (1990), which must certainly be recognized as a landmark not only in Milbank's work but also in late twentieth-century theology more generally, Metz figures as an important background figure, often simply lumped together with Rahner, against which Milbank develops readings of Aquinas and of Christian socialism. In his attempt to reconsider the post-Kantian character of modern theology, Milbank develops a reading of Aquinas's doctrine of analogy that explicitly aims to eradicate the pervasive transcendentalist presuppositions that have rendered it finally incomprehensible. At pains to emphasize that for Aquinas the possibility of analogy "is *only* comprehensible in terms of the absence of any 'critical,' transcendentalist claim to have surmounted finitude," Milbank explicitly develops his argument *contra* Metz.[23] Properly understood for Milbank, a defense of Aquinas's doctrine of analogy must be grounded in a metaphysics of participation without making recourse to some version of the good that consists in a self-transcending rational nature—precisely what he believes Metz's theological anthropology fails to accomplish.[24] This strenuous objection to what may be called a transcendentalist anthropology is, likewise, mounted in Milbank's sharp distinction between Christian Marxism and Christian socialism, albeit with further important nuances. The crux of the issue for Milbank lies in a series of displacements with respect to the critique of capitalism. Simply put, for Christian Marxism, unlike Christian socialism, freedom displaces justice, anthropology displaces ecclesiology, and dialectics displaces ethics.[25] While certainly still important for Milbank's

---

Milbank identifies three contexts in which the phrase "political theology" re-emerged in the twentieth century: in the Schmitt-Peterson debate, in the German "political theology" of the 1960s, and in relation to the question of "political Augustinianism." See Milbank, "Political Theology," 1251–53.

23. Milbank, "'Between Purgation and Illumination,'" 171 (emphasis added). Reprinted in *Word Made Strange*, 7–35. Milbank's Schmittian theo-logic is exemplified again in the manner in which he plays Aquinas off Kant: "Knowledge of God for Aquinas is change within the circumstances of a certain formal, 'beautiful' constancy of teleological development; knowledge of God for Kant is confirmation of this world as it is, or else a sublime aspiration which is a contentless bad infinitude, unrelated to actual social behavior" (ibid., 172). Note also the role of the aesthetic that, as we will see, comes to play a central role in Milbank's reconfiguration of political theology.

24. Milbank gives no textual support for his claim here that Metz's theological anthropology is insufficiently theological despite the fact that Metz's *Christliche Anthropozentrik*, in which Metz develops a highly relevant reading of Aquinas, would have been a natural and interesting point of engagement. This tendency plagues Milbank's work generally and is in evidence even in cases where he does indicate supplementary evidence to support his claims insofar as he often simply cites books or articles *in toto*.

25. Milbank, "On Baseless Suspicion," 9. Reprinted in *The Future of Love*, 112–32. Milbank credits Hauerwas with impressing upon him the importance of this distinction. See Hauerwas, "Some Theological Reflections on Gutierrez's Use of 'Liberation,'" 67–76.

argument, Rahner fades more distantly into the background and Metz's recourse to Marxism is foregrounded to highlight the sense in which, for Christian Marxism, the critique of capitalism is indirect, that is to say, insufficiently Christian. Milbank reads Metz's positive evaluation of Enlightenment freedom as a consequence of his recourse to Marxism, which is, as we have seen above, historically inaccurate since it is present much earlier in the development of his Christology such that the Marxist influence is, at best, an intensification of a tendency *already present* in his work. That aside, it is particularly instructive that Milbank characterizes Christian Marxism, and along with it Metz's *new* political theology, as subscribing to a "myth of apocalyptic negativity" that simply substitutes "a theoretical story in which history gradually unravels a condition of absolutely spontaneous peace and freedom" for a conception of practical reason rooted in the importance of "already-existing communities."[26] Taken together, these two essays certainly provide a warrant for reading Milbank's earlier work in the wake of Metz.[27] Moreover, it is also clear that Milbank is employing a kind of Schmittian theo-logic to construct his arguments since they are predicated upon the creation of enemies against which a constructive theological proposal is asserted, a procedure that represents, as we will see, a major component of his apocalyptic reconfiguration of political theology.

In a characteristically sweeping and programmatic essay, Milbank has more recently claimed that today "it is the debate within Catholic theology that is the vital one, to such a degree that a definitively Protestant theology is now extinct."[28] With apologies to Stanley Hauerwas, whose writings are apparently still "decisive" in some now nonvital way, Milbank's argument here is really just a more explicit acknowledgment of long-held intuitions and a continuation of his earlier work. The extent to which this is the case can be helpfully seen, for our purposes, in Milbank's parsing of what he calls the Catholic integralist revolution, into which the two earlier essays discussed above fit beautifully. Tipping his hand, Milbank claims that:

---

26. Milbank, "On Baseless Suspicion," 7–8. It is also instructive to note here that the stress on justice coupled with an emphasis on *phronesis* is what enables Milbank to argue that "Christian socialism has often been a mode of ecclesiology" (ibid., 8).

27. It is noteworthy that the first essay was written for inclusion in a Festschrift for Donald MacKinnon and that the second was reprinted in the section that ostensibly treats "theology and British politics" in *The Future of Love*, which suggests not only that they form part of what Milbank will later call his abiding interest in the minority report of British intellectual history but also, curiously, that Metz (and Rahner) play a significant negative role in this minority report. This is but further evidence of a Schmittian theo-logic operative in his work.

28. Milbank, "New Divide," 26.

> Once the dialogue with Marxism as an "autonomous" science is ended, and we return to the more important matter of Christian socialism, then it can be seen that the French, not the Rahnerian version of integralism, provides the basis for a true political theology: that is to say, a theological critique of society and politics. Only the French version truly abandons hierarchies and geographies in theological anthropology, because it refuses even to "formally distinguish" a realm of pure nature in concrete humanity.[29]

While it is clear that Milbank strongly prefers the so-called French version of integralism over the German, or Rahnerian, version, what is fundamentally at stake here is Milbank's insight that a truly revolutionary theological politics has everything to do with how the relationship between nature and grace is understood. We will return to this in greater detail below, particularly with respect to Milbank's revisionary reading of Henri de Lubac, so it will suffice to see here the great chasm opened up between these two versions of integralism. Explicitly aware of the crudeness with which his turn of phrase summarizes the argument, Milbank makes his differentiation by claiming that "the French version 'supernaturalizes the natural,' whereas the German version 'naturalizes the supernatural.'"[30] The heart of the problem with the Rahnerian version, which Milbank claims is accepted universally by both political and liberation theologians, is that it formally re-inscribes a neoscholastic account of grace that is superadded to a self-sufficient concept of pure nature already complete within itself despite appearing to reject such an account with recourse to the idea of a supernatural existential that is meant to preserve the gratuity of grace while avoiding extrinsicism.[31] This way of putting the matter clearly owes much to Maurice Blondel since, as de Lubac reminds us, "he is the one who launched the decisive attack on the dualist theory which was destroying Christian thought."[32] However, on Milbank's reading, Rahner's attempt pays insufficient attention to Blondel and merely reworks "the neo-scholastic scheme of two parallel supernatural systems, but in the terms of transcendental philosophy."[33] As we have seen

---

29. Milbank, *Theology and Social Theory*, 208.

30. Ibid., 207.

31. For Rahner's account of this relationship and his proposal of the supernatural existential, see Rahner, "Antwort," 141–45. This article was translated, revised and reprinted as Rahner, "Concerning the Relationship between Nature and Grace," 297–317. See also Rahner, "Nature and Grace," 165–88. For Blondel's account of extrinsicism, to which Milbank's argument is indebted, see Blondel, *History and Dogma*, 226–31.

32. De Lubac, *Brief Catechesis*, 38.

33. Milbank, *Theology and Social Theory*, 222.

above, here again it is precisely this transcendentalist residue from Rahner's account of grace to which Milbank vehemently objects because it bequeaths to all subsequent political theologies an inability to offer a truly theological critique of society and politics in its uncritical embrace of Marxist social theory as the basis upon which theology itself must be founded. The upshot of all this is that political theologies that follow Rahner's version of integralism become locked into a kind of Weberian inspired vision of the political in which cataclysmic social revolution is the means for the promotion of ever greater individual liberties and thereby tend to become little more than a "faint regulative gloss upon Kantian ethics" based on an "ahistorical metaphysics of human subjectivity."[34] For Milbank, this kind of theopolitical optics trades in a "methodological atheism" that short-circuits the sought-after unity between theory and practice despite the strong emphasis on foundational *praxis* characteristic of political and liberation theologies.[35] In stark contrast, the French version, which Milbank unfolds by way of an immensely significant excursus on Blondel that is subsequently modified with recourse to de Lubac and Balthasar, is able to overcome these difficulties by inseparably fusing thought and action together in a "supernatural pragmatism" that is finally able to found a truly theological ontology.[36] Milbank accomplishes this by using Blondel's phenomenology of action not simply to highlight the sense in which the question of the supernatural must be raised within philosophy itself but also, more significantly, to argue "that all thought is participation in divine creative action and, at the same time, that all creation is *kenosis*, a self-emptying mediation."[37] Coupled with de Lubac's stress on the irreducible paradox of an always already graced nature that can never be demanded but always comes to us as gift, this represents, so Milbank tells us, *the* definitive overcoming of the grace/nature duality that has plagued modern theology.[38] Helpfully elucidating the

34. Ibid., 208 and 223, respectively.

35. Ibid., 249. Again, this way of putting the matter owes much to Blondel, who claims that "every separated philosophy will remain deceived by false appearances." Blondel, *Action (1893)*, 442. Not incidentally, this quotation finds pride of place atop the homepage of the Centre of Theology and Philosophy website (http://theologyphilosophycentre.co.uk/), a research center directed by Milbank at the University of Nottingham.

36. Milbank, *Theology and Social Theory*, 209. Indeed, for Milbank it is "Blondel, more than anyone else, [that] points us beyond secular reason" (ibid., 219).

37. Ibid., 215.

38. Ibid., 219. It is worthwhile to note here that Milbank subsequently softens his position with respect to Rahner and concedes that he was able to overcome the nature/grace duality only "in a very flawed manner" in Milbank, "Intensities," 492n75. However, even in this later essay it is clear that it is de Lubac, not Rahner, who recommences

issue here with respect to de Lubac's theological anthropology, Balthasar argues that it is "the paradox of the spiritual creature that is ordained beyond itself by the innermost reality of its nature to a goal that is unreachable for it and that can only be given as a gift of grace."[39] Thus cleansed of the transcendentalist residue that plagued Rahner's account and coupled with Balthasar's theological aesthetics that insists much more strongly on the concrete historical form that this "supernatural pragmatics" must take if it is to be genuinely capable of a theological critique of society and politics we are now in a position to see in more detail how Milbank fills out the content of his theopolitical vision as an apocalyptically inflected Trinitarian metaphysics.[40]

However, before moving on to this task we must briefly pause to take account of the consequences of this mode of argumentation. The difference here cannot be underestimated since Milbank hangs the success or failure of his argument precisely on the extent to which this dualist reading of the Catholic integralist revolution can be maintained and, moreover, seeks to strengthen his reading by entrenching the great chasm he opens up between the French and German versions. Indeed, with regard to their sociopolitical implications these two versions of integralism become *opposites* and it is here, precisely, that the force of Milbank's argument finds its greatest purchase.[41] On the one hand, the foundational *praxis* that follows the Rahnerian version merely baptizes Marxism as "that consoling doctrine which can appear to suggest that the aims of Christian ethics and of Christian socialism can be achieved, indeed *must be* achieved, through the apparently alien workings of secularization and politicization."[42] On the other hand, the supernatural pragmatics that follow the French version alone enables a "directly theological discourse about the socio-historical" and is thereby able to avoid the pre-theologically determined site of a transcendentalist metaphysics.[43] Thus we can see here an explicit outworking of Milbank's Schmittian theo-logic insofar as his argument is predicated on a fundamental distinction, indeed

---

"the real theological revolution of the twentieth century" (ibid, 464). The category of paradox so central for de Lubac has become increasingly important for Milbank as well, as we will see in greater detail below.

39. Balthasar, *Theology of Henri de Lubac*, 13.

40. Ironically, Milbank's development of a Trinitarian metaphysics prescinds from this insight precisely insofar as he does not follow Balthasar's radical christocentrism. Milbank's move beyond Balthasar will be investigated in more detail below.

41. Milbank, *Theology and Social Theory*, 223.

42. Ibid., 243.

43. Ibid., 249. Or, again, "the 'priority of praxis' . . . has nothing to do with such a 'pragmatism': on the contrary, by rendering insignificant any specifically Christian practice, it makes the content of Christianity essentially theoretical, and prevents a unity of theory and practice altogether."

on an antithesis that lives out of what it opposes and in this way mirrors Schmitt's famous friend/enemy distinction and its concomitant need for decision.[44] Moreover, should we not regard it as more than a little ironic that the definitive overcoming of the nature/grace duality that Milbank argues for is unfolded on the basis of a dualist reading of the Catholic integralist revolution? Perhaps more significantly, if Milbank's Schmittian theo-logic informs and shapes his ontology, as we have briefly seen above, then what effect does this have on his development of his theopolitical vision? What becomes evident as we investigate his Schmittian theo-logic further is that his interpretive reification of friends reinforces the sense in which his political theology is motivated by the need for a formal conflictual symmetry insofar as possible alternative readings that may weaken the degree of intensity between antitheses are decisively foreclosed upon.

Bursting the Bonds of Nature: Blondel, de Lubac, and the Possibility of a Political Theology of the Supernatural

To be sure, Milbank is not uncritical in parsing the arguments in his reading of the Catholic integralist revolution. Indeed, Blondel is criticized for failing to take seriously enough the confrontation and refusal of nihilism, de Lubac retains too many ambiguities with respect to the concrete form the priority of grace takes in shaping our lives, and, most seriously, Balthasar's ontology remains insufficiently capable of incorporating the postmodern insights toward which Blondel's supernatural pragmatics point.[45] Perhaps even more to the point for our purposes, Milbank contends that "de Lubac and von Balthasar do not fully follow through the implications of their integralism, precisely to the degree that they fail to develop a social or a political theology."[46] Despite these reservations, Milbank is quite consistent in stressing that following up on the theological revolution of de Lubac, which he claims "was as real as it was stealthy," holds out the most promise for the development of a political theology that fully embraces a participatory Trinitarian metaphysics.[47] Thus I suggest that it will be most instructive

44. For Schmitt's famous distinction, see Schmitt, *Concept of the Political*, 26. Commenting on Milbank's affinities with Joseph de Maistre, but without mentioning the obvious connection to Schmitt, Douglas Hedley notes that "the temper of Milbank's work is deeply indebted to the German antihumanistic pathos of *Entscheidung* (decision) of the 1920s and 1930s" in Hedley, "Radical Orthodoxy and Apocalyptic Difference," 100.

45. Milbank, *Theology and Social Theory*, 213–20.

46. Ibid., 209.

47. Milbank, "Last of the Last," 13. This essay is revised and reprinted in *Being Reconciled*, 105–37.

to see how Milbank develops this trajectory in particular and, moreover, that the way in which Milbank draws out the consequences of the theological revolution recommenced by de Lubac represents an overlooked yet very significant intervention into the debates surrounding the category of the gift, which we will touch on here only in a tangential way.[48]

To understand Milbank's unfolding of de Lubac's theological revolution we must begin by investigating the background against which it is set, namely, the phenomenology of action developed by Maurice Blondel.[49] The reason for this is twofold: first, because Milbank's creative use of his work is of immense significance to his broader project—indeed, Fergus Kerr rightly recognizes that Blondel "remains the hero of *Theology and Social Theory*"—and second, because de Lubac himself is so profoundly influenced by and appreciative of Blondel's work.[50] Perhaps the most helpful entry to understanding Blondel's significance, especially with respect to the use Milbank makes of his work, is to note that his phenomenology of action can be profitably read as a confrontation with Hegel's *Phenomenology*.[51] Although this comparison is not without its difficulties, it is instructive because Milbank too acknowledges that "*Theology and Social Theory* is a kind of initial

---

48. Milbank himself gestures toward this kind of reading in his comparison of de Lubac and Marcel Mauss in Milbank, *Suspended Middle*, 88–92. Milbank's foray into the debates surrounding the much-discussed category of the gift cannot be dealt with here in any comprehensive way, but a series of articles that span more than a decade testify to its importance. See, for example, Milbank, "Can a Gift Be Given?," 119–61; "Only Theology Overcomes Metaphysics," 325–43; "Socialism of the Gift, Socialism by Grace," 532–48; "The Soul of Reciprocity Part One," 335–91; "The Soul of Reciprocity Part Two," 485–507; "The Gift of Ruling," 212–38; and "Fictioning Things," 1–37. It is not insignificant that Milbank's development of an ontology of the gift represents a shift in emphasis from his earlier focus on an ontology of peace in *Theology and Social Theory*.

49. The most comprehensive account of the life and work of Blondel is Blanchette, *Maurice Blondel*. For more succinct overviews, see Dru, "The Importance of Maurice Blondel," 118–29; Bouillard, "The Thought of Maurice Blondel," 392–402; and Baum, "The Blondelian Shift," in *Man Becoming*, 1–36.

50. Kerr, "Catholic Response," 57. Indeed de Lubac claims that "Latin theology's return to a more authentic tradition has taken place in the course of the last century. We must admit that the main impulse for this return came from a philosopher, Maurice Blondel" in *Brief Catechesis*, 37.

51. In his very helpful introduction to Blondel's *Letter on Apologetics and History of Dogma*, Alexander Dru notes that Blondel was explicitly aware of this parallel and was not disconcerted by it in "Introduction," 16–17. Additionally, Henri Bouillard notes similarities in the dialectic enacted by both Hegel and Blondel, albeit not without significant differences, in Bouillard, *Blondel and Christianity*, 212–13. See also the extensive comparison made by the Swiss Jesuit cousin of Balthasar, Henrici, *Hegel und Blondel*. Also helpful here is McNeill, *Blondelian Synthesis*, especially 237–64.

Political Theology and the Persuasions of Beauty 69

attempt to re-do Hegel in a non-gnostic fashion."[52] Blondel's phenomenology begins polemically by asking:

> Yes or no, does human life make sense, and does man have a destiny? I act, but without even knowing what action is, without having wished to live, without knowing exactly either who I am or even if I am. This appearance of being which flutters about within me, these light and evanescent actions of shadow, bear in them, I am told, an eternally weighty responsibility, and that, even at the price of blood, I cannot buy nothingness because for me it is no longer. Supposedly then, I am condemned to life, condemned to death, condemned to eternity! Why and by what right, if I did not know it and did not will it?[53]

There is an intense yearning here that lies at the heart of Blondel's philosophical enterprise since he recognizes that in all of our acting there is an attempt to reach beyond the simple objects that we will. Again in a manner not unlike Hegel, Blondel develops his phenomenology of action by successively passing through a series of insufficiencies and ultimately arrives at the conclusion that "all that has gone before results in making us conscious of an incurable disproportion between the *élan* of the will and the human end of action."[54] For Blondel, then, we are faced with a supreme option, what he calls the "one thing necessary" that is the key to the genesis of the idea of the supernatural, which is where he decisively parts company with Hegel, whom he considers the modern immanentist philosopher *par excellence*.[55] Henri Bouillard helpfully notes that Blondel's phenomenology of action successively establishes not only the insufficiency of the natural order but also, significantly, "the absolute necessity of remaining open to the divine action."[56] Thus we should not be surprised that the ultimate conclusion that results from the immanent journey of the human will enacted by Blondel's phenomenology is that "the fullness of philosophy consists, not in a presumptuous self-sufficiency, but in the study of its own powerlessness."[57] It is precisely this insight that leads Milbank to highlight the sense in which "Blondel associates all action with self-immolation and sacrifice: by acting/

---

52. Milbank, "Preface to the Second Edition," xv. The interaction with Hegel, or rather the use of some interpretation of Hegel, becomes even more significant in Milbank's more recent work, which will be discussed below.
53. Blondel, *Action (1893)*, 3.
54. Ibid., 358.
55. Ibid., 314.
56. Bouillard, *Blondel and Christianity*, 60.
57. Blondel, *Action (1893)*, 361–62.

thinking we grope towards a synthesis which seems 'right' to us, and yet is not originally intended by us, but only 'occurs' to us out of the future plentitude of being."[58] Here already we can see Milbank pushing the limits of Blondel's thought because he takes the logic of action to imply two things: first, that the self-surpassing supernatural character of every action means that there is a more than merely arbitrary synthesis of divine grace with the human will, and second, that this synthesis is rightly understood as the ever-renewed mediation of love.[59] To be sure, this is not an unfair characterization, especially given Blondel's comment that "we cannot arrive at God, affirm Him truly . . . except by belonging to Him and by sacrificing all the rest to Him."[60] However, Milbank understands this ever-renewed mediation of love, which is constituted by offering ourselves to others, in Trinitarian terms as that which founds an "ontology of supernatural charity" and thereby goes beyond Blondel's phenomenology of action in implying that supernatural grace is not simply required but rather always already present.[61] In this way it becomes clear that Blondel anticipates and opens the door for de Lubac's theological revolution since what is required is a transposition of his supernatural pragmatics into the more specific practice of the tradition of Christianity, which, as Milbank tells us, "can now assume all the traditional tasks of philosophy as metaphysics."[62]

Before moving on to see how Milbank accomplishes this, however, it is necessary to attend to the political context in which these arguments are embroiled, especially since Blondel's supernatural pragmatism was further developed in the context of a renewed understanding of the relationship between nature and grace that was to become so central for de Lubac. Given the immense significance that Milbank attributes to Blondel

---

58. Milbank, *Theology and Social Theory*, 214. That this remains central for Milbank, and again argued for in contradistinction to Rahner, is in evidence also in Milbank, *Beyond Secular Order*, 213 and 224.

59. Milbank, *Theology and Social Theory*, 214–15. Following Blondel, Milbank argues that this kind of mediating action is the key to understanding Leibniz's notion of the *vinculum substantiale* but, curiously, he does not cite Blondel's secondary Latin thesis submitted alongside *Action (1893)* or its subsequent French translation. For a helpful overview of Blondel's thesis on the *vinculum substantiale*, see Blanchette, *Maurice Blondel*, especially 95–97 and 346–53. David Grumett argues, to great effect, that attention to the often overlooked influence of Leibniz allows us to understand more fully the connection between the theopolitical motivations at the heart of both Blondel's phenomenology of action and de Lubac's paradox of the supernatural and their eucharistic foundations, in Grumett, "Blondel, Modern Catholic Theology and the Leibnizian Eucharistic Bond," 561–77.

60. Blondel, *Action (1893)*, 404.

61. Milbank, *Theology and Social Theory*, 215.

62. Ibid., 217.

in paving the way for the development of a truly theological politics in the twentieth century, it is more than a little curious that he devotes so little attention to the sociopolitical context that shaped much of his work. Indeed, all Milbank sees fit to tell us is that Blondel was utterly opposed to the nationalist-monarchist program developed by Charles Maurras and the *Action Française*.[63] While it is clear that a Schmittian theo-logic is again operative, what is especially illuminating in Milbank's discussion are the Blondelian tendencies that he sees exemplified in the Italian Catholic opponent of Mussolini, Luigi Sturzo. Still highly critical of what he calls a "residual positivism" in Sturzo's sociology of the supernatural, Milbank sees him following up on Blondel's insights just to the extent that he argues a true sociology must speak of the supernatural community, that is, of the Church. As with his reading of Blondel, Milbank pushes this insight well beyond any intention Sturzo might have had in his seemingly audacious claim that "there can only be sociology if an explanation is offered for the modes of human association, but this depends . . . on the recognition of one particular mode of association as normative, and as the goal towards which all human societies are tending. From this perspective, *that of the Church*, one is able to read all human society as 'supernatural' or as groping towards the 'true life' of proper relation to God and to fellow human beings."[64] What we can see in Milbank's assessment here is a significant insight that comes to light much more explicitly in his discussion of de Lubac and, indeed, one that punctuates all his work, namely, that any true theological politics will always be a mode of ecclesiology.

Turning back to Blondel, much of his work after his controversial thesis on *Action (1893)* is devoted not simply to defending it against the reigning neo-Thomism of the day but also to working out more precisely how nature and the supernatural could be reintegrated. Particularly at issue was

---

63. For a helpful historical account that places Blondel firmly within the context of French social Catholicism and highlights his disputes with the Jesuit Pedro Descoqs, who offered a defense of a Catholic alliance with the *Action Française*, see Bernardi, *Maurice Blondel, Social Catholicism, and Action Française*. Bernardi is right to note the sense in which there are striking similarities between the Blondel-Descoqs debate, on the one hand, and some of the current criticisms leveled against Milbank's project, on the other; however, his own criticisms of "Milbank's integralism" (ibid., 266) are almost wholly based on a cursory reading of secondary material and are tendentious at best. See also Dru, "From the Action Française to the Second Vatican Council," 226–45.

64. Milbank, *Theology and Social Theory*, 224–25. See also Sturzo, *The True Life*. Indeed, Milbank sees his subsequent promulgation of theology itself as a social science (and, moreover, as queen of the sciences) as a properly theological extension of Sturzo's work. See, for example, Milbank, *Theology and Social Theory*, 380–82.

Blondel's method of immanence, and his 1896 *Letter on Apologetics* helpfully clarifies what is at stake:

> In a phrase which must be explained but which indicates at once the seriousness of the conflict, modern thought, with a jealous susceptibility, considers the notion of *immanence* as the very condition of philosophizing; that is to say, . . . that nothing can enter into a man's mind which does not come out of him and correspond in some way to a need for development and that there is nothing in the nature of historical or traditional teaching or obligation imposed from without which counts for him, no truth and no precept which is acceptable, unless it is in some sort autonomous . . . On the other hand, nothing is Christian and Catholic unless it is *supernatural*, not only in the simple metaphysical sense of the word . . . but strictly supernatural, that is to say, beyond the power of man to discover for himself and yet imposed on his thought and on his will.[65]

Thus despite the worry that Blondel's method of immanence somehow occludes the transcendent, Balthasar is right to point out that his "purpose was to burst the bonds of the whole sphere of nature to reach that of revelation—which had already occurred in fact and was the very foundation of the whole sphere of nature in the first place."[66] Thus, as Blondel says, "when we study the close-knit system of our thoughts, it becomes apparent that the very notion of immanence is realized in our consciousness only by the effective presence of the notion of the transcendent."[67] For Milbank, the key to unlocking the political potential of these insights is the recognition that Blondel's phenomenology of action is focused on a kind of emanative *poiesis* in which our thought is, as he says, "entirely dependent upon its participation in a transcendent plentitude of *realized action, of thought as word and deed*."[68] It is precisely this notion of *poiesis*, of action as the gateway to transcendence, that is able to exceed the much-vaunted "priority of *praxis*" characteristic of political and liberation theologies which, so Milbank tells us, render Christian practice insignificant and make the

---

65. Blondel, *Letter on Apologetics*, 151–52.

66. Balthasar, *Theology of Karl Barth*, 341.

67. Blondel, *Letter on Apologetics*, 158. Oliva Blanchette helpfully notes that Blondel's method of immanence, which is nothing but the unfolding of the dialectic enacted in his phenomenology of action, creatively combines Spinoza and Hegel in a "critique of immanent critique" to show that thought "must go beyond itself and find its truth in something more than just itself," in Blanchette, *Maurice Blondel*, 115–16.

68. Milbank, *Theology and Social Theory*, 218 (emphasis added).

Political Theology and the Persuasions of Beauty 73

content of Christianity essentially theoretical because they sunder the unity of thought and action.[69]

Having thus established the significance of Blondel for Milbank's project we are now in a position to understand his highly controversial reading of de Lubac.[70] Interestingly, Milbank claims that "when one turns from Blondel to the later *nouvelle théologie* . . . there is a marked tendency to prescind from the political, and to insulate the Church from wider social processes."[71] This is a striking judgment, not least because Milbank sees political parallels between "de Lubac's wartime emergency *Surnaturel*" and "Dietrich Bonhoeffer's wartime emergency *Letters and Papers from Prison*."[72] Given Milbank's overt enthusiasm for rehabilitating the theopolitical potential of de Lubac's work, one would expect that he would seek to foreground its social, historical, and political embeddedness; however, as

69. See ibid., 249–52. Milbank directs his vitriol primarily toward the liberation theologians here. However, he fails to note that, at least for Gustavo Gutiérrez, the Marxist influence stands alongside an appreciation of Blondel such that his critique of Gutiérrez's notion of foundational *praxis* is more problematic than it would be if he had directed it primarily toward Metz, who has no such appreciation for Blondel. For Gutiérrez's approbation of Blondel, see Gutiérrez, *Theology of Liberation*, 53 and 98. David Grumett also traces a link between the Blondelian forms of social Catholicism embodied in the theologies of Pierre Teilhard de Chardin, Henri de Lubac, and Yves de Montcheuil and the liberation theologies of Gutiérrez, Leonardo Boff, and Juan Luis Segundo, in Grumett, "Blondel, the Philosophy of Action and Liberation Theology," 507–29.

70. Milbank's rather short treatise on de Lubac is an expansion of a brief overview for a reference work, which first adumbrated many of the themes he sketches in *The Suspended Middle*. See Milbank, "Henri de Lubac," 76–91. For our purposes, it is worth noting that the controversial nature of Milbank's reading of de Lubac is due, in part, to his vicious attack on the work of Lawrence Feingold, who in the first edition of *The Suspended Middle* Milbank consistently misidentifies as Lawrence Feinberg. Milbank's fierce excoriation of Feingold's work on the *desiderium naturale visionis Dei*, excluded from the body of his text and confined to a long footnote, highlights again the Schmittian character of his theo-logic. We will return to this in greater detail below.

71. Milbank, *Theology and Social Theory*, 225. In particular, Milbank points to the sense in which the final chapter of de Lubac's *Catholicism* allows for an autonomous private sphere that re-introduces a destructive dualism that he otherwise successfully avoids. See de Lubac, *Catholicism*, 351–66. To be fair, Milbank locates a greater difficulty with the French Dominican Yves Congar, whose "distinction of planes" model employed this dualism much more strongly than did de Lubac. Significantly, this objection also motivates Milbank's preference for de Lubac's *Surnaturel* over *The Mystery of the Supernatural*, as we will see below.

72. Milbank, *Suspended Middle*, 65. Despite the parallel conclusions that this comparison is meant to evoke, conclusions that are barely alluded to, Milbank complicates the matter by suggesting that Bonhoeffer's Lutheranism leads him to ultimately celebrate precisely what de Lubac's *Surnaturel* refuses: "an autonomous secularity grounded in a univocal ontology" (ibid.).

with his treatment of Blondel, he devotes precious little attention to this. It remains baffling, for example, why de Lubac's well-known resistance against the Nazis and his participation in the clandestine *Cahiers du Témoignage chrétien*, which placed him in real danger, does not inform Milbank's reading.[73] Instead, Milbank focuses on the extent to which, for de Lubac, the political question was inextricably bound up with the relationship between nature and the supernatural and his view that the long-standing separation between them theologically legitimized a separate autonomous secular realm of nature that could remain comfortably unencumbered by any claim the supernatural may wish to impose upon it. As evidence of this, de Lubac points out that the separation of nature and the supernatural so central for the neo-Thomist tradition had devastating sociopolitical effects:

> Theology had reigned as the queen of the sciences, and on occasion it had possibly taken unfair advantage of its title. Now it was beginning to lose its position; after dominating the whole of knowledge it was tending to become merely a separate branch. The supernatural end which is, so to say, the keystone of the arch, was no longer that of philosophy. The study of man was cut in two parts, the second of which no longer had roots in the first, and in this way an essentially good movement was dangerously perverted towards differentiation in the analysis of reality, and towards the recognition of an increasing autonomy at the various levels of human activity.[74]

Summing up this danger, Tracey Rowland notes that "for de Lubac, the idea of a pure nature contained dangerous Pelagian tendencies, since it meant that it would be possible to sever grace from nature and marginalize it under the category of the 'supernatural.' The supernatural could then be subsequently privatized and social life would then proceed on the basis of the common pursuit of goods associated solely with the 'natural' order."[75] Indeed, for de Lubac this separation was a fatal one and led him to ask, "Was not the relative autonomy which it granted to nature, as it defined it, a temptation to independence? Did it not encourage in this way the 'secularization' let loose at the Renaissance and already anticipated in the preceding centuries by the

---

73. See de Lubac, *Christian Resistance to Anti-Semitism*; *At the Service of the Church*, especially 44–59; and *Theology in History*, especially 367–504. Admittedly, de Lubac himself complicates this by suggesting that the spirit of the *Cahiers* "were in no way a political undertaking" in *At the Service of the Church*, 52. However, this claim must be understood more narrowly, as David Grumett's account of de Lubac's so-called "spiritual resistance to Nazism" helpfully illuminates in Grumett, *De Lubac*, especially 25–45.

74. De Lubac, *Augustinianism and Modern Theology*, 214–15.

75. Rowland, *Culture and the Thomist Tradition*, 94.

Averroist movement?"[76] De Lubac suggests that this juxtaposition of nature and grace resulted in "supernature," the term he claims was increasingly used, being understood only as "a vain shadow, a sham adornment."[77]

De Lubac sought to overcome this fatal separation by emphasizing that there is a natural desire for the supernatural that cannot be demanded and comes to us as a wholly gratuitous gift that is in no way owed as a *debitum*. The crux of the issue is de Lubac's own controversial understanding and development of the paradox of the supernatural. He explains that "the fact that the nature of spiritual being, as it actually exists, is not conceived as an order destined to close finally upon itself, but in a sense open to an inevitably supernatural end, does not mean that it already has in itself, or as a part of its basis, the smallest positively supernatural element."[78] Because of his attack on the system of pure nature that had come to prevail in neoscholastic thought, de Lubac's attempt at a unified vision had to make clear that in no way was the gratuity of grace thereby endangered. Thus especially in his later work, which he claims did not change the least point of doctrine, he is at pains to point out that "the desire itself . . . does not constitute as yet even the slightest positive 'ordering' to the supernatural."[79] Helpfully illustrating what is at stake here with reference to Aquinas, Milbank claims that de Lubac's paradoxical ontology of the supernatural can be understood through an analogical appeal to art: "Grace, one might say, is 'the art of spirit-governing.' Just as human beings fulfill, for example, the proper potential of wood by making a table and yet wood would never 'tablize' by itself, but needs to be 'given' the form of table, so we are elevated by a divine art that does not abolish but fulfills our nature, though in a contingent, unexpected way."[80] This example is particularly instructive for two reasons. First, it highlights the category of paradox that is so central for de Lubac, a category upon which Milbank also increasingly relies. With regard to the relationship between the natural and the supernatural we might say that, for de Lubac, it is paradoxically characterized as one of distinction in unity.[81] As Susan Wood helpfully notes, "the tension is continually between union

---

76. De Lubac, *Augustinianism and Modern Theology*, 233.

77. Ibid., 264. For a helpful account of the linguistic shift from the older usage of "supernatural" to the more common use of "supernature" that has prevailed since Suárez, see de Lubac, *Brief Catechesis*, 33–41.

78. De Lubac, *Mystery of the Supernatural*, 31.

79. Ibid., 85. See also de Lubac, *At the Service of the Church*, 62.

80. Milbank, *Suspended Middle*, 100.

81. Indeed, de Lubac claims that "the paradox is this: that the distinction between the different parts of a being stands out the more clearly as the union of these parts is closer" in *Catholicism*, 328.

and distinction, and one must not equate union with identification, there always being a distance between nature and the supernatural because of their incommensurability."[82] For Milbank, de Lubac's deployment of paradox in this way represents a significant advance over the negative dialectics of Blondel's philosophical account of grace.[83] Indeed, Milbank locates the failure of the Rahnerian version of integralism precisely in the sense in which it is finally unable to embrace the "paradoxical reaching of the finite towards the supernatural" and offers instead only a transcendentalist reworking of Thomas Cajetan's specific obediential potency.[84] The second reason Milbank's illustration is instructive is that it further develops the kind of emanative *poiesis* so central to his reading of Blondel. In fact, this notion of *poiesis* is intimately intertwined in Milbank's narrative with the notion of paradox because "it remains possible for poetry to claim to discern and elaborate paradoxical mediations and so to 'save' reality, which is the aim of science, in a way no longer possible for science itself."[85]

Apocalyptic Resonances in Milbank's Theopolitical Deployment of Paradox

Highlighting the political implications of denying de Lubac's paradox of the supernatural, Milbank notes,

> If grace now no longer fulfills the deepest longing of our nature . . . then it resembles a politics proclaiming (rather like that advocated by Hannah Arendt) that it is puristically "about the political" and not (as she would say, "improperly") about education, welfare, transport, the environment and defense, etc. If grace does not elevate nature in such a way that it further develops the natural (as not sufficient unto itself), then just what *is* grace after all? . . . Instead of grace being a participatory putting on of the divine nature it becomes a kind of purely nominal change in status.[86]

---

82. Wood, *Spiritual Exegesis and the Church*, 119. Elsewhere, Wood also helpfully points out that the problem de Lubac identifies with a *natura pura* is that "there is a tendency to see in the supernatural a continuation of the natural. That is, nature and supernature are conceived of as two species of the same genus" in Wood, "Nature-Grace Problematic," 395. For de Lubac this cannot be the case, which his citation of Pascal's description of the supernatural makes clear in de Lubac, *Brief Catechesis*, 29.

83. See Milbank, *Theology and Social Theory*, 219.

84. Milbank, *Suspended Middle*, 64.

85. Milbank, "Double Glory," 180.

86. Milbank, *Suspended Middle*, 21–22.

Political Theology and the Persuasions of Beauty   77

It is in this sense that Milbank claims that de Lubac's paradox of the supernatural "proposed a new sort of ontology articulated *between* the discourses of philosophy and theology."[87] It is clear that de Lubac's use of the concept of paradox is at its most potent in his discussion of the relationship between nature and the supernatural, as we have seen above. What is less clear and more pertinent for our purposes is the manner in which Milbank appropriates de Lubac's concept of paradox and, more important still, how he deploys it. There are at least two things to consider here. First, and perhaps most generally, it is important to note that Milbank's reading of de Lubac takes place within the context of his broad retrieval of a certain kind of Christian Neoplatonism, which is itself bound up with his theological critique of metaphysics.[88] This is played out in his reading of de Lubac in his reliance on Jacob Schmutz's thesis that there was a significant change in the meaning of the word *influentia* such that its earlier link to notions of participation in a divine plenitude gradually came to mean merely extrinsic conditioning.[89] Using a helpful illustration, Milbank explains that

87. Ibid., 5. Milbank explicitly draws on Balthasar's observation that "de Lubac soon realized that his position moved into a suspended middle in which he could not practice any philosophy without its transcendence into theology, but also no theology without its essential inner substructure of philosophy" in Balthasar, *Theology of Henri de Lubac*, 15. It is striking that Milbank can claim that Balthasar's summary of de Lubac is "wonderfully accurate" and, at the same time, go on to argue that Balthasar has, at least partially, misunderstood the radical potential of de Lubac's revisionary ontology. See especially Milbank, *Suspended Middle*, 62–78. For an astute criticism of Milbank's reading of Balthasar here, see Oakes, "Paradox of Nature and Grace," especially 681–92.

88. Milbank's wide-ranging critique of metaphysics drives much of his work and can profitably be read as, on the one hand, an overcoming of the ontotheological science of transcendental ontology diagnosed by Heidegger that Milbank claims has prevailed only since Suárez (*pace* Heidegger) and, on the other hand, a saving of the participatory ontology that runs from Plato to Aquinas. This double movement can be helpfully seen in Milbank, "Only Theology Overcomes Metaphysics," 325–43; and "Only Theology Saves Metaphysics," 452–500. Milbank's thinking here is heavily indebted to the French retrieval of neoplatonism in the twentieth century. For historical accounts that helpfully locate both Blondel and de Lubac within this retrieval, see Schmutz, "Escaping the Aristotelian Bond," 169–200; and Hankey, "One Hundred Years of Neoplatonism in France," 99–248. Especially relevant for our purposes is Schmutz's claim that for "most of the authors of the French thirties . . . modernity was seen not so much as an unfinished project, but as a largely failed one. The reasons for their dissatisfaction with contemporary metaphysics were closely linked with their dissatisfaction with modern politics. Most of them believed that more than politics, philosophy could provide us with an answer to what had gone wrong in modern life" (ibid., 170). This negative assessment of modernity is an important tributary of influence on Milbank's own narrative of decline, which will be investigated in more detail below.

89. See Schmutz, "La doctrine médiévale des causes et la théologie de la nature pure," 217–64; as cited in Milbank, *Suspended Middle*, 88–94; and Milbank, *Beyond Secular Order*, 42. Schmutz's article forms part of a special double issue of the French

on the newer view, a higher cause operating on a lower level is just "one other" causal factor—like homework set by a teacher for the evening which is only one factor, alongside the demands of boyfriends and girlfriends, what's on downtown, etc., determining how the evening will actually be spent. It is quite *unlike* the instructions of a mystical master which might "inform" the entire way one spent the evening.[90]

De Lubac sets off the decisive theological revolution of the twentieth century because what we have here, so Milbank tells us, is a paradoxical ontology that is so radical that it surpasses the contrast between free unilateral gift and gift exchange and inaugurates a "paradoxical unilateral exchange."[91] In this way, Milbank claims that if we follow through de Lubac's initial insights here then Christian theology itself is already the kind of "non-philosophy" of which François Laruelle speaks and inaugurates a kind of "non-ontology" or "ontodology" of the sort the French Catholic Claude Bruaire develops.[92]

The manner in which Milbank subsequently deploys this paradoxical ontology of the gift takes place mainly in work that follows his book on de Lubac; however, helpful comparisons persist, especially with respect to the relationship between paradox and dialectic. De Lubac contrasts paradox and dialectic by suggesting that "paradox has more charm than dialectics; it is also more realist and more modest, less tense and less hurried; its function is to remind the dialectician when each new stage is reached in the argument, that however necessary this forward movement is no real progress has been made."[93] This seems to indicate that, for de Lubac, paradox functions apophatically *alongside* dialectic such that it exposes as hubris any notion of ineluctable progress. In contrast to this, Milbank suggests that the truth of Christianity and its persuasive power is better understood in terms of a paradoxical logic *over and against* a dialectical logic. Indeed, Milbank provocatively argues that "paradox alone sustains both God and

---

Dominican journal *Revue Thomiste*, which has been translated into English and published in its entirety as Bonino, *Surnaturel*.

90. Milbank, *Suspended Middle*, 92.

91. Ibid., 91. See also Milbank, *Beyond Secular Order*, 47. The paradoxical unilateral exchange that Milbank articulates here also represents a radicalization of his previous and extensive work on the gift, which can be seen most clearly in Milbank, "Gift and the Mirror," 299ff. In this way it can be seen that the strenuous polemic against the notion of a pure gift takes on a new dimension hereafter in Milbank's work because it incorporates de Lubac's arguments against a pure nature.

92. See Milbank, *Suspended Middle*, 95–96. For an introduction to Laruelle's concept of "non-philosophy," see Laruelle, *Philosophies of Difference*. For a helpful overview of Bruaire's notion of "ontodology" in English, see López, *Spirit's Gift*.

93. De Lubac, *Paradoxes of Faith*, 9–10.

Political Theology and the Persuasions of Beauty 79

the reality of the world."[94] It is here that the second important consideration comes to light since looming in the background of Milbank's deployment of paradox is not Hegel but the Danish philosopher and theologian Søren Kierkegaard. In fact, de Lubac's recognition that Kierkegaard "wanted to save that 'shocking' element which is essential to Christianity, so in his struggle against Hegelianism he wanted to save the element of 'paradox'" is itself an apt description of Milbank's use of paradox that brings to light once again the decidedly apocalyptic inflection of his political theology.[95] Linking this insight back to Milbank's use of Blondel and de Lubac we are now in a position to see that it is Milbank's Kierkegaardian reading of de Lubac that allows him to make the move beyond the negative dialectics of Blondel's philosophical account of grace and arrive, finally, at a positively embraced paradox evinced most powerfully in the incarnation.[96] Milbank is quite clear that the logic of paradox, which he also describes as the analogical or, following the Irish Catholic philosopher William Desmond, the metaxological, "implies not an impossible contradiction that must be overcome (dialectics) but rather an outright impossible *coincidence of opposites* that can (somehow, but we know not how) be persisted with. This is the Catholic logic of *paradox*—of an 'overwhelming glory' (*para-doxa*) which nonetheless saturates our everyday reality."[97] In both its language and its

---

94. Milbank, "Double Glory," 193. See also Milbank, *Beyond Secular Order*, 47 and 223–24.

95. De Lubac, *Drama of Atheist Humanism*, 107. In this regard, Milbank's reliance on Kierkegaard here could well be read as a development of the kind of "converted Hegelianism" that de Lubac wonders about.

96. Milbank's earlier reading of Kierkegaard proceeds along similar lines. See Milbank, "The Sublime in Kierkegaard," 298–321. Reprinted in Blond, *Post-Secular Philosophy*, 131–56.

97. Milbank, "Double Glory," 163. Milbank's thought here is both too complex and not complex enough. On the one hand, his recourse to the concept of analogy and to Desmond's notion of the metaxological throws up a host of complex dynamics with respect to his deployment of paradox that remain unresolved. For example, it remains unclear how he can maintain an account of mediation, however paradoxical, without dialectic. On the other hand, his understanding of dialectic itself seems to be understood primarily as the antagonistic play between the one and the many, which rules out in advance a dialectic that is more than negative. If Milbank's paradox can be described as the metaxological, as he claims, then it is more accurately thought of not in contrast to dialectic, which would itself instantiate the kind of negative dialectic he abhors, but rather as a kind of doubling of the dialectic (in a nondualistic fashion) designed to prevent mediation, that is, the dynamic relating of beings, from lapsing back into self-mediation as Desmond claims happens in Hegel. In the moments when he is closest to Desmond, Milbank nearly admits as much in his claim that "only a metaxological framing allows all three other logical aspects [the univocal, the equivocal and the dialectical] to remain and not to be overruled" and, more strongly still, that

philosophical inclinations, this description comes very close to Schmitt's argument that a specifically Catholic logic—he doesn't use the language of paradox here—exists as a "*complexio oppositorum*" that is able to hold together all forms of life without synthesizing them in a Hegelian fashion to some "higher third."[98] Making the link to Schmitt here even stronger, Slavoj Žižek notes that underlying Milbank's concept of paradox is the need for decision, or, as Milbank himself puts it in his earlier reading of Kierkegaard, "the constant necessity for the event of decision."[99] More interesting still is

"because of the impossibility of truly thinking the paradoxical, this dynamic tension will even be conceived by thought in dialectical terms." Milbank, "Double Glory," 166 and 71, respectively. In this way, Milbank's notion of paradox might be better described as an analogical paradox or a paradoxical dialectic. For a very helpful introduction to Desmond's fourfold sense of being, see Desmond, "Being Between," 305–31. For his more developed work, to which Milbank refers, see Desmond, *Being and the Between*, especially 177–222. It is worth noting that Desmond occupies a unique and prized place among Milbank's interlocutors. Indeed, Milbank claims that "I agree with nearly everything that Desmond has to say, apart from some minor divergences or hesitancies that are scarcely worth discussing in print," in "*Glissando*," 217. Also relevant here is Gillian Rose's attempt, *contra* Adorno, to rehabilitate the speculative potential of Hegel in Rose, "From Speculative to Dialectical Thinking," 53–63. See also Milbank's brief assessment of Rose in this regard in Milbank, "Double Glory," 223n81.

98. Schmitt, *Roman Catholicism and Political Form*, 7–14. Milbank also notes that his paradoxical ontology of the gift must be "seen as a coincidence of opposites" in *Suspended Middle*, 90. The subtle difference in language here may well point to a significant difference with respect to the question of violence, however. Milbank's choice of "coincidence," which is a deliberate echo of Nicolas of Cusa, rather than Schmitt's choice of "complex," which itself is not unrelated to Cusa's formulation, is meant to highlight not "the agonistic, but rather an eschatological peace so extreme that even the incompatible are now at one, like the lion laying down with the lamb." Milbank, "Double Glory," 138. For Cusa's development of the *coincidentia oppositorum*, see Nicholas of Cusa, *On Learned Ignorace*, 85–206. Milbank's long-standing interest in Cusa can be traced back to a very early article in which he also wrestles with the question of whether dialectic destroys analogy. See Milbank, "Man as Creative and Historical Being," 245–57. For our purposes, it is also noteworthy that Milbank is often at pains to distance Cusa from the likes of Scotus and Descartes despite the widespread notion, variously held by Ernst Cassirer, Frederick Copleston, and Hans-Georg Gadamer, among others, that Cusa is the first modern philosopher. In this regard, see especially Milbank, "The Thomistic Telescope," 193–226; and *Beyond Secular Order*, 99–105. For an overview of no less than sixteen Cusan themes that can be understood as forerunners of modern philosophy, see Hopkins, "Nicholas of Cusa," 13–29. For a lengthy recent treatment of Cusa, positively endorsed by Milbank, which suggests, in constructive dialogue with Foucault and de Certeau, that Cusa offers resources to outflank postmodernism, see Hoff, *The Analogical Turn*.

99. Milbank, "Sublime in Kierkegaard," 316. See also Žižek, "Atheist Wager," 137. Helpfully complicating the nature of the decision in question here, Gavin Hyman suggests that Milbank's project out-narrates nihilism only through the sheer force of assertion and thus the decision remains fundamentally ungrounded and in need of a supplement for which it cannot give an account, in Hyman, *Predicament of Postmodern Theology*, 91–93. Milbank's response to this challenge is increasingly wedded to a more

the sense in which Žižek's initial response to Milbank in *The Monstrosity of Christ* can itself be read as an attempt to point out the katechontic structure of Milbank's vision of Christianity by asking, "What if the entire history of Christianity, inclusive of (and especially) its Orthodox versions, is structured as a series of defenses against the traumatic apocalyptic core of incarnation/death/resurrection?"[100] In this sense, it is not difficult to see that we are very close to the structural nature of the apocalyptic political theology seen in the debate between Schmitt and Metz. Indeed, Cyril O'Regan's intimation that the difference between Milbank and Žižek "forces a decision between apocalyptic discourses" also highlights the sense in which Milbank's use of paradox takes on an apocalyptic form that forces a decision between the reconfigurations of political theology we have seen in Schmitt and Metz.[101] To be sure, this is a more complex decision than that of simply choosing one over the other, but before we can see how Milbank in particular calibrates this decision we must return to investigate the second movement of what I have been calling Milbank's Schmittian theo-logic.

Milbank's Schmittian Theo-Logic II: Interpretive Foreclosures

Milbank's very creative reading of de Lubac and subsequent theopolitical redeployment of a paradoxical ontology of the gift are not the only significant pieces of the puzzle, however. Two issues in particular highlight, again, the operation of a Schmittian theo-logic in his work. First, it is worth noting that at least part of the controversial nature of Milbank's reading of de Lubac is due to his vicious attack on the work of Lawrence Feingold, who in the first edition of *The Suspended Middle* is consistently misidentified as Lawrence Feinberg. Milbank's fierce excoriation of Feingold's work on the *desiderium naturale visionis Dei* as "arch-reactionary" reaches dizzying heights for someone so proficient at gutting his opponents and is excluded

---

explicit acknowledgment that his theopolitical optics is inextricably bound up with an "agape of the aesthetic," to borrow Desmond's turn of phrase, that links not only beauty but all of the transcendentals much more closely with reason itself. We will return to this in greater detail below, but this move can be seen in two essays that respond to various critics, namely, Milbank, "On Theological Transgression," 145–76; and, especially, Milbank, "Invocation of Clio," 3–44. These essays are reprinted and appear consecutively in *Future of Love*, 145–220.

100. Žižek, "Dialectical Clarity," 260. See also Hoelzl, "Before the Anti-Christ Is Revealed," 98–110.

101. O'Regan, "Hegelian Death of God," 286.

from the body of his text and confined to a long footnote.[102] Reinhard Hütter's riposte is particularly apt:

> The readers of Milbank's treatise—most of whom in all likelihood are neither experts in the thought of Thomas Aquinas, Henri de Lubac, or Reginald Garrigou-Lagrange in particular nor of Catholic theology in general—are thus invited to entertain the suspicion of some sinister right-wing ecclesiastical conspiracy . . . Anyone willing seriously to consider Feingold's arguments . . . by the sheer dynamic of the connotations entailed, must be a supporter of the Spanish Inquisition, a defender of the Papal States, and an admirer of the Franco-, Vichy, and Pinochet regimes in addition to anything else implied by association as arch-reactionary.[103]

It is here, then, that we can see one instance where the diagnostic edge of Milbank's apocalyptic inflection of political theology can too easily slip into invective. For Milbank, Feingold's (mis)reading of de Lubac simply cannot be allowed to stand and must be thoroughly repudiated because, at least in Milbank's estimation, it represents a potential crisis within theology that must not be allowed to errupt.[104] In this sense, it is not difficult to detect strong Schmittian echoes in the formal registers of Milbank's apocalyptic inflection of political theology because, like Schmitt, he stresses the need for decision and his vision claims to separate the authentic Christian vision from mere simulacra.[105] Milbank's largely unjustified dismissal of Feingold's provocative work, which attempts to unsettle much of the received wisdom about the natural desire to see God, is evidence again of his need to create a formal conflictual symmetry, a practice that undermines his own ability

---

102. For Milbank's characterization of Feingold, see Milbank, *Suspended Middle*, 26–27n10. See also Feingold, *The Natural Desire to See God*. Feingold's text is somewhat difficult to get hold of and I must enter a personal note of thanks to him for sending me a copy of his book, which is not only a historical tour de force but also an eminently learned contribution to the commentatorial tradition that deserves more widespread attention than it has hitherto received.

103. Hütter, "*Desiderium Naturale Visionis Dei*," 88–89. This article forms part of a symposium that considers the implications of Feingold's work.

104. In this sense, then, Milbank's apocalyptic inflection of political theology is a kind of nonidentical repetition of Schmitt's apocalyptic resistance to civil war.

105. It is also interesting to note that "decision" has its etymological roots in the Latin suffix *-cisio*, which is related to the verb *caesum* meaning "to cut" or even "to kill." So, etymologically, incision is a "cutting in," precision is a "cutting before," and decision is a "cutting down or off." This certainly sheds some light on why a thoroughgoing *pathos* of decision of the kind that both Schmitt and Milbank offer can and does easily slip into invective.

to honestly argue for the coincidence of opposites that paradox is meant to evince. To be fair, the second, slightly enlarged edition of *The Suspended Middle* corrects the typographical misidentification of Feingold and does not simply dismiss Feingold's work in a footnote.[106] However, the sense in which Milbank claims his own reading of de Lubac is nevertheless the more incisive one is shored up even further against Feingold's reading that, so we are told, simply reduces the debate concerning the supernatural to two competing versions of Thomism and that exhibits "zero historical sense of far more fundamental conceptual shifts."[107] In this sense, then, Milbank positions himself as an apocalyptic seer of the highest order who is capable of discerning the meaning of these "fundamental conceptual shifts," whereas Feingold and a good many others besides simply remain unable to perceive the half-concealed meaning of these shifts and, arguably, may even remain blind to their existence in the first place.

Second, and coupled with his creation of enemies, we see interpretive foreclosures in his reading of de Lubac. Indeed, throughout his book on de Lubac, Milbank betrays a distinct preference for the arguments of *Surnaturel* (1946) rather than the "substantial modifications" he claims are in evidence in both *The Mystery of the Supernatural* (1965) and *Augustinianism and Modern Theology* (1965), which reproduce much of the same material. Milbank's worry is that the publication of the encyclical *Humani Generis* (1950) had a profound impact on de Lubac's subsequent work. He goes so far as to claim that after the encyclical "de Lubac came across as a stuttering, somewhat traumatized theologian, only able to articulate his convictions in somewhat oblique fragments."[108] However, this rather uncharitable judgment stands in stark contrast to de Lubac's own response to the encyclical in which he claims that "I have read nothing in it, doctrinally, that affects me."[109] Moreover, it fails to account for the very positive light in which de Lubac himself welcomed initial criticisms of *Surnaturel* and sought to take account of them by stressing more explicitly the "twofold gift of God."[110] To be sure, this is precisely the "concession" that worries Milbank since, as he notes, de Lubac now allows that there could be a spiritual nature *not* oriented towards grace. Making the contrast more explicit Milbank claims that

106. See Milbank, *Suspended Middle*, 2nd ed., 28–35.

107. Ibid., 87.

108. Milbank, *Suspended Middle*, 7. Milbank claims to have qualified certain statements that seemed "too bald" in the second edition; however, this pronouncement on de Lubac is not among them and is not only repeated verbatim but also expanded upon in Milbank, *Suspended Middle*, 2nd ed., 8.

109. De Lubac, *Theology in History*, 281.

110. De Lubac, *Mystery of the Supernatural*, 51.

84   *The Architectonics of Hope*

"de Lubac had earlier in *Surnaturel* said that the natural desire for the supernatural is 'something' of God, though it is not yet grace. But in deference to *Humani Generis*, de Lubac now *drops* from his re-worked 'The Mystery of the Supernatural' article the idea that there is a positive advance manifestation of the supernatural that gives the desire for the supernatural."[111] This "concession" has dire consequences in Milbank's view because it leads to "a Scotist exposition of his theory—which makes the natural desire for the supernatural not any longer participatory, but only vaguely aspirational."[112] It is here, again, that we can see the operation of a Schmittian theo-logic insofar as Milbank's strong preference for *Surnaturel* is representative of a larger interpretive reification that is motivated by the need to foreclose on alternative possibilities that may weaken his argument. It is no coincidence that Milbank also fails to mention the positive allusions that de Lubac himself makes to Rahner's friendly criticism of his thesis in *Surnaturel* since to do so would undermine the degree of intensity between the two versions of integralism outlined above.[113] In addition to this kind of foreclosing upon potential readings of de Lubac, Milbank also suggests that the inadequacies he points to in de Lubac—chiefly a tendency to treat spiritual matters as fundamentally inward and a concomitant inability to draw out the political implications of a proper understanding of the integral relationship between nature and grace—would, if de Lubac were alive today, be seen and addressed by him in much the same ways in which Milbank himself proposes to do so by stressing much more strongly the social and corporate nature of the church itself as the true human community.[114]

111. Milbank, *Suspended Middle*, 36. This represents a startling reversal from his earlier claim that "de Lubac consistently 'supernaturalizes the natural,' and, in his second work, restates his thesis more strongly, against the background of a more comprehending, post-conciliar climate" in *Theology and Social Theory*, 219. This reversal, however, is quite consistent with my argument that a Schmittian theo-logic is operative in his work since the drive in both cases is to argue for the same unified, even sanitized, version of de Lubac by foreclosing on possible alternative readings.

112. Milbank, *Suspended Middle*, 37.

113. For Rahner's critique, see Rahner, "Antwort," 141–45. For de Lubac's not uncritical appreciation of Rahner see, for example, de Lubac, *Mystery of the Supernatural*, 107–8.

114. This comes out most clearly in a long footnote in Milbank, *Beyond Secular Order*, 203–5n195. Milbank also intriguingly suggests that while de Lubac underappreciated the political implications of his integrative understanding of nature and grace, Schmitt had a particularly acute understanding of the importance of these despite his aberrant notion of how they are related in the first place. How Milbank conceives of this relationship is left vague here, but he promises more explicit engagement with Schmitt in *On Divine Government*. However, that de Lubac would have drawn such a conclusion is by no means clear and, indeed, could be called into question given

By foregrounding the extent to which the formal register of Milbank's apocalyptically inflected reconfiguration of political theology implicitly functions as a kind of Schmittian theo-logic I do not mean to suggest that there are not real divisions and conflicts at work here. Quite to the contrary, it is clear that there are significant differences that Milbank deftly picks up on and interprets with great effect. My concerns lie rather with the extent to which Milbank pushes these distinctions and, perhaps more importantly, the work he makes them do in the construction of his narrative. For if, as Milbank contends, his political theology wishes to unthink the necessity of violence, then will not a theological logic predicated on a friend/enemy distinction have deleterious effects on such a project? Like Hegel and Balthasar for whom there is no theo-logic that is also not an onto-logic, the Schmittian register unique to Milbank's theo-logic is parasitic upon his attempt to develop a truly peaceful political theology.

Christological Poetics and the Life of Jesus

Turning from the more formal register of his apocalyptically inflected reconfiguration of political theology to the visionary content that fills it out, it is clear that Milbank's theopolitical deployment of paradox, a brief overview of which he offers as the preface to the fragmentary political theology cobbled together in *The Future of Love*, could be chided for tending toward the kind of Hegelian abstraction he otherwise seeks to overcome. However, Milbank resists this by consistently reinvoking the poetic by claiming that "the balance is proclaimed with the most paradoxical extremity in the idea that reason itself has become incarnate, which means that the rational is now fully accessible only by the 'indirectness' of a poetic discourse concerning this event."[115] Here again, a Kierkegaardian influence is detectable

---

de Lubac's understanding of the degeneration of the mystical body of Christ and his attempt to prevent precisely what Schmitt takes as a given, namely, the sublimation of the *corpus mysticum* into a *corpus politicum*. See de Lubac, *Corpus Mysticum*, especially 101–19. Indeed, there is an important sense in which Milbank's worries about perceived inadequacies in de Lubac are simply the result of his failure to fully appreciate de Lubac's complex and indeed paradoxical notion of mystery that while not eschewing concrete form as the *ecclesia* nevertheless remains "obscure, hidden and 'mystical,' even once it has been described, signified and 'revealed,'" as de Lubac claims in *Corpus Mysticum*, 251.

115. Milbank, "Double Glory," 217. Or, again, "for a Catholic historiography, the narrative of Christendom is the contingent story of whether or not the balance of reason with poetry has held" (ibid., 218). Milbank's language of balancing here is somewhat problematic because it could be understood as a re-instantiation of a kind of Aristotelian mean that paradox itself is offered to unsettle. Apart from his

since the positive embrace of paradox constitutive of poetic nonidentical repetition is now linked much more strongly with reason itself. Indeed, Milbank argues that "when Kierkegaard says that he believes 'by virtue of the absurd,' he means 'by virtue of the incarnation,' and so for the best possible *reason*."[116] This same poetic linkage of faith and reason can be seen in Milbank's affinities for Pope Benedict XVI's "Regensburg Lecture" as well as in the refinement of his logic of persuasion in which he claims that "to opt for truth and peace is also to opt *for reason*."[117] However, this is to run ahead of the argument since in order to understand the dynamics involved in Milbank's linkage of reason with goodness, truth, and, in particular, beauty, we need to explore his account of *poiesis*. It is here, most explicitly, that we can see the aesthetic potentials that Milbank brings to bear on his apocalyptic reconfiguration of political theology.

While Milbank's stress on poetic existence can be found throughout his work, his development of "a christological poetics" in an important essay of the same name is most relevant for our purposes not only because it fleshes out his Kierkegaardian reading of de Lubac but also because it helpfully triangulates his reading with and beyond both Metz and Balthasar. Especially important for Milbank here is the sense in which *poiesis* involves much more than an account of human making since the overriding character of poetic action itself always outstrips any attempt to account for or contain it in terms of an original intention or purpose. For Milbank, "our products carry not only the charge of our own life and the presence of our human community, but also the ecstatic reach of our intention, although this is simultaneously and equally an intention of our products themselves,

---

academic work, Milbank's two published collections of poetry are evidence of the seriousness with which he takes this claim. See Milbank, *The Mercurial Wood* and *The Legend of Death*.

116. Milbank, "Sublime in Kierkegaard," 306. Supporting this claim, Milbank says that "readings of Kierkegaard as a simple fideist altogether overlook the point that it is primarily reason, not faith, which is 'absurd' and 'paradoxical'" (ibid., 319n26). However, Milbank goes on to claim both that repetition in Kierkegaard is the temporalization of analogy and that he "saves philosophy by transforming it, *without remainder*, into theology" (ibid., 307), all of which makes Kierkegaard into a natural ally for his own purposes. Interestingly, it is the constant necessity for the event of decision that prevents a lapse back into a nihilistic variant of recollection, which again highlights a curious proximity to Schmitt.

117. Milbank, "Invocation of Clio," 41. For Milbank's approbation of Benedict's "Regensburg Lecture," see Milbank, "Faith, Reason, and Imagination," 316–34. For our purposes it is also worth noting that Milbank understands Pope Benedict XVI to be a true heir of the *nouvelle théologie*. The connection here is so strong, in fact, that Milbank offers his reading of the pope's first encyclical as an appropriate way to frame his own political theology in Milbank, "Future of Love," 364–70.

which have already 'dispossessed' us."[118] What this amounts to is a poetic reworking of Hegel's "cunning of reason" that resists the technical reduction of *poiesis* not by admitting a certain tragic distortion into history but rather by introducing a "risky openness both to grace and the possibility of sinful distortion—for which one is both responsible and not responsible—within every action."[119] While Milbank explicitly makes a connection between the Hegelian "cunning of reason" and the "heterogenesis of ends" with respect to the poetic use Giambattista Vico makes of it, there is also a strong echo of Blondel here since poetic action "may be to create, to assert oneself, but it is equally to lose oneself, to place what is most ours . . . at a total risk."[120] Poetic action, then, "has the capacity to interrupt nature," and in the end Christ, the concrete universal, establishes the *telos* and poetic boundary for such interruptive action.[121] The incarnation is thus doubly important because "as the divine utterance, Jesus is the absolute origination of all meaning, but as human utterance Jesus is inheritor of all already constituted human meanings."[122] It is precisely here that the force of Milbank's theopolitical deployment of paradox finds its greatest purchase because the poetic and the ethical are fused on the cross such that beauty itself is redefined as the nonviolent incorporation and transfiguration of the ugly.[123] Significantly, this reconfiguration is not a pure negation since, as Milbank argues with reference to Paul Ricoeur, Jesus's death is "not other to his life," that is, the

118. Milbank, "Christological Poetics," 125.

119. Ibid., 127. For Hegel's narration of the "cunning of reason," see his Introduction in Hegel, *Lectures on the Philosophy of World History*; the explicit reference occurs on 96n44.

120. Milbank, *Theology and Social Theory*, 214. See also Milbank, *Religious Dimension*, 253–61.

121. Milbank, "Christological Poetics," 127. The language of "interruption" here is a clear echo of Metz.

122. Ibid., 136.

123. Significantly, there is no outright denunciation of dialectic here but rather a more careful nuancing of a particular kind of dialectic that is more than merely negative and definitively enacted by the absolute paradox of the incarnation. Making a link with Baroque music Milbank claims that "he [Jesus] refuses the violence which would actively distort his own work, yet allows to be incorporated into his own person ugly constructions which in their new context assume a different appearance. This is not, of course, the synchronic harmony of the whole as against the disorder of the parts, but the diachronic transfiguration of the parts in their new formal relationships" (ibid., 139). For an insightful reflection on the relation between music and theology that engages with Milbank's work, see also Begbie, *Theology, Music and Time*, especially 204–70. Significantly, Begbie positively draws on Metz's notion of "productive noncontemporaneity" to illustrate the improvisational capacity of music, which helpfully complicates some of Milbank's criticisms of Metz.

body of Christ as a supremely broken sign is informed by the life and work of a particular man.[124]

It is precisely here that Milbank's earlier criticisms of Metz's Christology are especially relevant, not least because his development of the poetic cunning of reason bears some resemblance to the interruptive character of Metz's *new* political theology. Milbank sums up his dissatisfaction with Metz this way:

> There is no appeal here to Hegelian *Sittlichkeit*, or to a substantive anticipation of the future community. For such an appeal, what would matter would be the past saints and holy communities in their lives and the modes of their deaths: the provocations which they gave to injustice, and not their mere passive enduring of it. In particular, why should one remember Christ, beyond all others, if his provocation were not recognized as supremely great? The *memoria passionis* has its context in the memory also of Christ's deeds and words.[125]

Two important interrelated issues are at stake here. First, and perhaps most significantly, Milbank identifies a lacuna in Metz's account of memory that fails to adequately account for the life and work of Jesus, which is crucial for the ongoing poetic repetition of the body of Christ. Second, he inveighs against Metz's account of the body of Christ itself because it remains too wedded to an account of apocalyptic negativity that inhibits the ability to positively imagine a sought-after future community. Milbank's reading of Metz here is certainly open to criticism, perhaps most seriously because there are points at which Metz seems to address, however tentatively, just the kinds of worries Milbank identifies.[126] What is most important to see, however, is that Milbank does not prescind from Metz's apocalyptic orientation; indeed, his claim that "the interruption of history by Christ and his bride, the Church, is the most fundamental of events" is evidence of an important continuity in this regard.[127] What Milbank wants to prevent is the artificial enclosure of the sacred that he claims occurs precisely "at the

---

124. Milbank, "Christological Poetics," 138. See also Ricoeur, *Essays on Biblical Interpretation*, 123–30.

125. Milbank, *Theology and Social Theory*, 239.

126. See, for example, Metz, *Followers of Christ*; and Metz and Moltmann, *Faith and the Future*. Part of the problem with Milbank's analysis of Metz is that he seems to be relatively unfamiliar with his work apart from *Theology of the World* and *Faith in History and Society*. While Milbank's criticisms are by no means wholly unfounded, there are certainly places where a wider reading would mitigate some of his worries.

127. Milbank, *Theology and Social Theory*, 388.

point where *poesis* is publicly defined as *techne*."[128] Thus it is here that we can finally see that Milbank's emphasis on the constitutive excess of human poetic activity harnesses the aesthetic potentials of political theology. In this sense, then, Milbank proceeds decisively beyond Metz's theopolitical vision with Balthasar.

Based on his development of a christological poetics and his criticism of Metz's Christology it would be reasonable to expect that Milbank would seek to offer a reading of the life and work of Jesus, since multiple and even competing readings would thereby open up a multiplicity of vistas that would, in turn, testify to the "plenitude of significance" that can be recovered from Jesus's concrete acts. After all, writes Milbank, "we need the stories of Jesus for salvation, rather than just a speculative notion of the good."[129] However, Milbank drops hints that no such account of the life of Jesus will be forthcoming. There seems to be a worry here that motivates Milbank's privileging of the *figura* of Christ over the concrete life and work of Jesus and that coincides with his critique of the primacy of *praxis* he sees as the motivating factor in Metz's work.[130] Candidly summing this up, Milbank proclaims that "the honest unabashed theoretician is better than the writer about practice who *displaces actual* practice."[131] Thus the aesthetic potential that Milbank harnesses, while significant because it positively risks the nonviolent incorporation and transfiguration of the ugly and hence holds out hope for a kind of healing of violence, remains in a curious proximity to the structural nature of the apocalyptically inflected aesthetics of violence seen in Schmitt and Metz insofar as form, albeit a more dynamic poetic form, is stressed over the development of a Christology that may have the power to concretely resist sliding into a tragic resignation to the present-day orgies of violence of which Metz speaks. In a manner not unlike Metz, Milbank claims that "the most formal answers will best preserve an apophatic caution" and this refrain is repeatedly displayed in his Christology.[132] Indeed,

---

128. Ibid., 242.

129. Milbank, *Theology and Social Theory*, 398. Significantly, Milbank also highlights the nonviolent work of Jesus here and claims that "an abstract attachment to non-violence is therefore not enough—we need to practice this as a skill, and to learn its idiom. The idiom is built up in the Bible, and reaches its consummation in Jesus and the emergence of the Church" (ibid.).

130. Floating just below the surface, there is some ambiguity with respect to the contrast Milbank wants to draw between *praxis* and *poiesis* since the Aristotelian and Marxist senses are at least partially in tension. For a helpful reflection on this distinction, see Agamben, "Poiesis and Praxis," 68–93.

131. Hauerwas and Milbank, "Christian Peace," 220.

132. Milbank, "Christological Poetics," 139. Elsewhere, Milbank seeks to avoid de-naturing the gift by suggesting that a certain sacred ineffability with respect to its

90 *The Architectonics of Hope*

Milbank insists that the identity of Jesus "does not actually relate to his 'character,' but rather to his universal significance for which his particularity stands, almost, as a mere cipher."[133] Emphasizing that Jesus's concrete acts are to be understood as signs of his universal significance, Milbank elsewhere claims that "precisely because Jesus escapes any general framework, given that any general set can always be subsumed in a further set, Jesus is universal. Christianity is universal because it invented the logic of universality; it constituted this logic as an event."[134] What the *Logos* become flesh means, then, is that "the specific *shape* of Christ's body in his reconciled life and its continued renewal in the Church provides for us the true aesthetic example for our reshaping of our social existence."[135] However, it is at this point that we are left to wonder if the formal aesthetic potential Milbank harnesses here amounts to a retreat from the inherent risk of poetic action that is always open to distortion and, concomitantly, if he thereby risks just the sort of technical reduction of *poiesis* he otherwise seeks to avoid. Put in christological terms, we are right to worry, with Frederick Bauerschmidt, about a monophysitism that absorbs Christ's humanity into his divinity.[136]

Beauty and Its Violences

Taken together, then, we are now in a position to see that Milbank's apocalyptically inflected reconfiguration of political theology takes on a mystagogical form that owes a great deal both to his theopolitical deployment of paradox and to his account of *poiesis*. As we have seen, Milbank's aesthetic reconfiguration of political theology proceeds beyond Metz with Balthasar; however, the ways in which he subsequently claims to move beyond

---

content must be allowed since the more it is "fetishized and confined to a narrow range of permissible forms, the more it becomes self-referring in a mode that is like a kind of concrete pre-figuration of the abstract self-reference of pure reason" in Milbank, "Politics of Time," 51.

133. Milbank, "Name of Jesus," 149. The qualifier "almost" is important here.

134. Milbank, "Materialism and Transcendence," 401.

135. Milbank, "Atonement," 103 (emphasis added). It is also worth noting that Milbank is here reworking Giorgio Agamben's use of Schmitt.

136. See Bauerschmidt, "The Word Made Speculative?," especially 422–26. See also Milbank's claim, which is at least semantically close to monophysitism, that "for reasons belonging to the logic of discourse, it is indeed true that incarnation cannot be by the absorbing of divinity into humanity, but only by the assumption of humanity into divinity" in Milbank, "Name of Jesus," 150. Milbank's desire to supernaturalize the natural without completely eviscerating Christ's humanity can also be seen in his recourse to the Russian sophiological tradition in general and to Sergii Bulgakov in particular. See, for example, Milbank, "Sophiology and Theurgy," especially 78–81.

Balthasar throw up a host of largely unanswered questions. Introducing an intriguing distinction that is left quite undeveloped, Milbank's parting shot in his christological poetics points toward the ongoing givenness of Christ constitutive of our collective poetic making as a decisive excess that exceeds the merely aesthetic givenness of Christ. This way of putting the matter highlights the proleptic and anticipatory character of Milbank's political theology since, as he writes, "only as makers may we look to the day when 'all flesh shall see him together.'"[137] However, this initial distinction between the aesthetic and the poetic, which seems to isolate a dynamic unfolding that is characteristic of the poetic but somehow absent in the aesthetic, reveals a worry that, in many ways, mirrors the development of Milbank's Christology and subsequently leads on to some significant assertions with respect to Balthasar that are especially relevant for our purposes. In what is perhaps the most striking example of his move beyond Balthasar, Milbank claims that

> under Balthasar's non-poetic view of action as something "in excess" of form, the aesthetic aspect of drama must inevitably be instrumentalized . . . This is confirmed by von Balthasar's view that the aesthetic, unlike the dramatic, is not interpersonal and interactive . . . But such a notion betrays a profoundly Kantian attitude to the aesthetic, where the paradigm of the beautiful is the lonely spectator looking at a picture, not the participant in a dance or the dweller within a building.[138]

Widening the gap between the aesthetic and the poetic even further, Milbank has more recently claimed, with recourse to the French Dominican Olivier-Thomas Vernard, that "Balthsar's need for a trilogy becomes redundant . . . because a poetics/aesthetics, unlike a *pure* aesthetics, is *already* a dramatics and a logic."[139] As in the case of his reading of de Lubac, Milbank's

---

137. Milbank, "Christological Poetics," 142.

138. Milbank, *Suspended Middle*, 71-72. Milbank's suggestion that Balthasar's understanding of beauty is fundamentally Kantian is tendentious at best and fails to appreciate the dynamism of Balthasar's vision. Indeed, Balthasar claims that "before the beautiful—no, not really *before* but *within* the beautiful—the whole person quivers. He not only 'finds' the beautiful moving; rather, he experiences himself as being moved and possessed by it" in *Glory of the Lord I*, 247. Balthasar's account of beauty is, in fact, far more dynamic than Milbank allows and is far closer to his own vision than he recognizes.

139. Milbank, "On 'Thomistic Kabbalah,'" 151. The strength of Vernard's work, according to Milbank, is that he offers a poetics rather than an aesthetics, which means he is able to more adequately do in three volumes what it took Balthasar fifteen volumes to do. This audacious claim, which can in no satisfactory way be dealt with here, fails to appreciate the sense in which Balthasar's *Aesthetics* are inherently participatory and

Schmittian theo-logic is at work here flattening out and foreclosing on possible alternative readings of Balthasar to open up a distinction that will serve as the basis upon which a positive theological program can be constructed.

Leaving aside the immense problems that this criticism of Balthasar raises, which Milbank attributes to certain unspecified "Bonaventurian tendencies" in his work, what is most relevant for our purposes is what is at stake for Milbank in his move beyond Balthasar.[140] In a particularly revealing statement, he claims that

> beauty, as Balthasar argued, is to do with glory, manifestation. But this means . . . that "the visible speaks"—that standing before the experience of the beautiful vision as something that terrifies us and commands us by manifesting something that is more than its visible self, we undergo a certain unsettling of the senses, whereby when we see, we seem also to "hear" something. The beautiful *is* the poetic uttering of nature. Inversely, the audible voices of nature, her music, compel us insofar as they seem to promise us unknown visions, unknown scenes of delight.[141]

Of central importance to the development of Milbank's harnessing of the aesthetic potentials of political theology here is the synaesthetic link between vision and hearing. If to see is also to hear, as Milbank contends, then aesthetics and rhetoric are inseparable, which, in turn, implies that the manifestation of the beautiful takes on a linguistic or, perhaps better, a liturgical form.[142] Indeed, this is precisely where Balthasar's fail-

---

fundamentally inseparable from the *Dramatics* and the *Logic*. Indeed, Balthasar argues that "the circumincession of the transcendentals suggests the necessity of a new discussion of issues that we have treated in the previous panels of our triptych. After all, there is simply no way to do theology except by repeatedly circling around what is, in fact, always the same totality looked at from different angles. To parcel up theology into isolated tracts is by definition to destroy it" in Balthasar, *Theo-Logic I*, 8. Moreover, Milbank also seems to miss the sense in which the sequence of Balthasar's trilogy itself can be read as a complete reversal of Kant's three *Critiques*. For Vernard's work, which is explicitly indebted to Balthasar, see Vernard, *Thomas d'Aquin poète théologien* (3 vols.). Milbank's afterword to Vernard's third volume is also relevant, as is Vernard's preface to his French translation of Milbank, *Le Milieu suspendu*. For a very brief overview of Vernard's work, see Burrell, "A Postmodern Aquinas," 331–38.

140. Milbank, "On 'Thomistic Kabbalah,'" 150–54. Interestingly, the influence of Bonaventure that Milbank derides here is much in evidence in Hart's theological aesthetics, as we will see below. See, for example, Hart, *Beauty of the Infinite*, 253 and 307–10.

141. Milbank, "On 'Thomistic Kabbalah,'" 150.

142. For the liturgical turn to which Milbank repeatedly refers, see Pickstock, *After Writing*, especially 169–76 and 213–19; and, with links to Schmitt, Pickstock, "Liturgy and Modernity," 19–40.

ure truly lies for Milbank, since he does not fully embrace the primacy of language as the integrating link between the true, the good, and the beautiful.[143] Even more to the point for our purposes, Milbank's coding of the transcendentals exhibits subtle differences with Balthasar's, the most significant of which involves the link with reason itself. Whereas Balthasar is at pains to emphasize that "the mysteriousness of being has absolutely nothing to do with *irrationality*," Milbank argues that "if glory is always *logos*, then it is impossible to speak of beauty without also speaking of the articulations of reason as such."[144] So while Balthasar remains "struck by boundless amazement at the structural complexity of the transcendentals," Milbank puts his coding of the transcendentals in the service of refining his logic of persuasion, and it is this point around which the themes of Milbank's theopolitical optics coalesce.[145]

If this link between reason and the transcendentals, and more specifically between reason and beauty, represents Milbank's move beyond Balthasar, as I have argued, then it reveals a significant shift in the theopolitical register that must be reckoned with. Indeed, I suggest that it is precisely from this vantage point that we can finally see how Milbank aesthetically reconfigures the structural displacement of violence characteristic of the apocalyptically inflected political theology developed by both Schmitt and Metz. Central here is the acknowledgment that beauty functions as an operation; "it *does* something rather than simply *is* something."[146] This insight allows us to see that Milbank's linkage of beauty with reason can be read as a theological reconfiguration of Schmitt's diagnosis of the ways in which the violent power of myth lurks behind *nomos*. Relying heavily on the French revolutionary syndicalist Georges Sorel, Schmitt helpfully articulates what is at stake:

> Out of the depths of a genuine life instinct, not out of reason or pragmatism, springs the great enthusiasm, the great moral

---

143. Milbank, "On 'Thomistic Kabbalah,'" 151. Milbank's claim here with respect to Balthasar, which, again, cannot be investigated in any depth, is but a reformulation of previous arguments about the primacy of language. See especially Milbank, "Theology without Substance: Christianity, Signs, Origins Part One;" and Milbank, "Theology without Substance: Christianity, Signs, Origins Part Two." Together, these essays form the bulk of Milbank, "The Linguistic Turn as a Theological Turn," in *The Word Made Strange*, 84–120. In the end, this claim gives short shrift to Balthasar's claim that "theology is a linguistic event" in *Theo-Logic III*, 359.

144. See Balthasar, *Theo-Logic I*, 9 (emphasis added); and Milbank, "On 'Thomistic Kabbalah,'" 151.

145. Balthasar, *Theo-Logic I*, 8.

146. Ward, "Beauty of God," 40.

94　*The Architectonics of Hope*

decision and the great myth. In direct intuition the enthusiastic mass creates a mythical image that pushes its energy forward and gives it the strength for martyrdom as well as the courage to use force. Only in this way can a people or a class become the engine of world history.[147]

Sorel himself is even more clear about the necessary violence that accompanies contemporary myths, which he argues "lead men to prepare themselves for a combat which will destroy the existing state of things."[148] For both Sorel and Schmitt this mythopoetic act is to be understood not as an intellectual product that can be endlessly debated, thus risking paralysis of the political itself, but rather as a "decisive struggle."[149] As we have seen, Milbank does not shrink from the apocalyptic character that lies at the heart of Sorel's and Schmitt's vision, nor does he break with the narrative of decline characteristic of their thought. Quite to the contrary, Milbank's political theology maintains strong apocalyptic echoes, especially in his theopolitical deployment of paradox, and likewise subscribes to an epic *Verfallsgeschichte*—a history of decline that manifests itself as an inverse Hegelianism that sits quite comfortably within the larger French retrieval of Neoplatonism in the twentieth century.[150]

At issue here for our purposes is the extent to which Milbank invests his *mythos* with additional persuasive power by linking his account of reason more closely with the transcendentals. This move begins as a response to various critics, in particular Gavin Hyman and Gordon Michalson, who argue that, in the end, Milbank's *mythos* remains fundamentally ungrounded and in need of a supplement for which it cannot give an account and thus remains "merely persuasive and not apodictic."[151] Confronting himself with this criticism, Milbank asks, "Do I not seem always to say that one may equally opt for the ultimacy of the agonistic—either in a resigned or a per-

---

147. Schmitt, *Crisis of Parliamentary Democracy*, 68.

148. Sorel, *Reflections on Violence*, 28–29. For a helpful introduction to Sorel that places him in the context of late nineteenth-century French political philosophy and grapples with his relation to fascism, see Vincent, "Interpreting Georges Sorel," 239–57. See also Kołakowski, "Georges Sorel: A Jansenist Marxist," 151–74, which helpfully highlights the apocalyptic character of Sorel's thought. Unsurprisingly, many of the arguments concerning the extent to which Sorel is accurately understood as a fascist closely resemble the arguments about Schmitt's relation to Nazism.

149. Sorel, *Reflections on Violence*, 28.

150. For a helpful overview of this narrative, see especially Hankey, "One Hundred Years of Neoplatonism in France," 97–248. See also Schmutz, "Escaping the Aristotelian Bond," 169–200.

151. Milbank, "Invocation of Clio," 41. For the critiques to which I am referring here, see Hyman, *Predicament of Postmodern Theology*, 65–94; and Michalson, "Re-reading the Post-Kantian Tradition with Milbank," 357–83.

versely celebratory tone? Here I feel I can now go a little bit further. To opt for truth and peace is also to opt *for reason*—the ultimate reality of reason."[152] Concomitantly, Milbank argues that "the 'choice' for peaceful analogy . . . is *not* really an ungrounded decision, but a 'seeing' by a truly-desiring reason of the truly desirable."[153] The linkage of reason with the transcendentals in this way, intensified in Milbank's move beyond Balthasar that highlights the particular role of beauty, results in an aesthetically reconfigured theopolitical vision that assumes a form that actively resists any kind of self-critique and thereby becomes a mythical power-structure that, as Sorel articulates, "cannot be refuted."[154] To be clear, the point here is *not* that beauty has nothing whatsoever to do with reason. On the contrary, issues of harmony, order, proportion, *and therefore of reason*, have been central in the reception of beauty in the Christian tradition and can be seen as far back as Augustine and Pseudo-Dionysius the Areopagite.[155] Particularly at issue here for our purposes is the extent to which Milbank's linkage seeks to control the operations of beauty and whether this, in fact, represents a misapprehension of beauty itself.[156] To ask the question this way is to enquire into the largely unexplored other side of Milbank's very significant forays into the logic of gift exchange; the question is not "can a gift be given?" but rather "how and in what ways can a gift be received?" or, to put it more sharply, "can a gift be refused?"[157] In other words, the question is whether the power Milbank invests in beauty could have a distorting effect and be potentially deceptive. By pressing the power of beauty into the service of refining his logic of persuasion, Milbank shores up his *mythos* against potential rivals and, in so doing, circumvents the residual liberalism of Schmitt's account of the decision and its attendant arbitrary character.[158] However, in the end, the aesthetic

152. Ibid.

153. Milbank, "Preface to the Second Edition," xvi.

154. Sorel, *Reflections on Violence*, 29.

155. See, for example, Augustine, *On Free Choice of the Will*, II.xiv; Augustine, *Confessions*, I.vii.12, II.v.10, IV.xii; and Pseudo-Dionysius, *Complete Works*, 596B, 701C–16D.

156. Comparison with Pseudo-Dionysius here is particularly instructive because he at least implicitly allows for the possibility that the divine beauty does not persuade absolutely, that is, he entertains the dangerous possibility that beauty might fail to persuade whereas Milbank's strategy seeks to foreclose on precisely this possibility. See, for example, his discussion of demons in *The Divine Names*, in Pseudo-Dionysius, *Complete Works*, 716A.

157. This provocative suggestion looms large in the background of Graham Ward's metaphysical ecclesiology as elaborated in Ward, *The Politics of Discipleship*, especially 260n81.

158. For a helpful account of the potential residual liberalism in Schmitt that is consonant with Milbank's work, see Pickstock, "Liturgy and Modernity," especially 32–40.

potentials that Milbank attempts to harness here are finally parasitic on his attempt to unthink the necessity of violence because it remains—perhaps tragically but nevertheless positively—committed to its educative function. Violence is thereby authorized to operate as more than merely a kind of "malign transcendental," and Milbank's aesthetic reconfiguration of political theology secretly participates in a manipulable economy in which peace, while certainly capable of being obscurely anticipated in time, is ultimately deferred and merely names the eschaton.[159]

To see more closely how this unfolds we must attend to Milbank's phenomenological reading of violence, which manages to be both deeply insightful and, at the same time, blissfully unaware of its own blind spots. Consistently disinterring as theologically incoherent the tradition of so-called radical evil, a tradition that roughly begins with Kant and continues through Schelling to Heidegger, Milbank's reading of violence proceeds on thoroughly Augustinian grounds.[160] That is, evil and violence, which are convertible but not synonymous, are denied any positive foothold in being and instead name the processes in which good is lost, processes in which we learn to see corruption.[161] What these processes of "learning to see" imply, then, is that the naming of violence is a complex and difficult task that requires judgment: "Is the crack of a whip a spur, a dishonouring, a rebuke or a caress?"[162] Milbank's phenomenology of violence is thus occu-

---

159. Milbank, "Violence," 28. Milbank's claim that because violence is an anti-transcendental peace is naturally a transcendental is problematic in itself for no other reason that it slides toward treating the transcendentals as attributes rather than names of God and thus threatens to domesticate transcendence. David Bentley Hart helpfully warns against this basic error by pointing to "a rule enunciated by Maximus the Confessor: Whereas the being of finite things has non-being as its opposite, God's being is entirely beyond any such opposition" in Hart, "Impassibility as Transcendence," 300. For more on the significant distinction between attributes and names, see Soskice, "Naming God," 241–54; and Hart, "The Offering of Names," 255–91. To be clear, I do not necessarily wish to deny that peace is a transcendental, only that it cannot be adduced to be so based on the positing of violence as an anti-transcendental since then peace would be little more than the absence of violence.

160. For Milbank's reading of the tradition of "radical evil," see Milbank, "Evil," 1–25. For the origins of the term, see Kant, *Religion Within the Bounds of Mere Reason*, especially 69–97. For a helpful summary of Augustine's account of evil, see Evans, *Augustine on Evil*.

161. For an account of the mediatory role of beauty and the convertibility of the transcendentals that is especially relevant to my argument here, see Pickstock, "Imitating God," especially 314–19. This essay was subsequently published as the first chapter of Milbank and Pickstock, *Truth in Aquinas*, 1–18. See also Robert Jenson's account of the essential trinitarian dynamics involved in the convertibility of the transcendentals in Jenson, *Systematic Theology I*, especially 224–36.

162. Milbank, "Violence," 26.

pied with the implications of spectatorship and takes seriously the fact that "we no longer carry daggers in our belts and whip them out at the slightest provocation—like, for example, the young J. S. Bach when faced with a recalcitrant viola de gamba player" but have become primarily "*onlookers of violence.*"[163] For Milbank this spectatorial gaze takes three forms: first, a quite straightforward and apparently passive watching of endless scenes of violence, whether simulated, filmed, or staged; second, a gazing upon the past with an air of detached moral superiority; and third, a refusal to participate in actual physical violence as the exercise of a supreme good. Relentlessly pushing each of these forms to their breaking point, Milbank's strategy performs the immense service of exposing as illusory the modern assumption that, because we are primarily watchers of violence, we are thereby at a safe enough remove from it so as to render its destructive effects relatively innocuous. Indeed, the strength of Milbank's phenomenology of violence lies precisely in its ability to expose new vistas that reveal the extent to which our supposed peaceableness "cannot avoid the taint of malice."[164] In this sense, we can read Milbank's analysis here as an echo of Jeremiah's indictment of the kings and priests of Judah who shouted "peace, peace" when there was no peace (Jer 8:11). The incisiveness of Milbank's vision goes some way beyond simply pointing to the ever-increasing technologization of war whereby combatants actually enter a simulated world wherein they are empowered to kill real people without any significant risk to themselves, as exemplified by the use of unmanned drones in Afghanistan.[165] Even those of us not remotely controlling what the Royal Air Force has described as the "staring eye" are, nonetheless, always already embroiled in the vicious dialectic of violence that, so Milbank tells us, "is like the regularity of breathing, which goes on all the time and is a fire so slow that we do not notice that it is fire."[166] This insight exposes the brutality of the marketplace, the commodification of knowledge and the pathos of modern politics and economics as nothing but a "slowed-down and distributed violence [that] is actually increased violence, like a torture that is all the more torture through being long drawn out."[167] In contradistinction to this radically unleashed and fundamentally ateleological violence that saturates our everyday reality, Milbank juxtaposes the admittedly more physical violence of the past that

163. Ibid., 28.
164. Ibid., 29.
165. For a prescient account of the changing nature of war, see Virilio and Lotringer, *Pure War*.
166. Milbank, "Violence," 36.
167. Ibid., 37.

was, nevertheless, a more measured and chastened form of violence that resulted only "accidentally" from the pursuit of peace. While we may wish to upbraid Milbank here for a callous indifference to centuries of martyrdom, we must not rush to dismiss his account because its basic motivating intuition, beneath its considerable conceptual sophistication, is that a restrained violence is preferable to one that knows no bounds, which is itself a thoroughly Augustinian intuition insofar as it seeks to limit violence through the self-giving operations of *caritas*.[168]

At issue here for our purposes is the manner in which Milbank subsequently puts his phenomenology of violence to work and the extent to which the work he makes it do illuminates a certain problematic slippage between what we might call retrospective description and formative prescription that results from an explicit endorsement of the necessary pedagogic function of an apocalyptic counterviolence. This dynamic comes to light most clearly in Milbank's critique of the pacifist gaze, which begins as a polemic against the "setting up of quasi-utopian communities in a removed wilderness" that, because they rigidly eschew any participation in actual physical violence, are thereby condemned to one of two possible courses of action: either to "stay and watch" or to "shrink quietly away to [their] prayers."[169] In either case, however, this seemingly pious posture of nonintervention is revealed to be nothing more than the instantiation of a failure of aesthetic judgment, of a failure to see that "both gazing at and averting one's gaze from violence are

---

168. For a history of the effects of Milbank's "chastened accidents," see, for example, the classic account of the Radical Reformation in van Braght, *Martyrs Mirror*. Milbank has developed a theological reading of sacrifice, for example in Milbank, "Stories of Sacrifice," 27–56; and "The Midwinter Sacrifice," 49–65. However, he seems unable or unwilling to countenance an account of martyrdom, which represents a significant lacuna in the development of his political theology. It is, perhaps, this aspect more than any other that illuminates the significant advance of Hart's theological aesthetics, as I will argue below. Admittedly, there are many additional thorny difficulties at work in the background here that simply cannot be investigated in any detail. Suffice it to say, however, that much of the issue revolves around how we understand, in particular, Book XIX of Augustine, *The City of God Against the Pagans*. For an immensely helpful reading of Augustine on this score, see Williams, "Politics and the Soul," 55–72.

169. Milbank, "Violence," 29. It should be noted here that while Milbank's critique of the pacifist gaze involves considerable conceptual sophistication it also displays a notable lack of any concrete specificity insofar as he describes it inconsistently as "phenomenological pacifism," "Christian pacifism," and "Christian pacifist idealism," all of which have different connotations that need to be unpacked. For a helpful typology of more than twenty different pacifisms, see Yoder, *Nevertheless*. Moreover, the only point at which any specificity is alluded to at all has the fortuitous effect, for Milbank, of secretly smuggling in to his critique perhaps the most well-known advocate of Christian nonviolence—Stanley Hauerwas—without having to engage his substantive position at all. This again is evidence of a Schmittian theo-logic at work.

intuitively complicit with its instance."[170] To miss this insight is to miss the profound sense in which this pacifist gaze, which Milbank rightly exposes as inherently incapable of participating in whatever "peace" it claims to have secured, emerges as yet another instance of the violence unleashed in the triumph of the sublime over the beautiful insofar as its logic reproduces, *in nuce*, a staged scene of horror.[171] This pacifist gaze, then, is inextricably linked with the modern society of the spectacle, which also turns on an absolute ban on reciprocal participation, and both therefore represent "a de-intensification of being that in itself *is* the spectacle of destruction."[172] Therefore, these unnamed pacifists are, at best, a manifestation of Hegel's figure of the beautiful soul that "lives in dread of besmirching the splendour of its inner being by action and an existence; and, in order to preserve the purity of its heart, flees from contact with the actual world [and] vanishes like a shapeless vapour that dissolves into thin air."[173] At bottom, then, what Milbank's critique of this pacifist gaze makes clear is that we retrospectively discover that there are no pure spaces into which we can safely retreat from the horrors of violence and that, as with Hegel's beautiful soul, a withdrawal into the void will not save us. What follows from this retrospective phenomenological description, however, is a formative prescription that positively endorses the educative function of violence as a "self-denying coercive ordinance" that naturally flows from our created, not fallen, desire to protect the innocent.[174] To be sure, this is no simple glorification of the efficacy of

170. Milbank, "Violence," 39.

171. Milbank names Edmund Burke as one of those who drove the interest in the aesthetics of the sublime in the eighteenth century, but it was arguably Immanuel Kant whose work brought to light most clearly the violent proclivities that resulted from the rupture between the beautiful and the sublime because, for Kant, the feeling of the sublime, as either "mathematical" or "dynamical," is an unrepresentable overwhelming of the senses that provokes not only awe but also terror. See Kant, *Critique of the Power of Judgment*, 128–59. Gilles Deleuze pushes this even further by claiming that in the feeling of the sublime "it is as if the imagination were confronted with its own limit, forced to strain to its utmost, experiencing a violence which stretches it to the extremity of its power" in *Kant's Critical Philosophy*, 50. Elsewhere, Milbank provocatively suggests that this rupture leaves only a "raped beauty . . . that is only violently surrounded and delineated" in "Beauty and the Soul," 6. As in his critique of the pacifist gaze, the issue here too is the refusal of reciprocity. See also Milbank, "Sublimity," 258–84.

172. Milbank, "Violence," 31.

173. Hegel, *Phenomenology of Spirit*, 400. It is worth noting that, in his earlier essay "The Spirit of Christianity and Its Fate," Hegel is more ambiguous about the figure of the beautiful soul, which he supremely identifies with Jesus. See Hegel, *Early Theological Writings*, especially 224–53. More helpful still is Charles Taylor's observation that Hegel uses the figure of the beautiful soul as a way to reflect on "the dilemma of purity versus efficacy" in Taylor, *Hegel*, 194ff.

174. Milbank, "Violence," 38. A similar line of reasoning is in evidence elsewhere in

violence, and subtle hints of tragic resignation are discernable here. Indeed, in what may be read as a chastened echo of Sorel's distinction between myth and utopia, Milbank claims that "we can only try to force force with reserve and with hopeful risk that distorted realities will come to repent. *This is the best we can do; our scenario is apocalyptic, not utopian.*"[175] Nor is this to dismiss out of hand the potential power of nonviolent interventions because, for Milbank, the Christian strategy is, as in Tolkien's *Lord of the Rings*, "a complex blend of double risk: renunciation of absolute power combined with occasional trickery of that power."[176]

Nonetheless, once the educative function of violence is positively embraced as that which is able to save our created desires to protect the innocent, beauty itself, as a form that evokes desire, is drafted and deformed into performing a function essentially alien to it. In this case, beauty secretly colludes with violence insofar as it evokes a necessary apocalyptic counterviolence that shapes our desire to intervene and is thereby no longer convertible with truth, goodness, and peace because it actively elicits violence itself, thereby causing injury, and thus departs from the form of Christ, which, as Balthasar reminds us, "can do no violence."[177] Put another way, Milbank's anxiety to save our created desires in this way enacts a separation of nature from its proper supernatural end and obscures the tangible difference of grace that he elsewhere insists must have priority in shaping our lives.[178] While it is indeed true that grace does not operate by "cancelling out animality," as Milbank protests, it is equally the case, as de Lubac argues, that "charity has not to become inhuman in order to remain supernatural; like the supernatural itself it can only be understood as incarnate."[179]

Milbank's suggestion that if we think of love in terms of "oscillating hierarchies, we can see how love educates the other" in Milbank, "Gift and the Mirror," 299. If space permitted, at this juncture it would be instructive to compare the roles creativity and hierarchy play in the relationship between beauty and violence with Jantzen, *Violence to Eternity*.

175. Milbank, "Violence," 43 (emphasis added). For Sorel's distinction, see Sorel, *Reflections on Violence*, 24–31.

176. Milbank, "Violence," 43. For the illuminating reading of Tolkien to which Milbank is in debt here, see Milbank, *Chesterton and Tolkien as Theologians*.

177. Balthasar, *Glory of the Lord I*, 482. Without wanting to make the same connections to the political philosophy of John Rawls, it is also worth remembering Elaine Scarry's observation that the word *fair* applies to both beauty and justice. See Scarry, *On Beauty and Being Just*, 86–93. For a helpful theological reading that outlines an anagogical imagination linking beauty and justice, see García-Rivera, *The Community of the Beautiful*, especially 182–86.

178. See Milbank, *Theology and Social Theory*, 220.

179. Hauerwas and Milbank, "Christian Peace," 222; and de Lubac, *Catholicism*, 365, respectively.

In the end, then, while the descriptive power of Milbank's phenomenology of violence cannot be gainsaid, the subsequent formative prescriptions he claims naturally follow rest on a fundamental misapprehension of beauty, that is, on a vision of beauty cut off from its proper supernatural end, which also has the effect of making grace a merely extrinsic conditioning of our created desires. The vision Milbank leaves us with, then, is not the beauty of violence, which glories in endless spectacles of horror, but the violence of beauty, which obscures our ability to "see in Christ the humiliation and offending of eternal love and in one's disfigured fellow human beings the glimmer of the grace of Christ."[180] Accordingly, this is one instance of a recognizably Hegelian gesture whereby Milbank sustains by sublation precisely what he reacts against.

THE RHAPSODIC LIVELINESS OF HART

Even if the foregoing analysis of the undulating terrain of Milbank's political theology has established that his lineage is tied to the apocalyptic reconfigurations begun by Schmitt and Metz, the further suggestion that David Bentley Hart's theological aesthetics can also be read in this vein seems a much more tenuous argument, to say the very least. After all, to my knowledge there is no juncture in his admittedly smaller body of published work in which he engages or even tangentially mentions either Schmitt or Metz.[181] And this despite the fact that it seems as though there are natural points at which Metz in particular could have figured as a prime target.[182] Moreover, Hart is not typically treated alongside political theologians, nor does he explicitly identify himself as such.[183] Indeed, the influences

---

180. Balthasar, *Glory of the Lord V*, 203.

181. Here we can only lament the fact that Hart seems destined to write only the first of what he originally intended to be a five-volume project treating in succession each of the medieval transcendentals. See Hart's admission of this in Hart, "Article Review," 101.

182. One such place might be his brief albeit vociferous denunciation of theologies that, in their attempt to "revise trinitarian doctrine in such a way as to make God comprehensible in the 'light' of Auschwitz, invariably describe a God who—it turns out—is actually the metaphysical ground of Auschwitz" in Hart, *Beauty of the Infinite*, 160. At issue here for Hart, however, is the careless distaste for divine impassibility displayed by a remarkably wide swath of modern theologians; thus, among those explicitly avowed political theologians, it is Jürgen Moltmann who comes under fire and not Metz, who, it must be noted, displays no such distaste. For more on this, see also Hart, "No Shadow of Turning," 184–206.

183. In *The Blackwell Companion to Political Theology*, for example, there is not a single mention of Hart, despite there being a chapter devoted to "Eastern Orthodox Thought." Moreover, the term "political theology" itself is not one that Hart routinely employs.

and interlocutors that populate Hart's work graphically bear this out: he is more influenced by Gregory of Nyssa and Maximus the Confessor than by Hobbes or de Maistre, more interested in Bonaventure and Balthasar than in Benjamin or Bloch. To put it this way is, in one sense, merely to highlight Hart's Eastern Orthodox pedigree; however, this should not be taken to imply, quite simplistically and inaccurately, a retreat into a spiritual and liturgical tradition ensconced with an endless glossing of the Fathers. Here we would do well to recall Rowan Williams's description of Sergii Bulgakov's political theology as demonstrating that "the Byzantine tradition is capable of engaging with modernity and post-modernity with unexpected vigour and integrity," which is a judgment that is also particularly apropos of Hart's work.[184] With that in mind and despite the more obvious reasons Hart does not fit neatly into the genealogy I am attempting to narrate, I suggest that the most significant reason for including him is that he mobilizes the resources of these patristic and contemporary figures in a spirited defiance of modernity's nihilistic drift, which for Hart is manifested supremely in Hegel. Even the considerable abuse Hart heaps on Nietzsche, who is resisted even more vigorously than Heidegger, is revealed to be a consequence of the violence unleashed by the "unrestrained and regal dynamism of the Hegelian system."[185] Thus just as the founding and refounding of political theology in Schmitt and Metz manifests itself as versions of right and left wing Hegelianism, as we have seen above, so too is Hart's political theology animated by an intense wrestling with Hegel, whose presence hovers over the entirety of *The Beauty of the Infinite*. A second reason for including Hart might suggest itself because of his proximity to and critical approbation of Milbank's work, and it is often the case that Hart's telling of the story of the "postmodern city and its wastes" is understood with, through and against Milbank's telling of a similar tale, not least because they are united against a common enemy.[186] While I wouldn't wish to deny the validity of these kinds of readings, especially because Hart invites such associations by explicitly beginning his narration with reference to Milbank, I suggest

---

184. Williams, *Sergii Bulgakov*, 18. It is clear that Hart wants more of this sort of social and political engagement from his own tradition and while, like Bulgakov, his body of work may not on the surface resemble typically Orthodox theology, it is nevertheless animated by a thoroughly Orthodox logic—seen perhaps nowhere more clearly than in his claim that "theology begins only in *philokalia*: the 'love of beauty'" in *Beauty of the Infinite*, 30. See also Hart, "Foreword," xi–xiv.

185. See Hart, *Beauty of the Infinite*, 38–43. Simply put, for Hart, Nietzsche's proclamation of the gospel of salvation from one violence by another is simply to turn the Hegelian logic of negation into an ethos of pure affirmation.

186. For an example of this tendency, see Loughlin, "Rhetoric and Rhapsody," 600–609.

that if we decouple Hart's narrative from Milbank's, which is by no means a procedure that rules out comparisons, we will be in a better position to see more clearly the radical nature of his provocations and how they sharpen and inflect the question of violence and its relation to apocalyptic in immensely helpful ways.

Thus situated as a slightly more distant satellite than Milbank in terms of the overall genealogy I am attempting to construct, Hart is nevertheless crucial in at least three ways. First, and perhaps most ineffably, Hart's rhetorical ontology attempts to perform a delicate act of subversion by entering ever more deeply into the quagmires of the Western metaphysical tradition and pointing toward the decisive Christian interruption of that tradition in which "the sorrows of necessity enjoy no welcome."[187] In this way, we shall see that Hart displays a significant counterpoint to the Schmittian theo-logic that infects Milbank's political theology. Second, Hart offers his rhetorical ontology as a "reorientation of vision that lifts one into another order of seeing" and takes "the form of martyrdom, witness, a peaceful offer that has already suffered rejection and must be prepared for rejection as a consequence."[188] In this way, I will argue that Hart's theological aesthetics helpfully push beyond Milbank and highlight a lacuna in his harnessing of the aesthetic potentials of political theology. Third, despite Hart's very persuasive account of Christian peace there remain, nevertheless, discernable vestiges of the logic of Hegel's "beautiful soul," which itself seems to play a role in inhibiting a robust account of the practices conformed to the peace of Christ. In this way, I will argue that Hart obliquely mirrors Milbank's critique of the pacifist gaze and suggest that an investigation of the unnamed pacifist that comes under Hart's interdiction is the most helpful way forward.

To begin with the first of these three, then, is to foreground the subtlety and nuance of Hart's rhetorical ontology, which is also to say, its riskiness. Hart unfolds the question this way:

> Christ is a persuasion, a form evoking desire, and the whole force of the gospel depends upon the assumption that this persuasion is also peace: that the desire awakened by the shape of Christ and his church is one truly reborn as *agape*, rather than merely the way in which a lesser force succumbs to a greater, as an episode of the endless epic of power. Christian rhetoric, then, is already a question to itself; for if theology cannot concede the

187. Hart, "Offering of Names," 276. Echoes of Metz are certainly audible here in Hart's appropriation of the language of interruption, which is deployed throughout *The Beauty of the Infinite*, 14, 22, 100, 128–31, 139, 221, 396–99, 421.

188. Hart, *Beauty of the Infinite*, 440–41.

intrinsic violence of rhetoric as such, neither can it avoid the task of framing an account of how its own rhetoric may be conceived as the peaceful offer of a peaceful evangel, and not—of necessity—a practice of persuasion for persuasion's sake, violence, coercion at its most enchanting.[189]

Understood in this way, Hart starkly articulates the difficulty of the Christian gospel as one that implicitly invites and justifies the "postmodern" narratives of suspicion it has, at least in part, given rise to and to which it can only respond by placing all hope on "the insane expectation that what was lost will be given back."[190] This way of putting the matter is important not simply because it highlights the centrality of the resurrection for Hart but also because it reveals the sense in which the many animated confrontations that populate his theological aesthetics are not primarily something to be dialectically overcome or even defended against but are rather opportunities for supplementation, qualification, revision and/or clarification of a theological vision that cleaves to the form of Christ. Put differently, we might say that Hart strives as far as possible to think analogically in a way that is hospitable to new insights, which is why he affirms that "however imperfect, or fallen, or degenerate one's vision of reality, still one cannot fail to see something of God's light."[191] This is not to say, however, that Hart is consistently successful in this endeavor, as there are moments in which he slides toward more recognizably dialectical expositions. Nevertheless, the rhapsodic liveliness of Hart's rhetorical ontology displays a deep concern for a form of generativity that is no simple battle of tastes and is subtly deployed in different forms that are responsive to the demands of particular contexts. For our purposes, an examination of two instances in which Hart displays this delicate act of subversion will suffice.

The first of these is perhaps best understood negatively as a kind of hole-punching exercise that problematizes overwrought caricatures of important interlocutors. Hart begins his telling of the story of the "postmodern city and its wastes" with reference to Milbank's reading of

189. Ibid., 3.
190. Ibid., 392.
191. Hart, "Response," 613. This conviction is central for Hart and is what prompts his claim that "whereas the story of violence simply excludes the Christian story of peace, the Christian story can encompass, and indeed heal, the city that rejects it: because that city too belongs to the peace of creation, the beauty of the infinite, and only its narrative and its desires blind it to a glory that everywhere pours in upon it" in *Beauty of the Infinite*, 34. It is important to recognize here that Hart's embrace of analogy is inextricably linked with a defense of Erich Przywara's understanding of the *analogia entis*. This is clear enough in *Beauty of the Infinite*, 241–49; but he has crystallized this in Hart, "The Destiny of Christian Metaphysics," 395–410.

Nietzsche in which we are presented with the development of a differential ontology that, in the end, can articulate itself as nothing more than the chaos of countervailing violences.[192] However, Hart understands this as a mere echo of "Dostoyevsky's prognostications of post-Christian 'nihilism's' ineluctable antinomianism" and it is immediately clear that he does not swallow Milbank's telling wholesale.[193] At issue for Hart in Milbank's narration is the way in which he treats the "major Nietzscheans . . . as elaborations of a single nihilistic philosophy."[194] Particularly problematic for Hart in this respect is Milbank's understanding of Heidegger's account of the ontological difference as a form of Scotist univocity.[195] To be sure, Hart's is a subtle criticism because he does not demur from Milbank's ultimate conclusion that Heidegger's ontology is univocal but merely from his deduction that it is so *because it is Scotist*.[196] Here I would suggest that Hart's point of interjecting this seemingly insignificant tangential remark is not so much to defend Scotus, or even Heidegger for that matter, but rather to highlight the sense in which if theology is to practice the peace it has been given in Christ it cannot proceed primarily on the basis of a staunch rejection of its enemies and must take far greater care of precisely those whom it considers most inimical to its own vision of reality. In this way, Hart's narrative displays little of the restlessness indicative of Milbank's account, which is at times anxiously overburdened by an intense desire to defeat the incipient nihilism of modernity, and is instead imbued with a creative liveliness that enables a deeper and more charitable engagement with enemies and friends alike.[197] Not only is Hart prepared to wade

192. See Milbank, *Theology and Social Theory*, 278–96.

193. Hart, *Beauty of the Infinite*, 37.

194. Milbank, *Theology and Social Theory*, 278. This is not to suggest that Milbank is unaware of important differences between Nietzsche, Heidegger, Deleuze, Lyotard, Foucault, and Derrida but rather to highlight the sense in which "he is more concerned that the Christian narrative (and its 'ontology of peace') be *distinguished from* and then *advanced against* the entire history of modern secular thought." See Hart, *Beauty of the Infinite*, 35–36 (emphasis added). I have argued above that this is the first movement of Milbank's Schmittian theo-logic.

195. See Milbank, *Theology and Social Theory*, 302–6.

196. See Hart, *Beauty of the Infinite*, 41n6. The precise details of this argument are less important for our purposes but, briefly, Hart argues that Scotus's account of predication is far more complex than Milbank's "hasty summary" allows and that his ontology is not univocal because he "understands being as the infinite coincidence of the transcendentals in God's *esse verum*." Hart makes this point again elsewhere by pointing out that Scotus "did not elevate being over God, nor assert that God and creatures *are* in the same way" in Hart, "Review Essay," 370. For a similar argument, see also Kerr, "Why Medievalists Should Talk to Theologians," 369–75.

197. This dynamic can be seen in Hart's differentiation of four narratives of the

106   *The Architectonics of Hope*

deeper into infested waters, so to speak, he also purposively seeks out the most dangerous glades, and it is one of the defining features of Hart's work that whatever "savagery" takes place there is of a definitively different sort than the kind in evidence in Milbank's work.[198]

Thus I suggest that the second instance in which we can visibly discern the generative proclivities of Hart's rhetorical ontology is in his critique of Robert Jenson's understanding of the Trinity. Setting up the debate by articulating it as a question of how we receive Karl Rahner's well-known axiom that "the 'economic' trinity is the 'immanent' trinity and the 'immanent' trinity is the 'economic' trinity," Hart contends that this maxim cannot be taken to imply any straightforward identity that abolishes a distinction between the two and privileges one at the expense of the other.[199] Lurking in the background here is the specter of Hegel's trinitarianism, and Hart is certainly aware that the most egregious case of the outworking of this logic is to be found in the work of Jürgen Moltmann, despite his own best intentions.[200] However, instead of pursuing what would undoubtedly be a

---

sublime: the differential sublime (Derrida), the cosmological sublime (Deleuze), the ontological sublime (Heidegger and Nancy), and the ethical sublime (Kant and Levinas). Hart also never gives the impression that these are the only four that could be identified or that they are not subject to correction or modification. Moreover, I would also suggest that it is precisely this dynamic that enables Hart to argue that "the forgetfulness of the difference between naming God and describing his attributes . . . is one and the same with the forgetfulness of the 'ontico-ontological' difference" in "Offering of Names," 258. It is because Heidegger does not need to be "overcome" that his thought can be valued "as a solvent of the decadent traditions of early modern metaphysics" as he also argues in Hart, "Impassibility as Transcendence," 323.

198. Hart claims the most savage remarks he has ever committed to print were directed at the Harvard bioethicist Joseph Fletcher; however, even in the short essay in which these comments appear Hart's vehemence enacts no simple death blow, which should be clear in his ascription to Fletcher of an intellectual honesty not found in the "new eugenists." See Hart, "The Anti-Theology of the Body," 139–47. Thus despite Fletcher's "meager intellectual gifts, grotesquely hypertrophied ego, and pestilentially sociopathic tendencies" we are nevertheless able to see something that is otherwise obscured. Put another way, Hart does not seek to silence those with whom he disagrees. Comparison with Milbank's treatment of Lawrence Feingold, as seen above, is instructive here.

199. Rahner, *Trinity*, 22.

200. For Hart's most sustained criticism of Moltmann, see Hart, "No Shadow of Turning," 188–93. See also Moltmann, *Trinity and the Kingdom of God*, 36–52, 80–83, 118–22, and 71–78. For a discussion of Hegel's trinitarianism that makes helpful connections to Moltmann, see O'Regan, *Heterodox Hegel*, 14, 77–78, and 221; and O'Regan, *Theology and the Spaces of Apocalyptic*, 34–44 and 102–12. For a comprehensive treatment of Hegel's trinitarian predilections, see also Schlitt, *Hegel's Trinitarian Claim*. It is also worth noting here that Hart's reading of Hegel is not supported by a great deal of close textual analysis and appears to owe a great deal to the French reception of Hegel as mediated by Alexandre Kojève, which is revealed nowhere more clearly than in his

relatively uncomplicated critique of Moltmann, Hart opts for a much more difficult and risky route by engaging Jenson, who, he claims, "might be said to speak for many when he writes: 'To reclaim Hegel's truth for the gospel, we need only a small but drastic amendment: Absolute consciousness finds its own meaning and self in the *one* historical object, Jesus, and *so* posits Jesus' fellows as its fellows and Jesus' world as its world.'"[201] For Hart, this "drastic amendment" to Hegel's logic simply isn't drastic enough, or, perhaps better, begins from premises that almost certainly doom it to fail not only because Hegel's expansive system cannot be tinkered with in this way but also for the more theologically significant reason that this move comes dangerously close to making history the theater in which God becomes or determines himself as God.[202] Hart makes it plain that the ensuing consequences of such an amendment are calamitous inasmuch as the God thus described, a God to whom must necessarily belong, as Jenson asserts, "an interplay between created regularities and evil," not only fails Anselm's test but also the test of Dostoyevsky's Ivan Karamazov.[203] For our purposes, the most remarkable aspect of Hart's critique is that he definitively attributes none of these consequences to Jenson and, moreover, acknowledges that he takes great pains to avoid these "Hegelian" traps. That in Hart's estimation Jenson's trinitarianism will inevitably fail if pushed to extrapolate its ultimate implications is in no sense a warrant for dismissing it but is rather an invitation to tarry a little while longer with the subtleties of its exposition.[204] In this sense, then, this second instance of the generative proclivi-

---

citation of Georges Bataille's essay "Hegel, Death and Sacrifice" in Hart, *Beauty of the Infinite*, 388n227.

201. Hart, *Beauty of the Infinite*, 157.

202. As with the first example of the generative proclivities of Hart's rhetorical ontology, the details of this argument are less important for our purposes and cannot be explicated here in any comprehensive way. However, very briefly, another way to put this might be to suggest that attempts to revise trinitarian doctrine after Hegel are always in danger of falling foul of Heidegger's critique of onto-theology where God becomes an ontic god, a mere supreme being among beings, possessing potential and thus in some sense finite and dispossessed of true transcendence. For Heidegger's critique, see Heidegger, *Identity and Difference*, especially 42-74. Hart alludes to the fact that he believes Heidegger's critique almost certainly holds against the entirety of Hegel's system in Hart, *Beauty of the Infinite*, 163. Part of the riskiness of Hart's critique of Jenson here is that he acknowledges that Jenson intends no such "pseudo-Hegelian thing," which is a position that Jenson explicitly articulates as a partial response to Thomas Weinandy, who, it must be said, seizes on Hart's criticism in a manner inconsistent with Hart's intention, in Jenson, "*Ipse Pater Non Est Impassibilis*," 117-26.

203. Jenson, *Systematic Theology I*, 73. For the details of this dual failure, see Hart, *Beauty of the Infinite*, 164-66. See also Hart's discussion of Dostoyevsky in Hart, *Doors of the Sea*, 36-44.

204. For a helpful overview of the sense in which Hart "celebrates" Jenson's work in

ties of Hart's rhetorical ontology enacts a kind of hospitality to conflict that purposively seeks out sites of productive disagreement not in an effort to overcome these once and for all but rather to enter ever more deeply into the mysteries of the challenges they pose.

Hart's Theopolitical Optics: A Martyr's Labor

These delicate acts of subversion characteristic of Hart's rhetorical ontology are by no means simply isolated moments confined to a more thoroughgoing negotiation of theological subtleties but are rather the very embodiment of a beauty that can really be *seen* even in innumerably imperfect creaturely imperfections. Hart helpfully articulates this metaphorics of vision by suggesting that

> what is at issue here is a species of vision that breaks down the rigid lineaments of a world that interprets itself principally according to the brilliant glamor and spectacle of power, the stable arrangement of all things in hierarchies of meaning and authority, or the rational measures of social order and civic prestige: a way of seeing that lights its way with no facile certitudes concerning the place of God above or of the human below, the orderly architecture of the cosmos and its immanent economies of power and truth, or the opposition of the finite and the infinite. It is a way of seeing that must be learned, because it alters every perspective upon things; and to learn it properly one must be conformed to what one sees. Vision here is inseparable, even indistinguishable, from practice: faith, which is the form this Christian optics must take, lies in the surrender of one's actions to the form of Christ.[205]

For Hart, this labor of vision is articulated by no one more clearly than Gregory of Nyssa, whose recurring motif of the mirror describes a "beauty that perdures in the midst of the world's ceaseless becoming [that] excites in the soul a longing for the infinite beauty it reflects."[206] Indeed, as a helpful summary of Hart's theopolitical optics, the former dense description is but one attempt to flesh out the multifarious implications of Gregory's

---

this way, see also Hart, "The Angel at the Ford of Jabbok," 156–69. I submit that Jenson is also aware and appreciative of this dynamic of productive disagreement, as is evident in Jenson, "Review Essay: David Bentley Hart, *The Beauty of the Infinite*," 235–37.

205. Hart, *Beauty of the Infinite*, 337.
206. Hart, "Mirror of the Infinite," 548.

understanding of the infinite. For our purposes two interwoven dynamics in evidence here are particularly important.

The first of these is the eschatological interruption of time, which is made visible within history supremely in the resurrection of Christ and breaks open every discourse of power that claims for itself a necessary or self-sufficient status. Articulating this radical reorientation of vision in a manner at least vaguely reminiscent of Metz, Hart claims that three things are axiomatic for any Christian eschatology: first, that it "comes suddenly, like a thief in the night, and so fulfills no immanent process, consummates none of our grand projects, reaps no harvest from history's 'dialectic'"; second, that it "impends upon each moment" like a "word of judgment falling across all our immanent truths of power, privilege, or destiny"; and, third, that it thereby "opens the future as a horizon of hope."[207] This "optical inversion" is graphically displayed in the narrative of scripture itself where orderings of power are not only exposed but reversed: the powerful are brought down from their thrones, the lowly are lifted up, the hungry are filled and the rich are sent empty away (Luke 1:46–55). For Hart, it is precisely this eschatological consummation of creation that interrupts every "self-aggrandizing saga of origins" and, from the more "secure" vantage of a stable metaphysics, must appear "at best an insane act of speculative expenditure, one that casts aside all the hard-won profits of history's turmoils and tragedies at the prompting of an impossible hope."[208] This is precisely how

207. Hart, "'Whole Humanity,'" 55. This earlier essay is folded into Hart's treatment of eschatology in *Beauty of the Infinite*, 396–402, although without the immensely illuminating discussion of slavery. Hart's similarities with Metz here go some way beyond simply employing the language of interruption. Indeed, without any explicit acknowledgment whatsoever, Hart's condemnation of forms of idealism, whether in Platonist or Hegelian guise, as myths that seek to root the world in a primordial struggle proceeds in a manner close to the negative-critical structure of Metz's *new* political theology that, likewise, condemns as "mythological gnosis" all those forms of metaphysics that attempt to theoretically ground *Dasein* apart from the concrete vagaries of history. While Metz's critique is largely dependent on his earlier reading of Heidegger, he also has both Hegel and Kierkegaard in his sights as his discussion of the relation between theology and metaphysics indicates in Metz, "Theological World and the Metaphysical World," 257 and 61n12. While both Hart and Metz emphasize the role of analogy this emphatically does not mean that their respective visions are congruent, nor does it suggest that Hart flirts with the kind of transcendental Thomism bequeathed to Metz through Rahner. If space allowed, an investigation of their respective readings of Heidegger would begin to parse the similarities and differences in play, although even here it should be abundantly clear that, despite his criticism, the kind of *aggiornamento* Metz recommends still concedes far too much to the legacy of the Kantian critical project for Hart. Additionally, whereas Metz isolates the *memoria passionis* as the crucial moment in the Christian narrative, Hart's emphasis is decidedly on the resurrection and the disorienting rhetoric of the empty tomb.

208. Hart, "'Whole Humanity,'" 55.

110 *The Architectonics of Hope*

Hart imagines Jesus must have been seen from the perspective of the empire the last time he stood before Pilate: "merely absurd, a ridiculous figure prating incomprehensibly of an otherworldly kingdom and some undefined truth, obviously mad, oblivious of the lowliness of his state and of the magnitude of the powers into whose hands he has been delivered."[209] But by the light of the resurrection, in and through the visibility of the empty tomb, we are enabled to *see* that the Christian interruption of history has reversed all worldly teleologies. Hart's remarkable reading of the eschatological nature of Gregory's condemnation of slavery in his fourth homily on Ecclesiastes is especially illuminating at this juncture.[210] Throughout his discussion, Hart is at pains to emphasize that while Gregory's eschatology might, on the surface, seem indistinguishable from one or another species of metaphysical closure, it is, in fact, not only much more than a baptized Platonism but also resists in advance the idealism of Hegelian dialectics. The crucial moment that sets Gregory's eschatology apart is the collapse he effects of the interval between the ideal and the historical. As Hart explains, "Gregory submerges the ideal in the historical (rather than the reverse), while still allowing the 'ideal' (which should now be read as the 'eschatological') to prevent the historical from assuming the aspect of an enclosed order oriented towards an immanent end."[211] It is this radical eschatological vision that makes sense of Gregory's denunciation of slavery, the force of which went well beyond the practice of manumission officially authorized by Constantine in 321 and ferociously sought the outright abolition of slavery as an institution on the grounds that it divides human nature and thereby claims for itself a power that, at least for Gregory, does not belong even to God.[212] While lamenting the fact that the force of Gregory's sermon, which he evocatively suggests had the "blinding brilliance of a lightning flash,"[213] quickly faded in the centuries that followed, Hart powerfully argues, along the same eschatological lines as Gregory, that

---

209. Hart, *Beauty of the Infinite*, 337. See also his discussion in Hart, *Atheist Delusions*, 171–74.

210. For an English translation, see Gregory of Nyssa, *Homilies on Ecclesiastes*, 72–84.

211. Hart, "'Whole Humanity,'" 58–59.

212. Gregory of Nyssa, *Homilies on Ecclesiastes*, 74. Gregory cites Paul's proclamation that God's gifts are irrevocable in Romans 11:29 in support of his view that even God does not have the power to enslave humanity and the point is equally well made by asking, as he does, after the cost of the likeness of God.

213. Hart, *Atheist Delusions*, 181. Hart's turn of phrase here is all the more interesting because it recalls Metz's reliance on Benjamin's sixth thesis on the philosophy of history.

so long as human power continues to exercise mastery, violence or coercion over souls and bodies, God's saving purpose is resisted. And there is inevitably a social provocation in Gregory's eschatology; if Christ has assumed to himself the human *pleroma*, the eschatological fulfillment of our shared nature has entered our history and left us no time any longer for the provisional employment of unjust but "necessary" arrangements of political or social order. We are already condemned and raised up together, in him in whom there is neither Jew nor Greek, free nor slave, man nor woman; and so our nature's redemption is neither an abstraction nor even only a promise, but is even now a practice, a church, a newness of life in which we participate only insofar as we really enact a redeemed society.[214]

Importantly, the collapse Hart identifies between the ideal and the historical in Gregory is not absolute, that is, the eschatological is not simply identified with the unfolding of history, which would mistakenly attribute to Gregory merely a kind of proto-Hegelian gesture. The continuing tension between the ideal and the historical, as nevertheless two sides of the same coin, two sides of a single reality, is precisely what gives the eschatological its power to disrupt all immanent teleologies, all regimes of "necessity," all the violences we continue to legitimate, however reluctantly. In this way, Hart's powerful interdiction against all worldly "necessities" surely gives the lie to Milbank's theology of justified coercion and reveals it to be yet another instance of the futile attempt to legitimate and perpetuate our own regimes of violence. Perhaps even more significantly, for Hart this eschatological interruption is not simply a negative judgment or a rupture that intrudes into time but rather one that "makes every moment in time one of discrimination, a *critical* moment."[215] It is at this point that we can see that Hart articulates a theopolitical vision with an apocalyptic inflection of a more precise and particular sort than Metz, who, as we have seen above, tends to conflate eschatology and apocalyptic and stresses the negative-critical structure of his *new* political theology above all else.[216] Whereas with Metz we are left

214. Hart, "'Whole Humanity,'" 67. For the details of Gregory's theological anthropology in evidence here, and particularly the significant and novel coincidence of *physis* and *pleroma*, see Balthasar, *Presence and Thought*, especially 71–88 and 133–52; and Ladner, "The Philosophical Anthropology of Saint Gregory of Nyssa," especially 80–85.

215. Hart, "'Whole Humanity,'" 59.

216. It should be noted that while the centrality of eschatological interruption in the development of Hart's theopolitical optics certainly provides a warrant for linking him with the overall trajectory of apocalyptic political theology at issue here, Hart nowhere describes himself as an apocalyptic theologian. Indeed, in the few places he deploys the term, Hart is decidedly more reticent about its potential and tends to employ it

gazing squarely at the ongoing suffering of others, the critical edge of Hart's theopolitical optics opens out onto "the possibility of creative gestures of reconciliation, to a power of discrimination strong enough to distinguish between death camps and hospices," that is, possibilities that Metz's account seems finally unable to countenance.[217] Quick to distinguish these gestures of reconciliation from an Hegelian account of *Aufhebung* that eviscerates the particular in its ceaseless march of "progress," Hart echoes Balthasar by claiming that the redemption in question here integrates all of creation into the story of God's peace as a *symphonia*.[218]

Inextricably linked with the eschatological interruption of time, the second interwoven dynamic that is significant for our purposes is the form Hart finally claims the Christian gospel must take if it is to be a gesture of peace: martyrdom. Without explicit acknowledgment here, Hart again follows Balthasar's claim that "martyrdom is the normal condition of the professed Christian," which by no means implies that Christians will always and everywhere be persecuted.[219] Rather surprisingly, given the radical nature of his provocations here, Hart devotes precious little space to fleshing out the ways in which his theopolitical vision can be said to be inseparable from the practice of the peace it proclaims. What he does provide, however, is a brief account of the difficulty and danger of all Christian persuasion, which highlights the sense in which his theopolitical vision is, in the last analysis, a martyr's labor. Because, as we have seen, the eschatological interruption of time unleashes a power of discrimination and of judgment, it is fundamentally linked to a concrete condition of justice, which is what rules out the institution of slavery for Gregory, that can very easily be usurped by or subordinated to some other regime of power masquerading as truth. The difficulty that Hart starkly faces up to is that Christianity has "no interest in the passivity of an impossible pluralism" and "means to embrace all creation, and so must seek to evoke love from the other, the aesthetic rapture that captivates (or liberates) by its splendor."[220] As Hart graphically puts it, this "comes perilously close to the imagery of seduction or even of rape" and only remains conformed to the peace of Christ if it offers itself as

---

pejoratively to describe the damaging predilections of Hegel, Nietzsche, and their heirs. See, for instance, *Beauty of the Infinite*, 52, 87, 94, and 418.

217. Hart, *Beauty of the Infinite*, 397.

218. Ibid., 401–2. See also Balthasar, *Truth Is Symphonic*, 7–15. If space allowed, it would be instructive here to compare Balthasar's account of the decisive moment and its suspension with Metz, whom he tangentially mentions in connection with Rahner in the Afterword, and with Schmitt.

219. Balthasar, *Moment of Christian Witness*, 21.

220. Hart, *Beauty of the Infinite*, 440.

a gift that is prepared to suffer rejection as a consequence.[221] The precipice at which the practice of the peace of Christ stands, then, cannot be secured in advance and is always at risk of compromising its own witness, which, moving some way beyond Hart's brief reflections, is a prospect made even more complex by the difficulty of distinguishing between the figure of the martyr and others that can, at least on the surface, look very similar. Helpfully elucidating this difficulty, Terry Eagleton suggests that "the martyr and the demoniac are sometimes hard to distinguish, since both are steadfast for death. Both see living in the shadow of death as the only authentic way of life."[222] The difference, which is nevertheless exceedingly difficult to see, as Eagleton goes on to explain, consists in the fact that "the demoniac is the living death of those who feed like vampires or scavengers on the ruin of others," whereas "the martyr . . . offers her death as a gift to the living," all of which comes close to Hart's conclusion that the martyr's labor consists in embodying the audacious hope of a return of the gift that it is powerless of itself to effect.[223]

Unnamed Pacifists and the Specter of Hegel's Beautiful Soul

Given that Hart's theopolitical vision rests on both the eschatological interruption of time and on martyrdom as the only authentic form the practice of the peace of Christ can take if it is not to betray its own witness, it should come as no surprise that a theology of justified coercion of the sort Milbank advocates has no place in his account. While Hart's account of martyrdom itself serves to highlight a lacuna in Milbank's political theology, his critique of "pacifism" is, nevertheless, strangely complicit with Milbank's critique of the pacifist gaze. Significantly placed within the very brief section devoted to the practice of the form of Christ, Hart articulates his critique this way:

> There is small room in theology for political "realism" of the sort advocated by Reinhold Niebuhr, which chooses to accommodate itself to the "tragic" limits of history on the grounds that the church of Christ is not of this world, and that Jesus—in his

---

221. Ibid., 442.

222. Eagleton, *Sweet Violence*, 269. Indeed, this way of putting the matter also helpfully recalls Metz's recommendation of an *ars moriendi* as a preparation for death in Metz, *Followers of Christ*, 18–22.

223. Eagleton, *Sweet Violence*, 270. For a helpful reading of the intricate relationship between tragedy and hope at work here that also makes illuminating connections to Balthasar's theology of Holy Saturday, see Ward, "Steiner and Eagleton," 100–111.

perfectionism and strictly "interpersonal" morality—could not understand the harsher conditions or more insoluble perplexities of political existence. A less obvious implication to many, however, but one that seems to me to follow every bit as ineluctably, is that there is also small room in theology for that passive collaboration with evil that often only flatters itself with the name of "pacifism." However primary the path of nonviolence is for the Christian, the peace of God's kingdom is exhaustively described in scripture, and it is the peace of a concrete condition of justice; it is neither the private practice of an "ethical" individual, jealous of his own moral purity, nor the special and quaint regime of a separatist community that stands aloof from (in ill-concealed contempt for) its "Constantinian" brethren. Where the justice of the kingdom is not present, and cannot be made present without any exercise of force, the self-adoring inaction of those who would meet the reality of, say, black smoke billowing from the chimneys of death camps with songs of protest is simply violence by other means.[224]

For our purposes, this passage is significant precisely insofar as it repeats the linkage Milbank makes between the pacifist gaze and the figure of Hegel's beautiful soul, a link that is made all the more remarkable in coming from a theologian who goes to great lengths to defend the doctrine of divine *apatheia* as having nothing whatsoever to do with apathy but, in the end, cannot entertain the possibility that the pacifism he so easily dismisses may have nothing whatsoever to do with a passive complicity with evil. What this passage finally reveals, then, is that despite his battle with Hegel, Hart has not been able to wrest from his account the dialectical logic of purity versus efficacy. All this is to the good for our purposes, however, because it is precisely at this point that the final piece of the genealogy I am attempting to narrate suggests itself since this presents a providential opportunity to explore and practice what the unnamed pacifist who comes under Hart's interdiction calls the "utility of being misunderstood."[225] It is to this task that we now turn.

---

224. Hart, *Beauty of the Infinite*, 341. To be fair, Hart has subsequently acknowledged that he especially regrets this passage in particular for both its tone and for not naming John Howard Yoder as his intended target. See Hart, "Response," 618. This regret notwithstanding, this passage is made all the more remarkable because Hart's language itself and the very brief critique of Niebuhr are so evocative of Yoder's much more extensive criticisms in, for example, Yoder, "Reinhold Niebuhr and Christian Pacifism," 101–17; and "Reinhold Niebuhr's 'Realist' Critique," 285–98.

225. Yoder, *To Hear the Word*, 47–70.

CHAPTER 4

Political Theology and the Power of Nonviolence

Introduction

THE SUGGESTION THAT THE work of John Howard Yoder, the unnamed pacifist who elicits Hart's consternation, represents the culmination of the genealogy I am attempting to narrate will undoubtedly indicate to some that my analysis has gone badly awry and come off the rails at a critical juncture. Surely even a lamentable condemnation of the sort Hart engages in cannot simply mean that a more charitable reappraisal of a decidedly minor target, and one that is so tangential that it does not merit even a footnote, could somehow figure significantly in the reconfigurations of political theology with which we have been concerned. Moreover, Hart's criticism aside, there seems to be precious little, at least upon first examination, to link Yoder with any of the interlocutors that have played a significant role in the genealogy I have been attempting to construct. Indeed, as we have seen, one of the major undercurrents that lurks in the background of the reconfigurations of political theology itself is a quarrel with Hegel or, perhaps more accurately, some later reception of Hegel. While Yoder does occasionally parachute Hegel's name into his arguments at various junctures there is no significant engagement, and his fleeting references are peripheral and caricatured at best, all of which leaves the distinct impression that the proper name "Hegel" is more of a placeholder for a problematic kind of grand philosophical synthesis for

Yoder than anything else.[1] More generally, while Yoder studied philosophy during his years as a doctoral student at the University of Basel, taking individual seminars on Augustine, Peter Lombard, Thomas Aquinas, and Immanuel Kant, among others, as well as at least one course taught by Karl Jaspers, his work is marked by a persistent suspicion of the motivations and usefulness of philosophy in general and of the search for first principles in particular.[2] Moreover, it is also clear that Yoder's work is not primarily devoted to indicting the philosophical tradition that remains wedded in various ways to the search for first principles but is rather animated most powerfully by an intense engagement with scripture and sixteenth-century Anabaptism.[3] In this respect, Yoder's worries about the motivations of philosophy seem to be broadly aligned with his one-time teacher, Karl Barth, when he wrote that "the great temptation and danger consists in this, that the theologian will actually become what he seems to be—a philosopher."[4] As if his misgivings about philosophical system building and his reliance on radically different source material weren't already enough to make him a thoroughly unlikely candidate to figure within a genealogy that traces the reconfigurations of political theology, Yoder also explicitly sought to distance his work from what he

1. Yoder's references to Hegel are few, but see, for example, Yoder, *Priestly Kingdom*, 130; *For the Nations*, 126; *Royal Priesthood*, 73 and 120; *Politics of Jesus*, 10n16 and 168; *War of the Lamb*, 175; and *Nonviolence*, 44. Taken together, however, there is certainly a sense in which Yoder's theological instincts predispose him to think, with Metz, Milbank, and Hart, that there is something in the Hegelian philosophical system that must be broadly resisted.

2. For the details of Yoder's coursework while at the University of Basel, see Nation, *John Howard Yoder*, 18n69. Yoder's worries about what he called "methodologism" are best described in Yoder, "Walk and Word," 77–90; and "'Patience' as Method in Moral Reasoning," 24–44. This is not to suggest, however, that Yoder's work is somehow "unphilosophical" but only to highlight the sense in which he "saw no reason to pursue philosophy in the interest of theory," as Stanley Hauerwas remarks in "Introduction: Lingering with Yoder's Wild Work," 13. Put another way, Yoder's work often displays the kind of exactitude prized by analytic philosophers but does not find it necessary to engage Wittgenstein, for example, to accomplish its tasks.

3. Yoder's commitment to scripture is woven into the very fabric of his work, as is amply demonstrated in what is still his best-known book, *The Politics of Jesus*. Additionally, Yoder's interest in sixteenth-century Anabaptism went well beyond his doctoral work—translated and published in English as Yoder, *Anabaptism and Reformation in Switzerland*—and continued throughout his career in his involvement on the editorial council of the Classics of the Radical Reformation series published by Herald Press, which saw Yoder directly involved in translating and editing material for three of the nine volumes.

4. Barth, "Fate and Idea in Theology," 29. It is worth briefly noting that, although he does not explicitly mention him, Barth's silent interlocutor here is Erich Przywara.

characterized as the "faddist approach to theology" in the late sixties that dealt with "'the revolution in theology' or 'theology for the revolution,' with politicking as a theological concern or with theology as a political event."[5] Even though Yoder has in mind here a broader notion of what I have referred to, with respect to Schmitt, as the refounding of political theology, his "relaxed confidence" that this theological fad would likely have abated by the time *The Original Revolution* was first published in 1971 seems, in retrospect, to have been turned on its head in important ways.[6] Far from falling out of fashion, the complex interrelation of theology and politics has continued apace, building up steam to such an extent that disciplinary boundaries that were once thought to be all but inviolable have been exploded and we now have atheist philosophers reading the Apostle Paul as a radical political figure.[7] Thus to link Yoder, however tenuously, with this trajectory might seem to some to run counter to Yoder's own wishes. Making his inclusion yet even more precarious, Yoder substantively engages none of the four major voices at the center of this book, although he shows an awareness of Metz in the course of a distinction between German political theology and Latin American liberation theology.[8] Indeed, the closer connection is certainly with the so-called theologies of liberation given the themes that populate Yoder's work, the sources on which he draws, and his own experience teaching and lecturing across South America.[9] Taken together, then, these seven

5. Yoder, *Original Revolution*, 8.
6. Ibid.
7. I am thinking of Badiou, *Saint Paul*, in particular, but the contributions of Slavoj Žižek and Giorgio Agamben to the philosophical interest in Paul could also be mentioned here.
8. The clearest examples of this are Yoder, "The Wider Setting of 'Liberation Theology,'" 285–96; and Yoder, "Political Theology," 1–7. In addition to an awareness of Metz, Yoder's footnotes in these essays and elsewhere reveal that he read very widely indeed in both political and liberation theology.
9. The lectures Yoder gave on his inaugural trip to Latin America have been published as Yoder, *Revolutionary Christianity*. Yoder's initial experience evidently had a strong impact on him, and his interest in Latin America continued throughout his career. At the invitation of José Míguez-Bonino, Yoder returned to Argentina to teach for the 1970–71 academic year and while the theme of liberation can be found scattered throughout his work, several essays in particular exemplify its importance, including Yoder, "Biblical Roots of Liberation Theology," 55–74; "The Anabaptist Shape of Liberation," 338–48; "Withdrawal and Diaspora," 76–84; and "Orientation in Midstream," 159–68. Yoder himself notes that some reviewers of *The Politics of Jesus* understood it to be "an especially valid expression of 'liberation theology'; others read it as a critique of that movement" in *Politics of Jesus*, 15n23. For our purposes this reinforces the view that his work has been received in some relation to liberation theology.

objections are surely more than enough to question the suggestion that Yoder's work could represent a significant contribution to a genealogy that purports to trace the reconfigurations of political theology with which we have been concerned.[10]

Despite this list of objections, which could undoubtedly be deepened and expanded along multiple overlapping lines of inquiry, I will argue that Yoder's work is indispensable for the genealogy I am attempting to narrate precisely because, as with the other four major voices at the heart of this essay, he continues to wrestle with the relationship between violence and apocalyptic but, unlike the others, does so in a way that embodies a nonviolent way of seeing that opens out onto possibilities of reconciliation by creatively orchestrating conflict. It is worth recalling here, as has been the case with all of the other reconfigurations of political theology with which we have been concerned, that the reading of Yoder that follows is in no way offered in an authoritative manner or even as a hermeneutic key that claims Yoder must be understood in the light of the apocalyptic element that undoubtedly infuses his thought. This is not only the case because of the quite self-conscious, though nonarbitrary, selectivity with which I will engage Yoder's work, which itself is necessary for a book that does not aim toward a kind of comprehensiveness, but also because Yoder explicitly qualifies the range and scope of apocalyptic within theology himself. Indeed, Yoder claims that "apocalypse is only one of many modes of discourse in the believing community. We should not prefer it; we should use them all."[11] Despite this important qualification, Yoder goes on to say that apocalyptic is "one of those [modes of discourse] with which we have the most trouble, and for that reason it may have more to teach us," and in this sense even a limited investigation of the kind that unfolds below holds out the potential of illuminating and reconfiguring the ongoing developments

---

10. This list of objections to Yoder's place in my genealogy is by no means exhaustive; there are more, perhaps most glaringly the routinely marshaled charge of sectarianism. The impetus for this charge begins with Troeltsch, *The Social Teaching of the Christian Churches*, and is refined in Niebuhr, *Christ and Culture*. For Yoder's devastating critique of Niebuhr's categories, see Yoder, "How H. Richard Niebuhr Reasoned," 31–90. The reason I have not included this objection above is that I consider it to be overturned to such an extent that even a very partial and cursory reading is able to discern the sense in which Yoder's position is genuinely political and his ecclesiology does not imply an ascetic withdrawal of some sort. For one such reading, see Žižek, *Living in the End Times*, 129.

11. Yoder, *Royal Priesthood*, 129–30. Elsewhere, Yoder makes the claim that a multiplicity of discourses has the laudable effect of preventing serious mistakes that may result from a too exclusive focus on only one "as some crazies use the Apocalypse or as some conservatives use the Davidic kingship" in *For the Nations*, 89.

of political theology in a way that follows up on Yoder's own insight.[12] With this significant proviso in mind, then, it is precisely in his development of what I call the generative capacities of nonviolence that I will argue Yoder is alone among the major voices at the interpretive heart of the book to subvert the fundamentally violent aporetics originally defined by Schmitt. This emphatically does not imply, however, that Yoder consistently embodies his own best insights, nor that the reconfigurations of political theology enacted by Metz, Milbank, and Hart should be understood as fungible stops on the way to the truly visionary and therefore peaceful political theology to which Yoder points. A helpful preliminary way to understand this is through Yoder's own metaphor of the vine, which he claims is like "a story of constant interruption of organic growth in favor of pruning and a new chance for the roots" that crucially involves "a 'looping back,' a glance over the shoulder to enable a midcourse correction, a rediscovery of something from the past whose pertinence was not seen before, because only a new challenge enables us to see it speaking to us."[13] The language of interruption here is already reminiscent of Metz and Hart, but in Yoder's hands political theology is apocalyptically inflected in such a way that we are enabled to see that dissonance creates space for renewal or, to continue with the vine metaphor, that pruning provokes new growth. So to be clear, I am not suggesting that Yoder is the next step or final stage in my argument that Milbank and Hart are helpfully read as reconfiguring the political theology initially founded and refounded in late modernity in the work of Schmitt and Metz. Put another way, the reconfigurations of political theology that I have been tracing are not a simple matter of historical progress, as if a line could be drawn from Schmitt through Metz, Milbank, and Hart to Yoder. The matter is more complex, and although Yoder occupies a more distant place with respect to his immediate historical relation to the four major voices at the center of this book, his work, nevertheless, allows us to see more clearly than anyone else the "'power' of 'nonviolence.'"[14] What follows, then, is emphatically *not* a defense of Yoder's "position" in the face of Hart's

12. Yoder, *Royal Priesthood*, 130.
13. Yoder, *Priestly Kingdom*, 69.
14. See Yoder, "'Power' of 'Nonviolence,'" 1–18. This paper was presented to the Section on Religion, Peace and War at the American Academy of Religion conference in Philadelphia in 1995. The phrase is taken from Gregg, *The Power of Non-violence*. Gregg was an American lawyer and social philosopher who is generally credited with introducing the thought of Mohandas Gandhi to a wider Western audience through his development of the notion of nonviolent resistance and influenced Martin Luther King Jr., among others. See also Yoder, "Jesus and Power," 447–54. In one sense, Yoder's distance from Schmitt, Metz, Milbank, and Hart is at least part of what enables his work to open up sites of productive disagreement, as we will see below.

criticism, nor a grand synthesis of some kind, but rather an attempt to think with and beyond Yoder in ways that highlight the insights of his nonviolent mode of vision that will, in turn, enable a productive "looping back" to the other voices that have contributed to the transformation of political theology. In one sense, and to continue with a minor thread that is woven into the previous chapter, what I want to suggest is that Yoder's work can helpfully be read as another of Balthasar's "theological styles," as yet another "reflected ray of glory" that illuminates the reconfigurations of political theology in immensely helpful ways.[15] To see how and in what ways this is the case is the burden of this chapter.

Yoder's Apocalyptic Politics of Jesus: Seeing the Generative Capacities of Nonviolence

Lest the foregoing give the impression that a theopolitical reading of Yoder of the kind I am attempting is something novel or even new, it is worth noting that much of Yoder's own work as well as the secondary literature that engages his work in various ways is focused squarely on the significance of the sociopolitical. Indeed, to cite only two well-known examples, Yoder begins the first chapter of *The Politics of Jesus* by asking whether a messianic sociopolitical ethic is possible and writes much earlier that "the church is properly a political entity, a *polis.*"[16] Following up on and complicating these themes in helpful ways, many of the most interesting of the burgeoning engagements with Yoder's work find in it a "compelling vision for pursuing justice and political engagements in heterogeneous societies."[17] And un-

---

15. For Balthasar's introductory discussion of theological style, see Balthasar, *Glory of the Lord II*, 11–30. Importantly, this comparison rules out in advance any separation between form and content since, as Balthasar elsewhere argues, "Christ is the form because he is the content" in *Glory of the Lord I*, 463. The way I am using it, then, a theological style is simply the expression of an impression of the form of Christ, as Balthasar makes clear in his discussion of Bonaventure in *Glory of the Lord II*, especially 270–308. Among the figures that populate Balthasar's discussion of theological style, Yoder is closest to those with a more distinctly kenotic flavor where Christ is at the center and divine glory is manifested supremely in suffering love as Balthasar claims is the case with the "lay styles" of Pascal, Hamann, and Péguy in *Glory of the Lord III*. This comparison resonates with Yoder's description of his own work as a "tone of voice" or "style or stance" in Yoder, *For the Nations*, 1.

16. Yoder, *Christian Witness to the State*, 18. See also Yoder, *Politics of Jesus*, 1–20.

17. Coles, "Wild Patience of John Howard Yoder," 306. I cite Coles in particular because, as will become clear, my reading of Yoder is indebted to him in important ways. Although there are simply too many other very interesting readings of Yoder to mention, two recent collections display the depth and range of engagement. See Bergen and Siegrist, *Power and Practices*; and Dula and Huebner, *The New Yoder*.

doubtedly these kinds of readings have been and will continue to be spurred on by efforts to posthumously publish ever more of Yoder's work.[18] Even without this steady stream of new material, however, there is something about Yoder's work itself that is endlessly productive of new and diverse encounters with others. While this creative generativity certainly reflects Yoder's own deep commitment to ecumenical and interfaith dialogue and is inseparable from his practice of working under assignment, it is also inextricably bound up with his understanding of nonviolence as a way of seeing that "explode[s] the limits that our own systems impose on our capacity to be illuminated and led."[19] For our purposes, it is precisely Yoder's creative negotiation of this complex interrelation between violence and apocalyptic that makes his inclusion in the genealogy of the regonfigurations of political theology invaluable.

Long before the now widespread interest in addressing what Jacques Derrida referred to as a "newly arisen apocalyptic tone in philosophy,"[20] Yoder memorably raised the issue of apocalyptic this way:

> When read carefully, none of the biblical apocalypses, from Ezekiel through Daniel to Mark 13 and John of Patmos, is about either pie in the sky or the Russians in Mesopotamia. They are about how the crucified Jesus is a more adequate key to understanding what God is about in the real world of empires and armies and markets than is the ruler in Rome, with all his supporting military, commercial, and sacerdotal networks.[21]

Continuing the strategy with which he began *The Politics of Jesus*, Yoder's attempt here is to unsettle the sense in which biblical apocalyptic is held captive to interpretations that, in various ways, either set it aside or use it as opiate, associate it with visions of violent destruction at the end of history or relegate its meaningfulness to secondary pastoral or therapeutic concerns.[22] Yoder does this not by adopting a strategy of "demythologization," which in

18. To my knowledge there have been at least eleven such publications since Yoder's death in 1997, the most important of which for our purposes are Yoder, *The War of the Lamb* and *Nonviolence*.

19. Yoder, *Royal Priesthood*, 129. For an example of Yoder's commitment to ecumenical and interfaith dialogue, see, for example, the essays collected in Yoder, *The Royal Priesthood* and *The Jewish-Christian Schism Revisited*. For a discussion of the importance of understanding Yoder's work as working under assignment, see Hauerwas and Huebner, "History, Theory, and Anabaptism," 391–408.

20. See Derrida, "On a Newly Arisen Apocalyptic Tone in Philosophy," 117–71.

21. Yoder, *Politics of Jesus*, 246.

22. For a helpful review of interpretive problems with apocalyptic literature, see Rowland, *The Open Heaven*; and Schüssler Fiorenza, *The Book of Revelation*.

an important sense simply ends up hijacking the understanding of apocalyptic by subjecting it to its own *a priori* assumptions, but by emphasizing the strangeness of biblical apocalyptic itself and by articulating what it might mean to enter ever more deeply into that strange and unsettling world.[23] Expanding this even further, Yoder notes that "it is not merely apocalyptic that is odd; it is the Bible whose world is strange."[24] For Yoder, bumping up against this strangeness may provide an opportunity for precisely the kind of mid-course correction that fosters new growth. Indeed, as Yoder writes, apocalyptic "does us the service of ignoring and thereby striking down our confidence in system-immanent causal explanations for the past, and, even more, in system-immanent causal descriptions of how the future is sure to unfold."[25] While this way of putting the matter certainly has affinities with what Derrida called "deconstruction," in Yoder's hands the "striking down" of our own interpretive grids opens the future as a horizon of hope because apocalyptic "inserts into our present setting a fulcrum capable of being leaned on to pry us away from the assumption that the world as we see it is the only way it can be."[26] Helpfully elucidating the difficulty of accomplishing this, Yoder recounts a classroom encounter:

> I was visiting a small Roman Catholic theological seminary in South Africa, discussing the moral resources for nonviolent social struggle, a vision which was born in that country in the work of Gandhi. One of the students immediately appealed to the action of John F. Kennedy in the 1962 Cuban missile crisis, as having proven the rightness of armed conflict. What is striking is not the status of the arguments for or against violence, or for or against the American policies in 1962, but the assumption made by a poor black man in South Africa that the settings in which the President of the United States makes decisions are more paradigmatic than his own.[27]

23. Yoder is thinking especially of Bultmann's project here. See, for example, the essays collected in Bultmann, *The New Testament and Mythology*.

24. Yoder, "Ethics and Eschatology," 127n7. Yoder's emphasis on the productive capacity of the strangeness of scripture here has certain affinities with Milbank's project of "making strange" in, for example, Milbank, *Word Made Strange*, especially 1–4.

25. Yoder, "Ethics and Eschatology," 122. This way of putting the matter resonates with the critical operations characteristic of Hart's theopolitical optics in which "the sorrows of necessity enjoy no welcome." See especially Hart, "Offering of Names," 276.

26. Yoder, "Ethics and Eschatology," 119. Without mentioning Derrida, Yoder specifically appropriates the language of deconstruction in Yoder, "Armaments and Eschatology," 53. For a helpful introductory account of Derrida's use of the term that highlights its "messianic ring," see Derrida, *Deconstruction in a Nutshell*.

27. Yoder, "Ethics and Eschatology," 122.

Political Theology and the Power of Nonviolence 123

As this encounter clearly illustrates, breaking through the crust of such entrenched interpretive grids will indeed continue to prove an onerous yet necessary task. However, for Yoder, that the present power constellation is not the last word is precisely the "good news" that attention to apocalyptic can "reveal."

It is important to note here, however, that in drawing attention to the strangeness of apocalyptic Yoder is not suggesting that its novelty as a genre is what makes it worthy of attention, nor that we should "play off an 'apocalyptic' cosmology as a whole against 'reality,' in order to study its oddity as we do an exotic culture."[28] Alternatively, Yoder asks whether "it is possible to specify certain elements of the 'apocalyptic' world-view which might in their setting be held to be not odd or irrational, but rather appropriate reactions to the way the world really is?"[29] Thus despite whatever flights of fancy we might read into or off of God's judgment of Rome as recounted by John of Patmos, for example, Yoder emphasizes again and again that the metaphors employed in no way remove us from history but rather highlight the way God acts within history. As Yoder puts it,

> The substantial assumption which moves the seer is that God is an actor. *How* God acts can be expressed only in metaphors which our mechanically formed world vision can only consider fantastic or poetic. Nonetheless, the addressees of "revelation" are expected or commanded to behave differently, *within* the system of the real world.[30]

Significantly situated between what Balthasar calls "the interplay of veiling and unveiling," Yoder's retrieval of an apocalyptic idiom certainly possesses a critical-disclosive edge, but what is especially important for our purposes is that it also takes on a specificity that has heretofore been largely absent in the reconfigurations of political theology with which we have been concerned.[31] Indeed, the manner in which Yoder tarries with this apocalyptic interplay is precisely where his unique contribution to the reconfiguration of political theology is to be found, for it eschews a theological logic that would seek to manage and manipulate violence in favor of one that seeks to cleave ever more intimately to the form of Christ, which, as Balthasar reminds us, "can do no violence."[32]

28. Yoder, "Armaments and Eschatology," 51.
29. Ibid.
30. Yoder, *Politics of Jesus*, 245.
31. Balthasar, *Theo-Logic I*, 206.
32. Balthasar, *Glory of the Lord I*, 482.

As Yoder himself subsequently confirms, the concluding chapter of *The Politics of Jesus*, which sought to make historical sense of the meaning of the apocalyptic vision of the seer of Patmos in the book of Revelation, seemed to provoke the most offense because it was mistakenly received as an argument for social withdrawal.[33] This erroneous reception aside, the connections Yoder makes here between cross and resurrection, ends and means, power and nonviolence, and the meaning and direction of history are no less scandalous. For Yoder, the apocalyptic politics of Jesus are linked from beginning to end with the question of violence and what form Jesus's kingship will take, which is why he suggests that the cross is "not a ritually prescribed instrument of propitiation but the political alternative to both insurrection and quietism."[34] Noting that the debate in Christian social ethics is particularly obsessed with the meaning and direction of history, which is by no means simply an idle philosophical concern but is itself a corollary of the biblical claim that God is active in history, Yoder offers up what he calls a "biblical philosophy of history" that is "nothing more than a logical unfolding of the meaning of the work of Jesus Christ himself, whose choice of suffering servanthood rather than violent lordship, of love to the point of death rather than righteousness backed by power, was itself the fundamental direction of his life."[35] While the first eleven chapters of *The Politics of Jesus* are devoted to a close reading of the Gospel of Luke and of the apostolic tradition primarily in the letters of Saint Paul, what is most important here for our present purposes is Yoder's reading of the series of visions and hymns as recounted by John of Patmos:

> Then I saw in the right hand of the one seated on the throne a scroll written on the inside and on the back, sealed with seven seals; and I saw a mighty angel proclaiming with a loud voice, "Who is worthy to open the scroll and break its seals?" And no one in heaven or on earth or under the earth was able to open the scroll or to look into it. And I began to weep bitterly . . .

---

33. Yoder, *War of the Lamb*, 64. Indeed, a sectarian reading of Yoder on this score, perhaps the most influential of which can be found in the work of Reinhold Niebuhr, was prevalent throughout Yoder's life. See, for example, Niebuhr, "Why the Christian Church Is Not Pacifist," 1–25; and "Love and Justice and the Pacifist Issue," 241–301. Yoder himself spent much energy showing a sectarian withdrawal has nothing whatsoever to do with his account of nonviolence—an argument that is reflected in the secondary literature. For Yoder's account of this argument with respect to Niebuhr's critique, see especially Yoder, *Reinhold Niebuhr and Christian Pacifism*, as well as chapters 18 and 20 of Yoder, *Christian Attitudes to War*, 285–98 and 309–20.

34. Yoder, *Politics of Jesus*, 36.

35. Ibid., 232–33.

> Then I looked and I heard the voice of many angels ... singing with full voice,
>
>> "Worthy is the Lamb that was slaughtered
>> to receive power and wealth and wisdom and might
>> and honor and glory and blessing!" (Rev 5:1–4, 11–12)

For Yoder, the question of the meaningfulness of history is here laid bare, and that the slaughtered lamb alone is able to open the scroll is, as he writes, "a meaningful affirmation that the cross and not the sword, suffering and not brute power determines the meaning of history."[36] The scandal here is, as Yoder himself spilled much ink attempting to clarify, not a simple refusal of power, a Nietzschean glorification of weakness, nor a dualistic choice between obedience and effectiveness, but rather that "the kind of faithfulness that is willing to accept evident defeat rather than complicity with evil is, by virtue of its conformity with what happens to God when he works among us, aligned with the ultimate triumph of the Lamb."[37]

Key to this understanding of the apocalyptic politics of Jesus is the biblical virtue Yoder singles out as perhaps the most crucial in a world where "part if not all of social concern has to do with looking for the right 'handle' by which one can 'get a hold on' the course of history and move it in the right direction": patience.[38] In this sense, Yoder's biblical philosophy of history is in deep sympathy with Balthasar's theology of history, which likewise highlights the centrality of patience in the New Testament. Indeed, in his illuminating discussion of Christ's mode of time, and also with apocalyptic echoes, Balthasar goes as far as to claim that patience

> becomes the basic constituent of Christianity, more central even than humility: the power to wait, to persevere, to hold out, to endure to the end, not to transcend one's own limitations, not to force issues by playing the hero or the titan, but to practice

---

36. Ibid., 232.

37. Ibid., 238.

38. Ibid., 228. This way of putting the matter is one way to identify a prominent narrative trope that punctuates Yoder's work, namely, "Constantinianism." The shape and development of Yoder's account of the Constantinian temptation is certainly not unimportant to the present discussion, but for reasons of space it simply cannot be dealt with in any explicit way here. For one of Yoder's succinct accounts of this shift, see his essay entitled "The Constantinian Sources of Western Social Ethics," in Yoder, *Priestly Kingdom*, 135–47. It is worth noting that the vicissitudes of this debate have recently been enlivened by the deliberately polemical and provocative work of Peter Leithart. See Leithart, *Defending Constantine*, as well as the special issue of *The Mennonite Quarterly Review* 85, no. 4 (2011), which engages Leithart's work and contains a response from him. If I have understood Yoder correctly, this is a debate that he would welcome.

the virtue that lies beyond heroism, the meekness of the lamb, which is *led*.[39]

It is perhaps here more than anywhere else that we can see a significant difference of the theo-logic that orients Yoder's apocalyptic politics of Jesus. Yoder encapsulates this powerfully and succinctly by claiming that "the relationship between the obedience of God's people and the triumph of God's cause is not a relationship between cause and effect but one of cross and resurrection."[40] Hence, he subsequently argues that the scandal of the cross is "one in which the calculating link between our obedience and ultimate efficacy is broken, since the triumph of God comes through resurrection and not through effective sovereignty or assured survival."[41] In Yoder's hands, then, apocalyptic does us the service of striking down whatever immanent strategic calculus might promise desirable effects and breaking open the future as a horizon of hope freed from such limiting possibilities. As Yoder writes elsewhere, "The image of a slaughtered Lamb is no empty cipher; it is the code reference to the simple narrative substance of the work and the words of that particular Palestinian populist, in all of his Jewishness and all of his patience."[42] The particularity of Jesus is essential here because "in Jesus we have a clue to which kinds of causation, which kinds of community-building, which kinds of conflict management, go with the grain of the cosmos."[43] This way of putting the matter importantly rules out any understanding of Yoder here that would simply relegate his apocalyptic politics of Jesus to the sectarian ghetto because the question is not centered

---

39. Balthasar, *Theology of History*, 37. As we will see below, Yoder's understanding of patience helpfully complicates Balthasar's view here with respect to humility since, for Yoder, patience is intimately bound up with repentance and fallibility. This dynamic can be seen in what Yoder calls the "contrite patience of repentance" and the "modest patience of sobriety in finitude" in "'Patience' as Method," 31. In his discussion of Dorothy Day and the Catholic Worker Movement, Yoder explicitly makes a link between active nonviolence and meekness when he argues that the renunciation of violence is "the active transformation of the ancient virtue of 'meekness,' that quality of self-emptying which makes one an apt subject for inheriting the earth" in *Nonviolence*, 112.

40. Yoder, *Politics of Jesus*, 232.

41. Ibid., 239.

42. Yoder, "To Serve Our God," 133. In what is his most explicit essay on patience, Yoder identifies nineteen distinctive yet overlapping kinds of patience, only one of which he labels the "apocalyptic patience of waiting in hope" in "'Patience' as Method," 33. At the risk of flattening out the distinguishing characteristics Yoder itemizes, I suggest that, in a broader sense, all of Yoder's forms of patience are apocalyptically inflected just to the extent that they exemplify a theo-logic that explodes the "limits that our own systems impose on our capacity to be illuminated and led" as he argues in *Royal Priesthood*, 129.

43. Yoder, *Politics of Jesus*, 246.

on a renunciation of power but on its very redefinition, or, perhaps better, on its reinscription within a doxological view of history that sees the cosmos itself in the light of the knowledge that the Lamb that was slaughtered is now living. This is precisely why the comparison with Balthasar here is particularly helpful because, like Yoder, he recognizes that to practice the virtue of patience is no simple refusal of action but is itself the outworking of a different kind of power—in his terms, a meekness beyond heroism. Yoder repeatedly returns to this dynamic throughout his work and, with unintentional echoes of Balthasar, highlights the "almighty meekness of the reigning Lord" by arguing that

> when the Christian whom God has disarmed lays aside carnal weapons it is not, in the last analysis, because those weapons are too strong, but because they are too weak. He directs his life toward the day when all creation will praise not kings and chancellors but the Lamb that was slain as worthy to receive blessing and honor and glory *and power* (Revelation 5:12–13).[44]

Again echoing this sentiment much later, Yoder readily concedes that nonviolence may, in some cases, refer to nothing more than a principled or pragmatic rejection of violence but argues instead for a form of nonviolent action that renounces violence "in order that other kinds of power (truth, consent, conscience) may work."[45]

Thus it should be abundantly clear that to understand Yoder as promulgating a politics of despair that simply renounces effectiveness is a gross misreading. His frankness in admitting that "we cannot sight down the barrel of suffering love to see how it will hit its target" highlights not some form of tragic resignation to the bloody theater of history but rather that, if hope is to be particularly Christian, it must be conformed to what it proclaims.[46] Put negatively, the cross is not a recipe for resurrection. In this way, we can see that Yoder's apocalyptic politics of Jesus takes on something of an apophatic function insofar as the exercise of patience has the effect of breaking through the mechanistic logic that dominates the workings of the interpretive grids through which we, to lesser and greater degrees, attempt to steer history in the right direction. However, the divine patience that Yoder is at pains to emphasize is not simply a *breaking through* but also a *breaking*

---

44. Yoder, *He Came Preaching Peace*, 29. Or, again: "Jesus chose the cross as an alternative social strategy of strength, not weakness" in Yoder, *War of the Lamb*, 41.

45. Yoder, *War of the Lamb*, 85. For Yoder's most systematic discussion of various types of pacifism, of which he identifies no less than twenty-nine, see Yoder, *Nevertheless*.

46. Yoder, *Nevertheless*, 137.

forth.⁴⁷ That is, alongside its power to "relativize both the gloomy and the confident determinisms to which we have been captive" is the production of a context for creativity that a commitment to nonviolence enables.⁴⁸ The "power" of "nonviolence," then, is co-constitutive with Yoder's apocalyptic politics of Jesus and not simply an optional appendage. Put differently, what Yoder calls the "pacifism of the messianic community" is subordinate to and arises out of a vision that puts its hope in the theological claim that Jesus Christ is Lord. For this reason, Yoder describes nonviolence as a "distinctive spirituality . . . [that] presupposes and fosters a distinctive way of seeing oneself and one's neighbor under God."⁴⁹ In what is perhaps his most complete description of this particular mode of vision Yoder argues that it is best understood as doxology, which is, as he writes, "a way of seeing; a grasp of which end is up, which way is forward."⁵⁰ In a particularly revealing passage Yoder helpfully connects his mode of vision with the *breaking forth* of hope by arguing that "to see history doxologically means that the criterion most apt for validating a disposition, a decision, an action, is not the predictable success before it but the resurrection behind it, not manipulation but praise. Hope is not a reflex rebounding from defeat but a reflection of theophany."⁵¹ Thus, in Yoder's hands, doxology, nonviolence, and patience are inextricably bound together and become something of a poetic art anchored in the apocalyptic politics of Jesus.⁵²

Bakhtin among the Anabaptists

In order to illuminate some of the less visible workings of the generative capacities of nonviolence constitutive of Yoder's apocalyptic politics of Jesus I suggest that a brief detour through the work of the Russian philologist Mikhail Bakhtin will be very helpful. The inclusion of Bakhtin here may seem, at least at first, like something of a jarring and unnecessary imposition;

---

47. In an explicitly apocalyptic context Yoder claims, "That this renewed breaking forth of light and truth goes on, and on, as much in the world as in the church, is both our history and our hope" in *For the Nations*, 88. This dynamic is what Romand Coles calls Yoder's "wild patience" in Coles, "The Wild Patience of John Howard Yoder," 305–31; and Yoder's "wild peace" in Coles, "The Wild Peace (Not) of John Howard Yoder," 22–41.

48. Yoder, "Armaments and Eschatology," 56.

49. Yoder, *Nonviolence*, 43.

50. Yoder, "To Serve Our God," 129.

51. Ibid., 137–38.

52. Indeed, Yoder himself describes this way of seeing as being "more like the artist than the strategist" in *Nonviolence*, 46.

Political Theology and the Power of Nonviolence 129

after all, what possible help could a once-exiled Soviet literary theorist offer to the genealogy of political theology with which we have been concerned? However, recourse to Bakhtin here is not as surprising as it might at first seem. The volume of scholarship on Bakhtin is immense, not least because his work seems endlessly productive in its anticipation of many key developments in so-called postmodern and post-structuralist philosophy, and his reception in the West has spawned a veritable industry with far-reaching effects that defy disciplinary boundaries.[53] Significantly for our present purposes, the persistence of Bakhtin's influence has had the effect of eroding the early reticence in the West of understanding the theological elements woven into his thought.[54] This erosion shows no sign of abating as ever more studies are given over to illuminating the often deliberately disguised theological undercurrents that animate his work.[55] Within the theological disciplines there seems to be a particular enthusiasm for utilizing a range of Bakhtin's key concepts in the field of biblical hermeneutics, which is precisely where a connection with Yoder has at least already been hinted at, even if only obliquely.[56] A closer connection of the kind I have in mind has been made by the political theorist and radical democrat Romand Coles, who provocatively argues that a rendering of Christianity in "Bakhtinian tones" can be seen in Rowan Williams's work.[57] My suggestion, then, is that similar

---

53. Julia Kristeva's development of the notion of "intertexuality" is but one early and influential example of how Bakhtin has been received and appropriated. See especially Kristeva, "Word, Dialogue and Novel," 34–61. Interestingly, Kristeva also wrote the introduction to the French edition of Bakhtin's *Problems of Dostoevsky's Poetics*.

54. For one such attempt to resituate Bakhtin with respect to Russian Orthodox theology, see Lock, "Carnival and Incarnation," 68–82. Though I am sympathetic with attempts such as Lock's to highlight the religious elements in Bakhtin's work, it is not my purpose here to argue that Bakhtin is, in fact, a kind of covert theologian, which is itself one of the many ongoing debates within Bakhtin scholarship. For a helpful treatment of this debate, see Morson and Emerson, *Mikhail Bakhtin*, especially 101–19.

55. The best book-length treatment of this that I am aware of is Coates, *Christianity in Bakhtin*.

56. For a helpful overview of the interest in Bakhtin in biblical scholarship, see Green, *Mikhail Bakhtin and Biblical Scholarship*. For the oblique connection between Bakhtin and Yoder, see Cartwright, *Practices, Politics, and Performance*, especially 145–68. Cartwright is intimately familiar with Yoder's work, having edited both *The Royal Priesthood* and *The Jewish-Christian Schism Revisited*, and remains one of the most able interpreters of Yoder; however, he makes no explicit connection between Bakhtin's sociolinguistic hermeneutics and what Yoder called the hermeneutics of peoplehood. As will become clear, I wish to push this analysis further and make a more explicit connection between Bakhtin and Yoder.

57. See Coles, "The Pregnant Reticence of Rowan Williams," 174–94. Coles explicitly suggests that this essay can be read as addressing the concerns he raised at the end of his essay on Yoder about whether even a "pre-Constantinian jealousy of Jesus Christ

"Bakhtinian tones" are also powerfully present in Yoder and, further, that by listening for these we might thereby illuminate some of the less visible workings of the generative capacities of nonviolence constitutive of Yoder's apocalyptic politics of Jesus.

Key to Coles's "infatuation" with Bakhtin is the dynamic interplay between centrifugal and centripetal forces that highlight the rough edges, the boundaries at which life itself vulnerably lives—what he elsewhere refers to as "tension-dwelling."[58] Bakhtin has illuminated this dynamic in the course of his influential reading of Dostoyevsky's novels, which, for him, come the closest to embodying what he calls the dialogic nature of the world. In Dostoyevsky's novels, argues Bakhtin, we come to see an analysis not of a single consciousness but of a complex interaction of many equally valid consciousnesses. As he writes,

> The most important acts constituting self-consciousness are determined by a relationship toward another consciousness (toward a *thou*) . . . Not that which takes place within, but that which takes place on the *boundary* between one's own and someone else's consciousness, on the *threshold*. And everything internal gravitates not toward itself but is turned to the outside and dialogized, and in this tension-filled encounter lies its entire essence. This is the highest degree of sociality . . . To be means to be for another, and through the other, for oneself. A person has no internal sovereign territory, he is wholly and always on the boundary; looking inside himself, he looks *into the eyes of another* or *with the eyes of another*.[59]

This dense description contains within it a host of key concepts—dialogic, double-voiced discourse, polyphony, unfinalizability—that Bakhtin unfolds with respect to close readings of Dostoyevsky's novels that display "not a multitude of characters and fates in a single objective world, illuminated by

---

as Lord" might slide toward postures that "erode the church's generosity from within." See Coles, "Wild Patience of John Howard Yoder," especially 325–28.

58. Without explicit reference to Bakhtin, this theme is prominent in Coles, *Beyond Gated Politics*. Moreover, Coles situates his understanding of tension-dwelling between "receiving the wisdom of a tradition and cultivating a readiness for reformation," which is suggestive of Yoder's work.

59. Bakhtin, *Problems of Dostoyevsky's Poetics*, 287. The dynamic and language here is reminiscent of Hegel's description of self-consciousness, particularly in Hegel, *Phenomenology of Spirit*, 104–19. That said, it is clear that Bakhtin's notion of dialogue decisively parts company from what he refers to as Hegel's "monological dialectic." See Bakhtin, "Toward a Methodology for the Human Sciences," 159–72. Indeed, Bakhtin claims that "dialectics is [merely] the abstract product of dialogue" in *Problems of Dostoyevsky's Poetics*, 293.

a single authorial consciousness; rather a *plurality* of *consciousnesses, with equal rights and each with its own world*, combine but are not merged in the unity of the event."[60] Following Bakhtin's lead, it is helpful to contrast Dostoyevsky with Tolstoy here. Particularly illuminating in this respect is Bakhtin's reading of Tolstoy's short story "Three Deaths," in which he argues Tolstoy's monologic position comes to the fore. Bakhtin describes the thematic unity of the story this way: "The coachman Seryoga, transporting the ailing noblewoman, removes the boots from a coachman who is dying in a roadside station (the dying man no longer has any need for boots) and then, after the death of the coachman, cuts down a tree in the forest to make a cross for the man's grave."[61] Thus the three deaths Tolstoy portrays in the story—that of a noblewoman, a coachman, and a tree—are, for Bakhtin, merely externally connected because they know nothing of one another, nor are they reflected in one another. In this way, each of Tolstoy's characters inhabits a kind of hermetically sealed world where "they do not hear and do not answer one another . . . they neither argue nor agree."[62] As such, there can be no dialogic relationships between them; each of the characters is ready-made and fits nicely into a predetermined plot with no resistance whatsoever. As a thought experiment, Bakhtin wonders what "Three Deaths" might have looked like had Dostoyevsky written it in his polyphonic style. In order for dialogic relationships to emerge, Bakhtin suggests that there must be a radical divestment of "authorial surplus," that is, each of the characters must be allowed to know what the author knows such that the author is thereby drawn into the dialogue as a participant without reserving the final word. In this way, "not only the pure *intonations of the author* would be heard, but also the intonations of the noblewoman and the coachman; that is, words would be double-voiced, in each word an argument would ring out, and there could be heard echoes of the great dialogue."[63] Thus, Bakhtin provocatively suggests that Dostoyevsky would not have depicted death at all because, in a dialogic frame, this kind of finalizing operation is disallowed. Instead of killing off the characters that populate his work, Bakhtin argues instead that Dostoyevsky depicts them "on the threshold, or, in other words, in a state of crisis."[64] Thus a dialogic rewriting would have the effect of breaking through the aggressive monological self-assertion of the author

60. Bakhtin, *Problems of Dostoyevsky's Poetics*, 6.
61. Ibid., 69. See also Tolstoy, "Three Deaths," 71–87.
62. Bakhtin, *Problems of Dostoyevsky's Poetics*, 70.
63. Ibid., 73.
64. Ibid., 292. Bakhtin describes the nature of this threshold as a breaking point of a life in *Dialogic Imagination*, 248.

not only by refusing to finalize the story but also by listening for the voice of the other, perhaps even in its silence.

Returning to Yoder, I suggest that these "Bakhtinian tones" resonate so strongly throughout his work that they are imbibed by some of his most astute interpreters without any explicit recognition.[65] That Yoder's work is in deep sympathy with the dialogic character of Bakhtin's reading of Dostoyevsky goes well beyond the confines of literary criticism, however. Indeed, for Bakhtin, and I would suggest also for Yoder, life itself is dialogic. Bakhtin puts it this way:

> To live means to participate in dialogue: to ask questions, to heed, to respond, to agree, and so forth. In this dialogue a person participates wholly and throughout his whole life: with his eyes, lips, hands, soul, spirit, with his whole body and deeds. He invests his entire self in discourse, and this discourse enters into the dialogic fabric of human life, into the world symposium.[66]

This dialogic dimension in Yoder is, perhaps, seen nowhere more clearly than in his early work on sixteenth-century Anabaptism, and my suggestion is that Yoder's understanding of the form of Anabaptism that emerges in a seemingly inexhaustible will to dialogue resonates with Bakhtin's reading of Dostoyevsky. Located within a larger medieval scholastic tradition of *disputationes*, Yoder's detailed investigation of the public debates of the Zürich Anabaptists with Huldrych Zwingli and his disciples is particularly revealing.[67] For our present purposes, we need not entertain the often fascinating details of these disputations but can confine ourselves to the significance Yoder makes of them. What is important here for Yoder is not simply the sheer number of dialogues in which the relatively small number of Zürich Anabaptists were involved, which he numbers at twenty-five in the formative period between 1523 and 1538, nor that the Anabaptists were themselves responsible for initiating the majority of these, either by explicitly demanding them or by their unsettling activities prompting the civil authorities to convene them.[68] While this reading of Anabaptist history certainly reveals the staggering extent to which they were committed

---

65. I am thinking of Chris Huebner in particular here. These "Bakhtinian tones" are especially evident in Huebner's development of what he calls Yoder's "pacifist epistemology" in Huebner, *Precarious Peace*, 97–113. This book itself forms part of a series entitled Polyglossia: Radical Reformation Theologies, which itself hints at a connection between Bakhtin and Yoder.

66. Bakhtin, *Problems of Dostoyevsky's Poetics*, 293.

67. For a helpful introduction to this tradition, see Donavin, Poster, and Utz, *Medieval Forms of Argument*.

68. See Yoder, *Anabaptism and Reformation in Switzerland*, especially 114–21.

to dialogue—often, it should be noted, at the price of their own lives—Yoder is keen to highlight what at first might seem to be the paradoxical form that dialogue took on for the Anabaptists.

> It is not as paradoxical as it might seem at first glance, to see the "recantation" of some Anabaptists as final evidence for their readiness for discussion. It actually was an open possibility for them that, in the course of a dialogue, they could change their position under the weight of a new understanding. The readiness "to let themselves be instructed" that was always expressed along with their pleas for dialogue was genuine.[69]

The open possibility of recantation, then, is not evidence for a kind of *a priori* weakness in one's own position but rather a positive refusal to allow it to have the last word. Put in Bakhtinian terms, Yoder is suggesting that Anabaptist practice displays precisely the kind of unfinalizability that is constitutive of the dialogic nature of the world. The real possibility of recantation, then, enables the operation of a particular kind of power that is made possible through vulnerable encounter with others.

Pushing this analysis further, Yoder suggests that "there begins to surface at this point something new in the course of the history of ideas. Between the simple condemnation, 'it must not be done,' issuing in withdrawal, and the simple acceptance, 'it cannot be helped,' which justifies compromise, there arises the 'it should not be' which refuses either to destroy the adversary or to withdraw from the struggle."[70] Here again I suggest that there are Bakhtinian resonant energies at work. To put it succinctly, Yoder's understanding of early Swiss Anabaptist practice enfleshes Bakhtin's understanding of Dostoyevsky's refusal to kill off the disagreeable characters in his novels. It is not difficult to imagine these Anabaptists as Dostoyevsky's characters, as living on the threshold in the midst of crisis.[71] As Yoder notes, "One of the most striking expressions of [the Anabaptist]

---

69. Ibid., 121.

70. Yoder, "'Anabaptists and the Sword' Revisited," 135. Yoder makes this claim with respect to the Schleitheim Brotherly Union, which he introduces and translates in Yoder, *Legacy of Michael Sattler*, 27–54. The debate surrounding this earliest Anabaptist confession continues. For a particularly helpful reading of it that draws on the resources of Ernesto Laclau and Chantal Mouffe's understanding of how antagonism functions, see Biesecker-Mast, *Separation and the Sword in Anabaptist Persuasion*, especially 97–132.

71. Indeed, Yoder suggests that whereas Zwingli wished to "end his battle with the bishop," one of Conrad Grebel's distinctive characteristics was to "welcome the battle"; furthermore, Yoder highlights Felix Mantz's judgment that Zwingli's rhetorical flourishes often had a silencing effect that would "choke off one's speech in the throat." See Yoder, *Anabaptism and Reformation in Switzerland*, 6 and 117, respectively.

conflictual initiative was interfering with other people's sermons."[72] Indeed, Yoder's understanding of Anabaptist practice is fundamentally dialogic just to the extent that it seeks to enter ever more deeply into that tension-filled space where life itself is called into question. The execution of many of these Anabaptists is a graphic reminder that to kill is to silence and that to silence once and for all is to kill.[73] What we have here, then, is a glimpse of the complex workings of the poetic act that binds together doxology, nonviolence, and patience in Yoder's apocalyptic politics of Jesus, which, again in Bakhtinian terms, is itself an attempt to dialogically reimagine a world held monologically captive.

The readiness for radical reformation, graphically displayed in early Anabaptist practice as a positive embrace of the open possibility for recantation, is woven into the very fabric of Yoder's work. The extent to which this is the case is perhaps seen nowhere more clearly than in his introduction to *The Priestly Kingdom*:

> . . . in contrast to other views of the church, this is one which holds more strongly than others to a positive doctrine of fallibility. Any existing church is not only fallible but in fact peccable. That is why there needs to be a constant potential for reformation and in the more dramatic situations a readiness for the reformation even to be "radical."[74]

Yoder understands "radical" here both in the etymological sense that derives from the Latin *radix*, meaning "root," and in the theological sense that faith itself is "rooted" in Jesus Christ (Eph 3:17). For Yoder, radical reformation names, then, not a particular denominational affiliation but a vision of "unlimited catholicity."[75] With further echoes of Bakhtin, Yoder describes his understanding of radical reformation "as a paradigm of value for all ages and communions, rather than as an apology for a denomination claiming

---

72. Yoder, *War of the Lamb*, 184. See also Fast, "The Anabaptists as Trouble Makers," 10–13.

73. Although I am not suggesting here that Bakhtin is something of a covert pacifist, it is clear in his discussion of monologue that violence is central to its operation: "Monologue is finalized and deaf to the other's response, does not expect it and does not acknowledge in it any *decisive* force. Monologue pretends to be the *ultimate word*. It closes down the represented world and represented persons." See Bakhtin, *Problems of Dostoyevsky's Poetics*, 293 (emphasis added).

74. Yoder, *Priestly Kingdom*, 5.

75. Ibid., 4. Yoder's understanding of catholicity is perhaps most succinctly understood as "a lived reality that will have its place or 'location' wherever all comers participate, in the power of the Triune God, in proclaiming to all nations . . . all that Jesus taught," as he argues in Yoder, *Royal Priesthood*, 320.

the last—or the best—word."⁷⁶ The positive embrace of fallibility, the open possibility of recantation, the refusal to silence the other are all ways of remaining on the threshold, of willingly entering into that tension-filled space where, to return to Yoder's metaphor of the vine, pruning provides a new chance for the roots. The contribution of Yoder's theopolitical vision to the overall genealogy that I have been attempting to construct, then, enables us to see more clearly that the "power" of "nonviolence" opens out onto creative possibilities for orchestrating conflict that are prematurely foreclosed upon when the possibility of violence, of silencing the other, remains as a viable option. Part of Yoder's provocative suggestion, then, is that the recourse to violence, even as a last resort, is a kind of convenient release valve that, when activated, expunges the context for creativity along with whatever expedient effects it promises.⁷⁷ As a distinctive way of seeing, then, Yoder's understanding of nonviolence is itself apocalyptically inflected just to the extent that it opens out onto a host of possibilities that break through a commitment to any one idiom or language. As he argues,

> We shall often be tactical allies of some apologetic thrust, when it rejects the results of a previous too-close identification of church and dominion. We may be tactical allies of the pluralist/relativist deconstruction of deceptive orthodox claims to logically coercive certainty, without making of relativism itself a new monism. We will share tactical use of liberation language to dismantle the alliance of church with privilege, without letting the promises made by some in the name of revolution to become a new opiate.⁷⁸

The interweaving of doxology, nonviolence, and patience that are constitutive of Yoder's apocalyptic politics of Jesus thus emerges in the midst of these tactical alliances as a poetic art that must continually discern "which historical developments can be welcomed as progress in the light of the Rule of the Lamb and which as setbacks."⁷⁹ For Yoder this poetic art is not merely idle speculation precisely because we can already see it operating in a multitude of circumstances and forms: in Leo Tolstoy's active strategy of

---

76. Yoder, *Priestly Kingdom*, 4–5.

77. See Yoder, *Nonviolence*, 47.

78. Yoder, *Priestly Kingdom*, 61. Yoder puts a slightly different emphasis on this in his discussion of Jeffrey Stout's book *Ethics after Babel* when he claims, again in Bakhtinian tones, that "there never was a homogeneous moral language, it only seemed like there was because the other voices were not heard" in "Meaning after Babble," 135. Elsewhere he suggests that there is no reason to prefer one moral language, whether based on ends, means, contract, virtue, etc., over another. Yoder, "Walk and Word," 81.

79. Yoder, *Royal Priesthood*, 132.

nonresistance and his support for acts of civil disobedience, in Mohandas Gandhi's active renunciation of violence as the key to restoring a fuller human community, in Martin Luther King Jr.'s conviction that the struggle for civil rights could not be solved though retaliatory violence, in the nonviolent spirituality of Dorothy Day and the Catholic Worker Movement.

As we have seen, then, Yoder's apocalyptic politics of Jesus intimately weaves together doxology, nonviolence, and patience into something of a poetic art that actively seeks out spaces of conflict by refusing to destroy the adversary. While some of Yoder's most incisive readers have argued that his understanding of nonviolence implies a particular epistemology, an epistemology of peace—an argument from which I do not wish to demur—what I want to suggest is that it also implies a particular metaphysics, a theological metaphysics that is distinguished by its subordination to the lordship of Christ.[80]

Between Politics and Metaphysics

The invocation of metaphysics here may well finally exhaust the patience of readers that have so charitably endured the construction of the genealogy of political theology that I have so far been attempting. After all, if recourse to Yoder is (wrongly) understood as little more than a retreat to the purity of a desert enclave, as it indeed seems to be for both Milbank and Hart, then a recourse to metaphysics may well be (mis)understood as yet another decision to desert this world for one beyond. In the context of the genealogy I have been trying to elucidate, this seeming double desertion is itself doubled because of the fact that many of Yoder's disciples espouse an innate suspicion of metaphysics itself, often on the grounds of its alleged violence, and because of the more general fact that it has been fashionable for some time to proclaim that we are living in a post-metaphysical age. Indeed, is it not quite self-evidently the case that metaphysics is precisely the kind of totalizing discourse that Yoder's apocalyptic politics is meant to explode? Moreover, how could it ever be the case that the concrete particularity of Jesus could be adequately understood in and through such an absolutely comprehensive system that subjects everything to its own regulative gaze? Is not such metaphysical abstraction better understood as a form of ideology that is ultimately corrosive for theology?

Flying in the face of what seem today to be these most self-evident of all proclamations, William Desmond notes, on the contrary, that "one does

---

80. For a reading of Yoder's epistemology of peace, see, in particular, Huebner, *Precarious Peace*, especially 97–113, and 33–44.

not have a choice about being an *animale metaphysicum*."[81] Pushing his case, Desmond rightly asks,

> Is it evident that we know what metaphysics is? If that is not so evident, how less evident will be the relations of metaphysics and politics. And whence the self-assurance about our identities as being postmetaphysical? . . . What space is there that post-metaphysical thinking might occupy, since all thinking, whether it attends to it or not, whether it knows or acknowledges it as such, is informed by basic presuppositions about, and orientations toward, the meaning of what it is "to be"? If this is so, to be postmetaphysical is to make a metaphysical claim.[82]

Following up on Desmond's insights here we can see that just as Hart's facile dismissal of Yoder reveals more about his own wrestling with the difficult nature of justice in a world racked by violence than a thoroughgoing indictment of the pacifism Yoder articulates, so too do the contemporary suspicions and denunciations of metaphysics, which include apocalyptic proclamations of its imminent end, reveal more about their own (metaphysical) presuppositions than about why metaphysics is itself apparently doomed and inescapably violent. Indeed, Desmond's own development of what he calls a metaxological metaphysics, which eschews any attempt to describe all of reality in the form a circumscribed totality, proceeds in some sympathy with the metaphysical implications of Yoder's apocalyptic politics of Jesus.[83] These similarities notwithstanding, we must attend to Yoder's own account to see how he unfolds the relationship between politics and metaphysics.

Before doing so, however, it is worth briefly noting that not all of those deeply influenced by Yoder have leapt to the conclusion that he is necessarily allergic to metaphysics *tout court*. Some have seen in Yoder's own reflections deep metaphysical implications. In one utterly powerful and succinct reflection Yoder suggests that

---

81. Desmond, "Neither Servility nor Sovereignty," 154. Put succinctly, what I mean by "metaphysics" is not univocal.

82. Ibid., 153–54. David Bentley Hart echoes this in arguing that "the critique of metaphysics is often only another metaphysics" in *Beauty of the Infinite*, 13.

83. The comparison between Desmond and Yoder may go well beyond this similarity, especially in Desmond's claim that nonviolence is essential to what he calls the "agapeic relation." That Desmond's understanding of the interrelation of metaphysics and politics enjoins "doing good even to one's enemy" certainly resonates with Yoder's apocalyptic politics of Jesus, and that Desmond articulates this point with reference to Schmitt's definition of the political makes his reflections all the more relevant for our present purposes. See Desmond, "Neither Servility nor Sovereignty," especially 177–81.

> the point apocalyptic makes is not only that people who wear crowns and who claim to foster justice by the sword are not as strong as they think—true as that is: we still sing, "O where are Kings and Empires now of old that went and came?" It is that *people who bear crosses are working with the grain of the universe.* One does not come to that belief by reducing social processes to mechanical and statistical models, nor by winning some of one's battles for the control of one's own corner of the fallen world. One comes to it by sharing the life of those who sing about the Resurrection of the Slain Lamb.[84]

Stanley Hauerwas leverages this claim in his Gifford Lectures to argue that Karl Barth's *Church Dogmatics* is a theological metaphysics that holds no pretensions about being more determinative than God.[85] Especially important for our present purposes, however, is Hauerwas's further suggestion that Yoder's understanding of Christian nonviolence exemplifies precisely the kind of witness that Barth's theological metaphysics requires. Indeed, Hauerwas provocatively argues that "Yoder forces us to see that the doctrines of God and nonviolence are constitutive of one another."[86] Further alleviating the sense in which there is an innate suspicion of metaphysics in Yoder, Hauerwas subsequently pushes his analysis even further by provocatively suggesting that Yoder would not object to the kind of Thomistic "natural theology" defended by Denys Turner in his *Faith, Reason, and the Existence of God*.[87] In addition to Hauerwas, an openness to a particular kind of metaphysics continues in the work of several of his students, including David Toole, who develops a Yoderian metaphysics of apocalypse, and Charlie Collier, who claims not only that Yoder did not shy away from metaphysics but that his work can be received as a radical form of Augustinianism that transformed the classical metaphysical tradition.[88] This trajectory also finds expression in Arne Rasmusson's admittedly underdeveloped suggestion that Yoder's theology implies a trinitarian metaphysics.[89] It is also

---

84. Yoder, "Armaments and Eschatology," 58 (emphasis added).

85. See Hauerwas, *With the Grain of the Universe*, 141–204.

86. Ibid., 220. Hauerwas subsequently makes a provocative link between the metaphysical implications of Yoder's understanding of nonviolence and John Paul II, who, he suggests, with recourse to George Weigel's biography, is the first "non-Constantinian Pope."

87. For Hauerwas's comments on the sense in which Yoder would not disagree with Turner, see Hauerwas, "End of Religious Pluralism," 297n29.

88. See Toole, *Waiting for Godot in Sarajevo*, especially 205–25; and Collier, "Nonviolent Augustinianism?," especially 182–86.

89. See Rasmusson, "Historicizing the Historicist," especially 241–43.

worth noting that Yoder is not wont to simply reject forms of discourse wholesale and often rather engages in painstaking analytical reconstruction of the effects of various forms such discourse might actually take, and in this sense it is not difficult to imagine Yoder drafting a list of the various forms and uses of metaphysics.[90]

While all of these instances of resistance to a wholesale allergy of metaphysics on the part of Yoder are helpful, the best way to see how the complex relationship between politics and metaphysics works in Yoder is to return to his understanding of the apocalyptic character of the politics of Jesus. The richness and provocative nature of Yoder's reflections here are worth quoting at length:

> Jesus' acceptance of the cross, from which we throw light on his rejection of both pietism and Zealot compulsion, was not, in the first analysis, a moral decision, but an eschatological one. It was dictated by a different vision of where God is taking the world. Or, we may say it was an ontological decision, dictated by a truer picture of what the world *really is* . . . The cross is not a scandal to those who know the world as God sees it, but only to the pagans, who look for what they call wisdom, or the Judaeans, who look for what they call power. This is what I meant when I stated that the choice of Jesus was ontological: it risks an option in favor of the restored vision of how things really are. It has always been true that suffering creates shalom. Motherhood has always meant that. Servanthood has always meant that. Healing has always meant that. Tilling the soil has always meant that. Priesthood has always meant that. Prophecy has always meant that. What Jesus did—and we might say it with reminiscence of Scholastic christological categories—was that he renewed the definition of kingship to fit with the priesthood and prophecy. He saw that the suffering servant is king as much as he is priest and prophet. The cross is neither foolish nor weak, but natural.[91]

The metaphysical character of Yoder's reflections here surely cannot be missed. As a distinctive way of seeing, Yoder's understanding of nonviolence is inextricably linked with and gives rise to a particular theological metaphysics that incessantly returns to the "root" from whom all blessings

---

90. D. Stephen Long suggests a list of five uses of the term "metaphysics" and charts the complex ways in which they overlap in Long, *Speaking of God*, 9–10. The initial list occurs on the aforementioned pages but Long weaves his discussion of how these are understood, appropriated, and deployed throughout the book.

91. Yoder, *For the Nations*, 211–12.

flow, that is, to the revelation of God in Jesus Christ. Again and again, Yoder differentiates his understanding of how nonviolence functions from other potential justifications by suggesting that, in the end, it is the outworking of a vision of how things are that arises out of the life, death, and resurrection of Jesus. Thus Yoder can claim that "to renounce violence is the first functional meaning of affirming creation or nature."[92] Yoder is quick to concede that the recourse to violence may well in some cases prove "effective" or "expedient"; however, the credibility of the vision he offers us does not place its hope in our ability to orchestrate desirable effects. As we have seen, this is precisely what Yoder means when he says that "the cross and not the sword, suffering and not brute power determines the meaning of history."[93] For Yoder, the credibility of the vision lies rather in the *kenosis* of God in Jesus Christ, that is, in what God is already doing. In this he makes common cause with Dietrich Bonhoeffer, who suggests that Christian ethics presupposes a decision about ultimate reality:

> All ethical reflection then has the goal that I be good, and that the world—by my action—becomes good. If it turns out, however, that these realities, myself and the world, are themselves embedded in a wholly other ultimate reality, namely, the reality of God the Creator, Reconciler, and Redeemer, then the ethical problem takes on a whole new aspect. Of ultimate importance, then, is not that I become good, or that the condition of the world be improved by my efforts, but that the reality of God show itself everywhere to be the ultimate reality.[94]

For this reason, Yoder suggests that this peculiar nonviolent mode of vision is properly understood doxologically. In Yoder's hands, then, the weaving together of doxology, nonviolence, and patience in the apocalyptic politics of Jesus implies a theological metaphysics that attempts, however precariously, to render the present world transparent to the lordship of Christ. Thus, Yoder claims that

> we are not called to love our enemies in order to make them our friends. We are called to act out of love for them because at the cross it has been effectively proclaimed that from all eternity they were our brothers and sisters. We are not called to make the bread of the world available to the hungry; we are called to restore the true awareness that it always was theirs. We are not called to topple the tyrants, so that it might become true that

---

92. Yoder, "Cult and Culture," 59.
93. Yoder, *Politics of Jesus*, 232.
94. Bonhoeffer, *Ethics*, 48.

the proud fall and the haughty are destroyed. It is already true; we are called only to let that truth govern our own choice of whether to be, in our turn, tyrants claiming to be benefactors.[95]

For Yoder, then, the renunciation of violence is neither simply pragmatic nor a matter of puristic legalism but is rather a product of its fundamental incompatibility with the nature of the kingdom of God. A commitment to nonviolence, then, is "a commitment to work with the grain of the cosmos."[96] It is important to note at this stage that in the light of this theological metaphysics we shall be no less concerned about making the world better but are freed from the belief that real power can be "boiled down to progress that can be extrapolated from intrasystemic potentials."[97] Thus the generative capacities of nonviolence come to the fore again here because, as we have seen above, this vision of the world seeks to enter ever more deeply into that tension-filled space by refusing to destroy the adversary. Indeed, in what I suggest must surely be counted as one of his most succinct and utterly powerful metaphysical affirmations, Yoder claims that "there is no enemy to be destroyed; there is an adversary to be reconciled."[98] The kind of theological metaphysics that I am suggesting is implicit in Yoder's work, then, enjoins neither a flight from this world nor the creation of a speculative grid that regulates the meaning of being and which necessarily squelches the inevitable interruptions of surprising otherness that attempt to break into its closed system. On the contrary, when understood in the light of his rendering of the apocalyptic politics of Jesus, the kind of theological metaphysics implied in Yoder's work remains perpetually, stubbornly open, unfinished, and, most importantly, subject to the lordship of Christ. Put differently, the particular theological metaphysics that I am suggesting is implied in Yoder's work is itself apocalyptically held open, that is, it is restrained from devolving into a kind of closed-system determinism that claims to have mastered the meaning of being. On the contrary, as Yoder writes, "apocalypse promises . . . that tyranny will not have the last word. It promises that the wholesome potential of creation will one day be fulfilled. It promises that diversity, and even conflict, will enrich human existence rather than destroying it."[99]

One of the clearest instances of the way the dynamic between Yoder's apocalyptic politics and the theological metaphysics it implies functions can

---

95. Yoder, *For the Nations*, 210–11.
96. Yoder, *Nonviolence*, 46.
97. Yoder, *War of the Lamb*, 62.
98. Yoder, *Nonviolence*, 46.
99. Yoder, "Cult and Culture," 61.

be seen in his understanding of the work of Christ in relation to the Pauline doctrine of the powers.[100] For Yoder, the powers are understood loosely as an essential collection of religious, intellectual, social, economic, and moral structures that, although created by God, have claimed for themselves an absolute value that oversteps the modesty required for them to participate in the divine ordering of creation and thereby also enslaves humanity.[101] Particularly important for our purposes is how Yoder conceives of the work of Jesus Christ in relation to these rebellious powers, which for him cannot be simply destroyed or evaded.

> Subordination to these Powers is what makes us human, for if they did not exist there would be no history nor society nor humanity. If then God is going to save his creatures *in their humanity*, the Powers cannot simply be destroyed or set aside or ignored. Their sovereignty must be broken. That is what Jesus did, concretely and historically, by living a genuinely free life and human existence. This life brought him, as any genuinely human existence will bring anyone, to the cross.[102]

For Yoder, then, the work of Jesus Christ on the cross has the effect of revealing the assumed sovereignty of the powers to be an illusion, a skewed vision of the way things really are. In this sense the unveiling or, as Yoder says, disarming of the powers accomplished by Jesus on the cross is, at the same time, a restoration of the creaturely capacity to see through the sovereign pretensions of the powers and a "declaration about

---

100. That Yoder himself considered his reading of the powers to imply a particular kind of metaphysics can be seen in his claim that "the Pauline cosmology of the powers represents an alternative to the dominant ('Thomist') vision of 'natural law'" in *Politics of Jesus*, 159. Moreover, Yoder's desire to give a biblical account of the relation of Christ and creation also led him to acknowledge the possibility of a uniquely biblical metaphysics as developed by the French Catholic theologian Claude Tresmontant, who, it is interesting to note, was a sympathetic interpreter of Maurice Blondel. I am not suggesting that Yoder uncritically or enthusiastically embraces the biblical metaphysics of Tresmontant—it is clear he prefers what he considers the critical sophistication of Paul Minear's "realism" to Tresmontant's more archaic style—but rather highlighting the sense in which Yoder considers his own work, particularly *The Politics of Jesus*, to be a "late ripening" in the same biblical realist tradition of which Tresmontant's development of a uniquely biblical metaphysics was an important part. That is to say, Yoder is willing to acknowledge, with Tresmontant, that certain metaphysical commitments are implied in scripture *and* that some forms of metaphysics may be inimical to the biblical vision of reality. For Yoder's location of his own work in this way, see Yoder, *Politics of Jesus*, x; and for his very brief engagement with Tresmontant, see Yoder, *To Hear the Word*, 141–44. See also Tresmontant, "Is There a Biblical Metaphysic?," 454–69.

101. See Yoder, *Politics of Jesus*, 134–61.

102. Ibid., 144–45.

the nature of the cosmos and the significance of history, within which both our conscientious participation and our conscientious objection find their authority and their promise."[103] It is in this particular sense, then, that Yoder's apocalyptic politics of Jesus implies a theological metaphysics that is neither servile nor sovereign, but rather one that is enabled to see through a parade of false similitudes by willingly subjecting itself to the lordship of Christ. As Yoder says, "In Jesus we have a clue to which kinds of causation, which kinds of community-building, which kinds of conflict management, go with the grain of the cosmos, of which we know, as Caesar does not, that Jesus is both the Word (the inner logic of things) and the Lord ('sitting at the right hand')."[104]

As a way of bringing together and making more explicit my understanding of the metaphysical implications of Yoder's apocalyptic politics of Jesus, I suggest that it will be instructive to place my reading alongside another recent reading of Yoder that highlights remarkably similar themes, albeit in quite a different register. In his traversal of twentieth-century theology, from Ernst Troeltsch through Karl Barth and Stanely Hauerwas to Yoder, Nathan Kerr takes as his point of departure the long-running "crisis of historicism," in which, particularly since Hegel, "history has itself come to be recognized as sovereign."[105] As Kerr sets up the debate, what is at stake is the difference between two "theological historicisms": one that "comes unhinged from the singular historicity of Jesus Christ and attains an ideological-critical function" and another that is a "renewed Christian apocalypticism which maintains that our only hope is to remain immovably fixed alongside Christ in his irreducible singularity."[106] The narrative Kerr weaves is both subtle and sophisticated, interrogating in turn the eclipse (Troeltsch), re-emergence (Barth), failure (Hauerwas), and promise (Yoder) of Christian apocalyptic. While Kerr's criticisms of Hauerwas are certainly not beside the point for our purposes, especially since he invokes Schmitt to argue that Hauerwas's ecclesiology is overdetermined by its reaction to Protestant liberalism, his understanding of the promise of Yoder's particular apocalyptic inflection is particularly helpful because it opens up a space of productive disagreement.[107] In order to get to the heart of the matter here, I would like to suggest that one way to profitably understand the genealogy Kerr constructs is to read it as a quarrel with a particular kind of idealist

103. Ibid., 157.
104. Ibid., 246.
105. Kerr, *Christ, History, and Apocalyptic*, 3.
106. Ibid., 6.
107. For this criticism of Hauerwas, see ibid., 116–26.

metaphysics bequeathed to modern theology principally, though not exclusively, through Hegel with deleterious effects that can only be thwarted by what he calls the singular apocalyptic historicity of Jesus Christ.

As Kerr unfolds the argument, what is principally at stake in Troeltsch's understanding of the crisis of historicism is the dual problem of, on the one hand, a prioritization of the absolute that can lead to ahistorical abstraction and, on the other hand, an overemphasis on radical historicity that can lead to what Troeltsch referred to as unlimited relativism. Kerr argues that the only way out of this crisis for Troeltsch is through the development of a new metaphysics that is itself rooted in the contingencies of history and thereby capable of serving as the backdrop against which the conditions for ethical, social, and political life are made possible.[108] For our purposes, the significant upshot of Kerr's analysis of the logic of what he descriptively, though rather cumbersomely, calls Troeltsch's teleologico-eschatological metaphysics is not only that it shapes Troeltsch's understanding of politics but also that it serves to ideologically constrain the political vision that is consequent upon such a metaphysics.[109] Anticipating the end of his argument, Kerr's critique hangs on his diagnosis that the logic of Troeltsch's metaphysics is, as he puts it, "structurally and ideologically Constantinian."[110] For Kerr, this leads to a double failure that relativizes both the political meaning of the Gospel and what he calls the "cosmic-historical significance of Jesus," which together amount to a refusal to acknowledge the fundamentally apocalyptic nature of Christ's lordship.[111] So while Troeltsch's metaphysics effects the eclipse of apocalyptic, what is significant about Kerr's reading of Barth is not simply that Barth's *Der Römerbrief* represents an unabashed re-emergence of apocalyptic but also, and particularly important for our purposes, that we should understand Barth's later apocalyptic Christology, as articulated in the *Church Dogmatics*, as a kind of overcoming of a residual idealist metaphysics that is, nevertheless, still held captive to ontological abstractions and thereby unwittingly repeats the failure of Troeltsch's metaphysics, albeit in an avowedly apocalyptic key.[112] Thus Kerr argues that while Barth's shift from "an apocalyptic-metaphysical perspective" to "an apocalyptic-historical perspecive" provides an "indispensable framework for conceiving Christ's relation to history . . . it [also] points up the need to work out that

---

108. See ibid., 26–29.

109. For Kerr's reading of Troeltsch's development of a new metaphysics of history,, see especially ibid., 29–57.

110. Ibid., 41.

111. Ibid., 53

112. For Kerr's reading of this shift in Barth,, see especially ibid., 63–90.

relationship even more narrowly in terms of concrete *historicity*."¹¹³ While Kerr moves on to discuss the ways in which the influential development of Hauerwas's narrative ecclesiology is finally unable to adequately carry forward the Barthian project of an apocalyptic Christology, his understanding of the way Yoder does so is of particular importance for our purposes.¹¹⁴ Whereas Hauerwas's project remains caught within "ideological modes of thinking" and thus represents, for Kerr, the failure of apocalyptic, Yoder's work shows us the way forward by stressing the "moral independence" and "apocalyptic singularity" of Jesus. For Kerr, Yoder alone is able to articulate a genuine apocalyptic politics precisely insofar as he "develops his account of Jesus's apocalyptic historicity by loosing key aspects of Barth's later, narrative Christology from the residual metaphysical formulations according to which Barth still related 'Jesus' to 'history.'"¹¹⁵ Kerr develops his reading of Yoder's particular apocalyptic inflection at some length; however, in the end, its significance lies primarily in the extent to which it disrupts any and all ideological schemes of meaning by cleaving ever more closely to what he calls the apocalyptic singularity of Jesus Christ. As Kerr writes, "Jesus is operative (that is, he *acts*) *in* history in such a manner as singularly to disrupt and transcend the universalizing function of all causal immanental systems and their corresponding teleo-eschatological frameworks."¹¹⁶ Again and again, Kerr emphasizes that a genuinely apocalyptic theology must proceed "in such a way that Christ's singular historicity is not itself falsely universalized in a manner that a priori and metaphysically severs the resurrected crucified one from ongoing history."¹¹⁷ This challenge, for Kerr, is also a danger—perhaps the most serious and insidious compromise theology goes on (unwittingly?) making—whose apocalyptic overcoming is represented in the concrete particularity of the death and resurrection of Jesus, which itself disrupts any and all attempts to metaphysically conceptualize the

113. Ibid., 78 and 92, respectively.

114. This is not to say that Kerr's reading of Hauerwas is not relevant. Indeed, I would suggest that, as is the case with Troeltsch and Barth, Hauerwas's embrace of a particular kind of metaphysics is at least as problematic for Kerr as is the difficulties he articulates with respect to his ecclesiology. On this score, it is fair to wonder whether Kerr's assesment that Hauerwas's ecclesiology is articulated as a mode of metaphysics that follows the insights of Milbank is precisely the kind of reductionism he elsewhere eschews. For this reading, see Kerr, *Christ, History, and Apocalyptic*, 107–16.

115. Ibid., 146. Kerr repeats this again on 151.

116. Ibid., 143.

117. Ibid., 145. Kerr emphasizes this challenge again in his reading of Yoder's apocalyptic politics as being finally able to break free from "a vision of history as the mere unfolding of an 'obscure metaphysics,'" which Barth had intended all along but ultimately failed to do.

relation of the *Logos* to God. In this sense, then, Kerr understands Yoder as a throughgoing apocalyptic postmetaphysical Barthian.[118]

It should be clear from the foregoing that although there are points where Kerr's account of Yoder's apocalyptic politics overlaps with my own account, especially with respect to the concrete particularity of Jesus, there are also significant differences that converge around the question of metaphysics. Although Kerr does not explicitly put it this way, I would suggest that it is not unfair to characterize his overall genealogy as a kind of apocalyptic overcoming of metaphysics—in the end, a tragic overcoming at that, because even Yoder—Kerr's ostensible hero—is unable to fully wrest from his account the "Constantinian" logic that, as Kerr narrates his genealogy, is endemic to the various forms of metaphysics that continue to plague modern theology.[119] However, it is here that Kerr's reading of Yoder begins to show signs of buckling under the enormous weight he asks it to bear. To begin with, the initial specificity of Kerr's description of Troeltsch's "teleologico-eschatological metaphysics" gradually gives way to become, in his reading of Barth, a problematic set of "ontologico-metaphysical commitments" that are further generalized in his reading of Hauerwas to become an adjectival qualification and critique of the way in which his ecclesial metanarrative functions.[120] To be clear, the problem I wish to identify here is not that Kerr fails to fully explicate the differences in the metaphysics articulated by the major voices in his genealogy, but rather that he seems either unable or unwilling to conceive of metaphysics as anything *other* than a totalizing ideological grid which acts as a condition of possibility for all meaning. Throughout his genealogy the problem Kerr consistently identifies with metaphysics is the seemingly unavoidable tendency for it to lapse into yet another form of ideology that is ultimately corrosive for theology and which therefore must be eliminated at all costs.[121] This is one

---

118. This is not the place to assess Kerr's reading of Barth, or of Troeltsch or Hauerwas, for that matter. Nevertheless, it is noteworthy not only that Kerr's reading of Barth faults him for being insufficiently postmetaphysical without significant reference to the work of perhaps the most influential of the postmetaphysical Barthians, namely, Bruce McCormack, but also that this reading itself is by no means uncontested. For McCormack's reading, see, for example, McCormack, "Karl Barth's Historicized Christology," 201–34. For a reading of Barth that vigorously and persuasively contests his postmetaphysical reception, see Stanley, *Protestant Metaphysics*, especially 160–235.

119. The extent to which this is the case in Kerr's reading of Yoder only becomes apparent in his analysis of the shortcomings of Yoder's ecclesiology, to which I will return in the final chapter.

120. For Kerr's specific description of the metaphysics of Troeltsch, Barth, and Hauerwas in this way, see *Christ, History, and Apocalyptic*, 30, 89, and 111.

121. See, for example, ibid., 41–52, and 116–25.

Political Theology and the Power of Nonviolence 147

form of an argument that has gained theological ascendency at least since Heidegger's critique of onto-theology, and Kerr gives no indication that he thinks a single governing ideological pathos does not reside at the core of all forms of metaphysics.[122] Indeed, Kerr's scorn seems to be without reserve on this point as his target extends well beyond any of the specific metaphysical commitments held by any of his particular interlocutors to what he boldly refers to as "the 'omnipotence of analogy' by which all discrete historical events are disambiguated within immanence for the purpose of teleo-ideological political construction."[123] A double protest must be lodged here. On the one hand, we must question what sense, if any, it makes to launch a critique that is, presumably, meant to apply to the entire history of metaphysics as perpetuating a form of ideology decisively at odds with theology without the labor-intensive work required to understand its traditions, discursive practices, and forms of life.[124] If I have understood Yoder correctly, he would have been uncomfortable being enlisted as an ally in such a grandiose and undifferentiated critique. On the other hand, Kerr's use of Yoder to illustrate the way in which the residual metaphysical formulations of Barth's later Christology can be overcome requires him to stretch his interpretation of some of the key metaphysical affirmations I have identified above in Yoder's work to breaking point and to avoid others altogether.[125] For example, Kerr understands Yoder's reading of the Gospel

---

122. For Heidegger's influential essay on "The Onto-theo-logical Constitution of Metaphysics," see Heidegger, *Identity and Difference*, 42–74. Another way to put this would be to question the extent to which Heidegger is a reliable guide to the history of metaphysics and to suggest that Kerr concedes far too much to Heidegger's account.

123. Kerr, *Christ, History, and Apocalyptic*, 57. Elsewhere Kerr suggests that Yoder's work represents an exemplary test case for a non-analogical mode of theological politics that "resists the ontological mechanizations of the *analogia entis*." See Kerr, "Transcendence and Apocalyptic," 144. In this sense, Kerr understands Yoder's work to more nearly follow through on Barth's famous statement that the *analogia entis* is the "invention of Antichrist" than even Barth himself was able to do.

124. Just to the extent that Kerr's genealogy makes such a critique—and I grant here that this is more a tendency than an avowed objective—it unwittingly repeats the very foundational gesture of the forms of metaphysics he rightly wishes to apocalyptically disrupt because it enacts a retreat from the intractable historical particularity that has always been central for the Christian tradition and that plays such a decisive role in his argument.

125. Perhaps the most significant of the omissions in Kerr's reading is Yoder's affirmation that Jesus's acceptance of the cross was an "ontological decision, dictated by a truer picture of what the world *really is*" in *For the Nations*, 211 (emphasis original). This omission is especially curious because Kerr cites this exact passage and uses it in his reading of Yoder's understanding of doxology in Kerr, *Christ, History, and Apocalyptic*, 162n3. Here Kerr emphasizes the eschatological nature of doxology but conveniently leaves out its ontological nature that Yoder immediately identifies and

of John to mean that "we can *only* speak of Jesus as God—but not only that, of the eternal Logos itself—from within the density and angularity of his constituent life-story."[126] As his subsequent quotations make clear, what this means for Kerr is that a metaphysical sense of the incarnation is definitively ruled out.[127] However, Kerr's reading here is very curious indeed, not only because his interpretation restricts the scope of Yoder's comments where Yoder does not but also because he does not seem to be aware that, in what is his most sustained reading of the Gospel of John, Yoder explicitly does not rule out a metaphysical understanding of the incarnation but rather suggests that the existing idiom is adopted and turned inside out.[128] Yoder is well aware that from its inception Christianity has borrowed freely from existing idioms of all kinds, and while he is certainly less appreciative of particular patristic and medieval borrowings he nevertheless locates himself in the Nicene and Chalcedonian tradition and asks that "the implications of what the church has always said about Jesus as Word of the Father, as true God and true Human, be taken more seriously than ever before."[129] To be sure, this borrowing is no simple uncritical adoption, entailing as it inevitably does a crucial subversion—as it has for the entire history of Christian thought—and, as Yoder emphasizes, is also not without serious dangers of compromising its central proclamation of the lordship of Jesus

---

emphasizes alongside it. To be fair, there are points where Kerr seems to recognize something of the difficulty in enlisting Yoder to overcome metaphysics in this way. See, for example, his concession that "for Yoder, the language of 'history' and of 'historicity' is *no less true* a way of talking about and conceiving eternity's relation to time than is the language of 'substance' and 'metaphysics'" in *Christ, History, and Apocalyptic*, 148n45 (emphasis added).

126. Kerr, *Christ, History, and Apocalyptic*, 147 (emphasis added).

127. See ibid., 147n45 where Kerr cites both Yoder, *Politics of Jesus*, 24; and Yoder, *Royal Priesthood*, 185. That Kerr's reading is articulated as a kind of apocalyptic overcoming of metaphysics is further supported in his subsequent suggestion that "Jesus' identity as the incarnate Son of God is unable to be expounded in terms of a metaphysically preconceived divine 'essence'" in *Christ, History, and Apocalyptic*, 155.

128. Yoder's most sustained reading of the Gospel of John is his essay entitled "Glory in a Tent," which Kerr does not cite, in Yoder, *He Came Preaching Peace*, 69–88. One way that Yoder enacts this kind of subversive acceptance of an explicitly metaphysical idiom, and one that directly confronts Kerr's assertions, can be seen in his claim that in the Gospel of John "it says first that what has come among us in the word and work of Jesus is far more than the work and word of a man, since what it brings us has the dignity of preexistence, of having shared in the divine work of creation" (ibid., 81).

129. Yoder, *Politics of Jesus*, 102. In his reading of the Gospel of John, Yoder makes this point by emphasizing the continuity of creation and redemption and suggests, "That the world is created, or that God is Creator, was not a new idea . . . but that that which comes to us in Jesus is no different from the truth and the power of creation is a new claim." See Yoder, *He Came Preaching Peace*, 81–82.

Political Theology and the Power of Nonviolence 149

Christ.[130] However, while Yoder explicitly remains willing to risk this danger, Kerr's reading of Yoder retreats from this precipice and is decidedly more anxious and calculating precisely insofar as it uses Yoder's work as a way to purify Barth's later Christology of any remaining residual metaphysical formulations. Concomitantly, Kerr repeatedly emphasizes what he calls the independence of Jesus and, whereas in the example noted above Kerr problematically restricted the scope of his interpretation of Yoder, in this second example he amplifies the significance of this independence, which has the effect of distorting Yoder's own reading of the powers such that it can be put to use in his genealogy. While Yoder does indeed claim that Jesus existed in the midst of these powers as "morally independent of their pretensions," he also affirms right alongside this claim that Jesus was nevertheless still "*subject* to these powers."[131] Given the manner and extent to which Kerr develops the theme of Jesus's independence, readers that are relatively unfamiliar with Yoder's work may be forgiven for thinking that this is also a major theme in his work when, in fact, it is manifestly no such thing.[132] Seemingly undaunted by this fact, Kerr devotes substantial space and energy to uncovering what he argues is the key link between Jesus's independence and what he calls the logics of singularity and excess, which work together to apocalyptically disrupt any and all "universalizing and ideological mechanisms of control."[133] However, despite all of his emphasis on the concrete particularity of Jesus, it is at this point that Kerr's reading itself becomes ever more formal—emphasizing the event of history breaking open "according to the *singular* logic of a concrete political *action*, which is operative in history as the *excessiveness of singularity itself*" while remaining curiously and problematically silent on precisely those kinds of action to which Yoder so often deliberately attended.[134] When taken together, these

---

130. Yoder identifies this danger as the temptation to "adopt the language of our doubting audience in order to say what they want to hear" in *He Came Preaching Peace*, 79–80. In this sense, I think it is fair to wonder whether and to what extent Kerr's reading of Yoder as a postmetaphysical Barthian does not fall into precisely the kind of faddist approach that Yoder explicitly warns against.

131. Yoder, *Politics of Jesus*, 145.

132. Indeed, the quotation in question of which Kerr makes so much is, to the best of my knowledge, the only time Yoder ever refers specifically to Jesus's independence in his work. Elsewhere, Yoder does advocate for what he calls the "moral independence" that is required to "speak truth to power," but even here this takes place within a redefinition of the cosmos as a way to "persevere in living against the stream when no reward is in sight." See Yoder, "Armaments and Eschatology," 53.

133. Kerr, *Christ, History, and Apocalyptic*, 145.

134. The quote is from ibid., 159. That Kerr's reading of Yoder's understanding of Jesus's independence is central for his wider argument is also in evidence elsewhere in

two problematic interpretive strategies reveal a wider tendency in which Kerr comes more and more to read Yoder's work exclusively through the lens of apocalyptic and thereby considerably elevates its status, perhaps not all the way to a kind of governing principle but certainly far beyond the much more qualified sense that, as I have highlighted above, Yoder grants it.[135] In this sense, Kerr's reading of Yoder is, at best, idiosyncratic, creatively pushing the boundaries of what Yoder's work can reasonably be understood to support and, at worst, to borrow a provocatively loaded term employed by another of Yoder's interpreters, truly heterodox.[136]

In contradistinction to Kerr, then, the theological metaphysics that I am suggesting is implied by Yoder's apocalyptic politics of Jesus is in no way a regulative or totalizing principle that can be abstracted from or more determinative than the concrete life, death, and resurrection of Jesus Christ. In this, Yoder's theo-logic is in sympathy with Balthasar, who argues that "Christology (as sketched in its outlines by Chalcedon) gives an account of an event that cannot be made subject to any universal law but that subjects all other laws (regulating the relationship between God and the creature, that is) to its own uniqueness."[137] Indeed, and as Kerr rightly notes, Yoder is critical of metaphysics precisely at the point where

---

his work. See, for example, Kerr, "Transcendence and Apocalyptic," 145; and "*Communio Missionis*," 330–31. Moreover, and particularly in the light of Kerr's repeated stress on concrete political action, it is remarkable that his reading of Yoder gives no account of the practices and forms of life—the body politics (baptism, the Eucharist, etc.)—that play much more of a role in Yoder's work than does the nature of Jesus's independence. This is also why I suggested above that Yoder is merely the *ostensible* hero of Kerr's genealogy because, in the end, it is Walter Benjamin's concept of Messianic time, which Kerr invokes at several key points, that captures just as well, if not far better, precisely the kind of apocalyptic inflection that Kerr is straining to articulate. Indeed, the logic of singularity and the emphasis on embodied action are articulated in connection with Benjamin much earlier on in Kerr's genealogy and are subsequently imported into his reading of Yoder, which itself also ends with reference to Benjamin. See Kerr, *Christ, History, and Apocalyptic*, 57–60, and 159–60.

135. To take but one example, Kerr claims that Yoder finds the "apocalyptic imagination" to be "at the heart of the Judeo-Christian prophetic tradition and literature" in *Christ, History, and Apocalyptic*, 135. It is difficult to square this assertion with Yoder's explicit qualification and warning that apocalyptic is only one mode of discourse and we should not prefer it, in Yoder, *Royal Priesthood*, 129–30.

136. See Martens, *The Heterodox Yoder*.

137. Balthasar, *Theo-Logic II*, 311. Indeed, Yoder explicitly claims that his development of the apocalyptic politics of Jesus is "more radically Nicene and Chalcedonian than other views" in *Politics of Jesus*, 102. See also his chapters titled "The Trinity and the Council of Nicea" and "Chalcedon and the Humanity of Jesus" in Yoder, *Preface to Theology*, 180–209, and 10–23, respectively.

it takes on a regulative function more determinative than and abstracted from what we find in Scripture.

> The concept of Incarnation, God's assuming human nature, has often made us direct our thought to metaphysics; asking how it can be that the human nature and the divine nature can be present together in one person. Whether this substantial miracle be joyously affirmed or found unthinkable, it seems agreed by all that metaphysics is the question. But when, in the New Testament, we find the affirmation of the unity of Jesus with the Father, this is not discussed in terms of substance but of will and deed.[138]

However, for Yoder this critique is more nuanced than Kerr seems to assume and cannot be understood as yet another proclamation of the end of metaphysics or even as a more circumspect argument that metaphysical speculation has a tendency to corrupt theology. Yoder's quarrel here is not with metaphysics *tout court* but rather with a particular kind of metaphysics that abstracts from the gospel narrative and thereby artificially separates Christology from discipleship, nature from grace, law from gospel. What Yoder does, then, is to resituate metaphysics within the gospel narrative or, perhaps better, to subordinate metaphysics to the authority of Jesus. Insofar as this is the case, the kind of theological metaphysics I am suggesting is implied in Yoder's work is neither antique nor modern but rather one that refuses the separation between scriptural and metaphysical modes of reflection.[139] Thus Yoder goes on to say that the unity of Jesus with the Father "is visible in Jesus's perfect *obedience* to the *will* of the Father. It is evident in Jesus that God takes the side of the poor. It is evident in Jesus that when God comes to be King, Jesus rejects the sword and the throne, taking up instead the whip of cords and the cross."[140] Understood this way, Yoder's apocalyptic politics of Jesus implies a theological metaphysics just to the extent that it

---

138. Yoder, *Royal Priesthood*, 185.

139. For an especially helpful account of the interaction of these modes of reasoning, see Levering, *Scripture and Metaphysics*. Yoder's refusal to choose between two sides of a debate already in progress, or, as he puts it, "traditional antinomies of which we must repent," is a hallmark of his work. See, for one example, the list he outlines in *Politics of Jesus*, 103–9. In the light of Kerr's reading of Yoder we might add to Yoder's list and suggest that, at least to some extent, Kerr's genealogy tells us we must choose between metaphysics and apocalyptic. If I have understood Yoder correctly, this is one more choice he would refuse.

140. Yoder, *Royal Priesthood*, 185. See also David Toole's account of what he calls Yoder's metaphysics of apocalypse, which he helpfully develops with respect to Yoder's reading of Paul's language of the principalities and powers, in Toole, *Waiting for Godot in Sarajevo*, especially 205–25.

too functions as a disruption of the world that can only seem "like a hammer that breaks rocks into pieces."[141] However, it also enjoins much more than the endless apocalyptic disruption indicative of Kerr's account because to say that those who bear crosses are working with the grain of the universe "risks an option in favor of the restored vision of how things really are."[142] To catch a glimpse of this theopolitical vision and, importantly, its limitations and seductions in the context of the overall genealogy I have been constructing is the task of the next and final chapter.

141. Yoder, *For the Nations*, 212.
142. Ibid.

CHAPTER 5

Retrospect and Prospect

A Theological Recapitulation

In the foregoing chapters I have attempted to excavate and to reconstruct the Schmittian seductions of political theology. On the basis of a reading of Schmitt's work that paid special attention to the theological elements that are inextricably woven into his articulation of political theology the argument proceeded to develop a genealogical account of some of its key contemporary reconfigurations that at least implicitly assume they have sufficiently overcome the violent aporetics characteristic of Schmitt's work, albeit without any sustained engagement with it. Particularly in the case of Metz, who is arguably the closest of any of the main interlocutors at the heart of the book to Schmitt, at least historically and geographically, and the only one who, to my knowledge, actually met Schmitt in person, there is a puzzling and troubling silence—at times even an active avoidance—with respect to Schmitt.[1] The non-demonstrative

---

1. The most Metz is ever explicitly able to muster with respect to Schmitt is one paragraph in Metz, *Passion for God*, 146. Even here, however, it is clear that although he considers his own development of the *new* political theology to be quite self-consciously and decisively opposed to Schmitt, he only reluctantly mentions him because it seems that Schmitt's version of political theology is, as he says, "gaining influence in the contemporary scene, and not just in Germany." Just to the extent that this silence is connected in some way with a reluctance to wade into the controversy surrounding the degree to which Nazism infected the political thought of its leading intellectual architects, this silence is, perhaps, less unusual when one takes into account the fact

character of the argument has also been highlighted at points throughout but it bears repeating: the genealogy presented here is not offered as the only or even the best way to read the transformation of contemporary political theology but rather one that, through patient and careful reconstruction of the manner and extent to which Schmitt's theopolitical vision is unwittingly repeated in subsequent debates, has the capacity to helpfully illuminate significant undercurrents that may otherwise remain hidden. In this sense, one way to understand the overall trajectory of the genealogy would be to suggest that it aims to trace the history of effects of failing to adequately engage the vision articulated by Schmitt, which has increasingly been recognized outside the discipline of theology for its contemporary significance and, indeed, prescience, in a way that arguably amplifies Metz's worries that Schmitt's vision is gaining influence. If Jürgen Habermas is right that the contemporary struggle for global order is now waged between the Kantian and Schmittian projects, then a theology that purports to be about more than simply inward devotion—that is, any genuinely *political* theology—cannot turn a blind eye to this ongoing battle and must actively engage its shifting terrain.[2] However, it is also important to note that, read as a whole, the genealogy is not simply a history of the *failure* to seriously wrestle with Schmitt's vision. Indeed, the genealogy is intentionally constructed such that it refuses any easy identification as a kind of *Verfallsgeschichte* that simply charts a precipitous decline from an idealized past because although Metz, Milbank, and Hart in various ways unwittingly and unwillingly repeat certain foundational Schmittian gestures, these repetitions can in no way be understood as simple capitulations and are not without their own forms of resistance. In the end, while none of these reconfigurations of political theology is finally up to the task of subverting the violent aporetics characteristic of Schmitt's thought, Yoder's theopolitical vision manages to do just this in certain key ways. Here, however, it is equally important to note that just as the overall genealogy cannot be characterized as tragic, neither can it be characterized as epic because although Yoder's vision holds crucial advantages with respect to refusing the Schmittian seductions that con-

---

that despite his criticisms of Heidegger, Metz likewise did not engage in the debate surrounding Heidegger's involvement with Nazism, a debate that has been reignited with the 2014 publication of Heidegger's so-called *Schwarze Hefte*. While this fact may make Metz's silence seem more consistent it is certainly no less troubling, particularly for a theologian who claims to do theology "after Auschwitz."

2. See Habermas, *Divided West*, 188–93.

tinue to bedevil political theology, it does not hold all the advantages. Admittedly, this latter aspect has only been fleetingly hinted at in the foregoing chapters and it is one of the explicit aims of this final chapter to bring this more clearly into focus. Before doing so, however, it is worth highlighting in a short ambit the progression of the argument itself.

The genealogy proper began in chapter 2 where I argued that, far from being diametrically opposed to one another as is so often simply assumed, Schmitt and Metz actually stand much closer to each other than is currently realized. Indeed, although certainly not identical, their respective theopolitical visions overlap in significant ways. As we saw, Schmitt's political theology is mobilized by an apocalyptically inflected aesthetics of violence concerned primarily with the maintenance of order through the structural power of the state, which he defines primarily in negative terms as the avoidance of civil war, and whose formalism makes the highest virtue of decision as such. Animated by a thoroughly negative theological anthropology, which comes to the fore in his reliance on Hobbes and the Catholic counterrevolutionaries, Schmitt's political theology struggles with all its might to effect a structured geographical displacement of the inherent violence between human beings on to a public enemy that is essentially alien and different. Despite the fact that Metz articulates his *new* political theology as a response to the horrors of Auschwitz, in which Schmitt's work is undoubtedly implicated, and despite what is arguably his most closely held conviction that unnecessary suffering must be apocalyptically interrupted with the explosive force of lived hope, he nevertheless regrettably acquiesces to the present-day orgies of violence that, on his reading, are coming more and more to attain a normative status. In the end, therefore, Metz's apocalyptic inflection, which emphasizes disruption over and against the preservation sought by Schmitt, unwittingly repeats the foundational gesture of Schmitt's political theology in the formal register. In this limited sense, I provocatively argued that when Schmitt and Metz are read in the light of the apocalyptic element that infuses and haunts their respective accounts of political theology, significant convergences emerge that otherwise remain hidden, and while Metz, significantly, points up the need to move decisively beyond Schmitt, his *new* political theology cannot, in the end, show us the way.

Given this unsettling conclusion, chapter 3 sought to find subsequent articulations of political theology that were able to confront and reconfigure the relationship between violence and apocalyptic in ways that moved beyond the impasse at which Metz's *new* political theology remained tragically stuck. Again, because of a distinct lack of explicit theological engagement with Schmitt, there are barriers to identifying potential candidates; however, I argued that while neither Milbank nor Hart articulates his political theology primarily with reference to Schmitt or Metz, it is nevertheless immensely helpful to read them as successors of the reconfigurations of political theology begun by these two German Catholics precisely because they continue to grapple with the complex relationship between violence and apocalyptic. Indeed, their respective aesthetic reconfigurations of political theology are audibly haunted by an attempt to reconfigure the Schmittian decision in apocalyptic terms that echo a kind of Metzian interruption. In Milbank's case, we saw that his political theology took on a mystagogical form that owed a great deal both to his theopolitical deployment of paradox and to his account of *poiesis*. However, his account of beauty threw up a host of problems with respect to the question of violence. While descriptively persuasive, Milbank's phenomenology of violence was implicated in manipulating the operations of beauty and thus secretly perpetrated its own form of apocalyptic counterviolence. Milbank's political theology also posed an additional difficulty because it takes the form of what I called a Schmittian theo-logic that proceeded on the basis of the creation of an enemy against which a substantive theological agenda could subsequently be positively constructed. In the end, then, Milbank's political theology was judged not only to have failed to subvert the fundamentally violent aporetics of Schmitt's political theology on the level of content—because it embraces the educative function of violence to protect our created desires to save the innocent—but was also found to have unwittingly repeated the foundational gesture of Schmitt's political theology formally. This double failure is precisely why I suggested that, in the end, Hart's theopolitical vision is arguably more significant to the overall argument, despite being prosecuted in a much shorter space than is Milbank's. Reading Hart's theological aesthetics against the grain of much of the received wisdom that links his telling of the tale of the postmodern city and its wastes much more closely with Milbank's telling of a similar tale, I argued not only that Hart's theopolitical optics manages to see through the theology of justified coercion Milbank leaves us with but also that whatever "savagery" takes place in his work is of a definitively different sort than the kind evidenced in Milbank's work precisely because it surrenders to the form of Christ and understands martyrdom as the normal condition of the Christian life. Read this way, and in spite of the fact that Hart does not explicitly consider himself to be a political theologian, I suggested that he nevertheless manages to avoid both of the failures evidenced in Milbank's work. However, in the end, while Hart's theopolitical vision comes tantalizingly close to subverting the Schmittian seductions of political theology, in its curious and scathing critique of some only vaguely specified pacifist commitments, which wallow in despair at the possibility of a corrupt humanity to justly struggle for peace and thereby obscenely choose martyrdom for others, it nevertheless remains unable to see the extent to which the power of nonviolence has nothing whatsoever to do with a passive complicity with evil and thereby, like Milbank's vision but to a lesser degree, falls victim to the logic of Hegel's beautiful soul.

Chapter 4 turned to examine the unnamed pacifist who is the object of Hart's vehement and polemical criticism. Despite the fact that Yoder arguably occupies a more distant place with respect to his relation to the other four major figures at the interpretive heart of the book, I nevertheless argued that his work is indispensable not only because it continues to wrestle with the complex relationship between violence and apocalyptic but also because it crucially does so in a way that embodies a nonviolent way of seeing that encourages the possibilities of creaturely reconciliation that are otherwise occluded. As we saw, for Yoder doxology, nonviolence, and patience are inextricably bound together and become a poetic art anchored in the apocalyptic politics of Jesus. By way of an excursus on Mikhail Bakhtin that highlighted the less visible workings of the generative capacities of nonviolence I suggested that Yoder's theopolitical vision enables us to see more clearly than anyone else that the power of nonviolence opens out onto creative possibilities for orchestrating conflict that are prematurely foreclosed upon when the possibility of violence, of silencing the other, remains as a viable option. In conclusion, I argued that in Yoder's hands the weaving together of doxology, nonviolence, and patience in the apocalyptic politics of Jesus implies a theological metaphysics that precariously attempts to render the present world transparent to the lordship of Christ. In stark contrast to Nathan Kerr's reading of Yoder's apocalyptic politics as promoting a decidedly postmetaphysical theopolitical vision, I argued that while the kind of theological metaphysics implied by Yoder's work does not secretly harbor some kind of alien governing ideological pathos, as Kerr fears that all forms of metaphysics necessarily must, it nevertheless risks compromising its own witness in its attempt to see things for how they really are, that is, how they are revealed—"apocalypsed"—in the light of the cross and ressurection.

Interwoven into this principal genealogical narrative, I have also argued that, right from its beginnings in Schmitt, all of the reconfigurations of political theology with which we have been concerned are articulated not only in an apocalyptic key but also in an aesthetic key. Indeed, throughout the genealogy the aesthetic dimension has at every turn closely accompanied the apocalyptic such that we might suggest that they are mutually implicative of one another. This way of putting it echoes an observation made by Cyril O'Regan, who notes that apocalyptic is a form of theology that "attempts to persuade by the power and beauty of its vision and in this respect there is in principle and not simply in fact an elective affinity between apocalyptic and aesthetic forms of theology."[3] In this sense, then, another way to understand the overall genealogy would be to suggest that it stages a confrontation between several different visionary options in an effort to theologically assess their relative strengths and weaknesses, particularly with respect to Schmitt's vision. What is revealed in the light of this analysis, then, is that each of the reconfigurations of political theology that have occupied the foregoing chapters can indeed be helpfully read, to varying degrees, as a contestation of Schmitt's vision *and* that explicitly articulating the manner and extent of the reconfigurations undertaken helpfully illuminates the relative successes and failures of each. In Schmitt's case I have suggested that his vision can be helpfully understood as an apocalyptically inflected aesthetics of violence, a vision that coalesces around the exceptional moment of decision, that is, the violent rupture of mechanized petrifaction characteristic of bourgeois normalcy in which the political itself is paralyzed in endless discussion. The extent to which Schmitt's vision can properly be identified as aesthetic is, perhaps, thrown into some doubt given his own criticism of political romanticism as fundamentally incapable of a genuine political decision precisely because it subsumes politically productive antitheses as mere aesthetic contrasts.[4] However, in spite of the fact that Schmitt castigates the paralyzing effects of political romanticism as both privatizing and "occasionalist," his own political theology aesthetically harnesses the interruptive potential of the antithesis between norm and exception and offers it as an apocalyptic vision capable of recognizing the enemy *as* enemy.[5] In light of the disastrous concrete consequences in which Schmitt's vision is undoubtedly implicated, Metz offers an apocalyptically expectant praxis of discipleship whose primary function is to interrupt the ongoing history of human suffering manifested most powerfully in the death camps of the Third Reich. Thus articulated, Metz's *new* political theology is certainly a refusal of Schmitt's vision and highlights the need to move decisively beyond it. However, despite Metz's explicit worries about a kind of "secret

3. O'Regan, *Theology and the Spaces of Apocalyptic*, 128.

4. For a general overview of this critique, see the Preface in Schmitt, *Political Romanticism*, 1–21.

5. For Schmitt, this recognition is the "high point of politics," as he asserts in Schmitt, *Concept of the Political*, 67. Without identifying Schmitt's vision as apocalyptic, the German literary theorist Peter Bürger links Schmitt's opposition to bourgeois society with what he calls an "aestheticist *Lebensphilosophie*" that itself repeats a characteristic romantic gesture in its search for an exceptional event or experience that comes to ground "real life." See Bürger, "Carl Schmitt oder die Fundierung der Politik auf Ästhetik," 170–76.

aestheticization of suffering," his insistence that what is most necessary is the constant development of a "more acute perception of others' suffering" nevertheless continues to operate within the categories of Schmitt's vision even as it rightly attempts to contest its violent boundaries.[6] This is precisely the sense in which Milbank's now well-known interpretive strategy of "outnarration," characteristic not only of *Theology and Social Theory* but his entire theopolitical vision, becomes particularly helpful, not least because it takes up a decidedly more assertive posture that not only explicitly critiques and refuses the political ontology of *bellum omnium contra omnes* that underwrites Schmitt's vision but also exposes the sense in which its very existence is in some sense an invention of certain corrupt modes of late medieval and early modern theology that depart from "the most authentic Christian tradition."[7] In one sense, then, Milbank's aesthetic simply aspires to a greater comprehensiveness of vision—indeed, a vision so powerful that it can see in the dark—that is able to subsume all other lesser visions within its own larger horizon and is thereby not simply persuasive but apodictic. Moreover, Milbank's political theology takes on an aesthetic hue not only in the form or style of its argumentation but also with respect to its content, which as we saw above drafts and deforms beauty into performing a function essentially alien to it insofar as it evokes a necessary apocalyptic counterviolence that shapes our desire to protect the innocent. That Hart's theopolitical vision can be properly identified as aesthetic hardly needs justification; however, I have argued that the manner in which Hart understands a Christian aesthetic represents a helpful corrective to Milbank's precisely insofar as he recognizes that the seductions of aesthetic rapture that are properly a part of any theological aesthetics can easily be subordinated to some other discourse of power and violence and must therefore take the form of martyrdom.[8] For Hart this means that beauty as a form that evokes desire "does not always immediately commend itself to every taste; Christ's beauty, like that of Isaiah's suffering servant, is not expressed in vacuous comeliness or shadowless glamor, but calls for a love that is charitable, that is not dismayed by distance or mystery, and that can repent of its failure to see."[9] If all of the foregoing reconfigurations of political theology are articulated to some degree in an aesthetic key it is, perhaps, Yoder's theopolitical vision that admits of this aesthetic dimension least of all. However,

---

6. Metz calls this continual process of becoming ever more attuned to the suffering of others a "mysticism of open eyes" in "Suffering unto God," 611–22.
7. Milbank, *Beyond Secular Order*, 3.
8. See Hart, *Beauty of the Infinite*, 439–43.
9. Ibid., 20.

despite the quite obvious fact that Yoder spends no time explicitly developing a theological aesthetics, my suggestion in the previous chapter was that we can understand Yoder's work as another of Balthasar's lay theological styles, as one more "reflected ray of glory" that has the capacity to illuminate the transformation of political theology in helpful new ways. The sense in which we can understand Yoder's theopolitical project as echoing distinctly Balthasarian tones goes well beyond a hermeneutical strategy though it is also that. Indeed, Yoder's development of the apocalyptic politics of Jesus, which, as Yoder himself claims, does not "advocate an unheard-of modern understanding of Jesus" but asks rather "that the implications of what the church has always said about Jesus . . . be taken more seriously than ever before" can be profitably read as a concrete example that tackles Balthasar's worry that the "centrality of Christ's figure has not been heeded emphatically enough" head-on.[10] Understood this way, the generative capacities of nonviolence and the kind of theological metaphysics I argued it implies in Yoder's work reveals that his theopolitical vision is habitually "seized by the beauty of Christ" such that he is able to see, with Balthasar, that disciples of the crucified one "suffer because of their love, and it is only the fact that they have been inflamed by the most sublime of beauties—a beauty crowned with thorns and crucified—that justifies their sharing in that suffering."[11] But this also complicates Hart's vision because for Yoder it is not only a case of being ready to repent of the (fleeting?) moments when we fail to see, that is, for our lack of vision, but also a case of becoming more acutely aware of the sense in which our creaturely modes of vision are always already in the grip of some form of self-deception. In this way, a positive capacity for self-criticism is built into Yoder's theopolitical vision, and this comes to the fore in his description of the apocalyptic habit of seeing doxologically as that which "demands and enables that we appropriate especially/specifically those modes of witness which explode the limits *our* own systems impose on *our* capacity to be illuminated and led."[12]

The extent to which an aesthetic dimension animates the whole of the genealogy of political theology with which we have been concerned and the

---

10. Yoder, *Politics of Jesus*, 102; and Balthasar, *Glory of the Lord I*, 154.

11. Balthasar, *Glory of the Lord I*, 33. The link between aesthetic and apocalyptic forms of theology are especially clear here in Balthasar's claim that the figure of Jesus Christ is the lightning bolt of eternal beauty whose appearance captivates and transforms. The theme of "sharing in the sufferings of Christ" can be found throughout Yoder's work, but see, for example, the extent to which he sees this theme being embodied in the epistles in Yoder, *Politics of Jesus*, 94–97.

12. Yoder, *Royal Priesthood*, 129. Here too Yoder makes the link between aesthetic and apocalyptic forms of theology.

preliminary connections I have made in particular to Balthasar's theological aesthetics can also serve as a useful analytic tool to further diagnose the relative adequacy of each of the reconfigurations of political theology that have occupied the foregoing chapters. Balthasar's insight that Christianity is the "aesthetic religion *par excellence*" is predicated on the fact that form and content are inseparable because, as he says, "the God whom we know now and for all eternity is Emmanuel, God with us and for us, the God who shows and bestows himself."[13] Again and again, Balthasar affirms that Christ is the center of the form of revelation because he is the content and that any attempt to separate these would radically depart from a properly Christian theological aesthetics.[14] For our purposes, this insight becomes analytically useful insofar as each of the reconfigurations of political theology with which we have been concerned articulates its own vision as a complex negotiation of form and content. In the most general sense, then, it would be tempting to suggest that the genealogy constructs a confrontation between a tendency to emphasize form at the expense of content in both Schmitt and Metz and, conversely, a tendency to emphasize a comprehensive content at the expense of form in both Milbank and Hart, and that Yoder finally represents the definitive coalescing of form and content. However tempting, this tidy way of putting the matter would simplify a much more intricate story, fail to do justice to the complex negotiation of form and content that occurs within each account, and would tend toward an epic rendering of the overall genealogy, which I explicitly disavow. Thus the analytic potential of Balthasar's insight that form and content are inseparable will not be deployed to summarily dismiss Schmitt, Metz, Milbank, or Hart or to elevate Yoder. Alternatively, then, what follows is an attempt to bring the foregoing reconfigurations of political theology to bear upon one another such that they are not only able to critique but also to supplement each other. This process of mutual critique and supplementation will occupy the remainder of the book and could proceed down a number of productive lines; however, I suggest that it will be most instructive to return first of all to the discussion of politics and metaphysics that occupied the concluding section of the previous chapter, particularly because it pushes the analysis into the realm of ecclesiology and thereby also opens up possibilities for concrete engagement that will serve to illuminate some of the relative strengths and

---

13. Balthasar, *Glory of the Lord I*, 216 and 154, respectively.

14. This claim is central to Balthasar's theological aesthetics. See, for example, his claim that "this is not a beauty which draws things into unity in accordance with an abstract scheme of 'infinity and perfection,' 'emanation and encapsulation,' but in the precise and unique mode of the Incarnation" in *Glory of the Lord I*, 477.

Between Metaphysics and Ecclesiology

It is worth recalling, as we saw above in the context of the kind of theological metaphysics I argued is implied in Yoder's apocalyptic politics of Jesus, that there is a complex two-way relationship between politics and metaphysics such that our understanding of one has consequences for the other. Our ability to discern the shape and extent of such consequences is, perhaps, made more difficult by the incessant and supremely confident claims that we are now denizens of a distinctly postmetaphysical world. While we may grant that some of these postmetaphysical claims are articulated precisely to critique or reject a problematic metaphysical vision that, to some significant extent, refuses to give way, the correlative suggestion that moving somehow "beyond" metaphysics will enable a clearer sense of concrete political actualities to come into focus is, nevertheless, blind to the sense in which any vision of the political already involves certain metaphysical presuppositions about what it means to be human. In the context of the genealogy I have been constructing this relationship is made more complex still because, again as we have seen particularly in the case of Milbank, any true theological politics is also a mode of ecclesiology. Likewise, to suggest as I did in the previous chapter that Yoder's apocalyptic politics of Jesus implies a theological metaphysics is already also to suggest that participation in the body of Christ is the true form of sociality, that is, an ecclesiology. Indeed, for Yoder discipleship is only conceivable as a mode of participation, as a sharing in the divine nature.[15] As was the case in the previous chapter, it is instructive to see how this unfolds in Yoder by contrasting my reading with Kerr's, which helpfully reveals the extent to which a desire to purge every last remnant of metaphysics from theology may well reveal a tendency toward articulating a remarkably reactive and disembodied form of theological politics.

Key to the promise Kerr sees in Yoder is his isolation of what he calls a "historicist apocalyptic logic that is at work in determining the life of the church in the world as an altogether different mode of political engagement and action."[16] Going some way beyond Yoder, Kerr's provocative suggestion is that participation in the apocalyptic politics of Jesus must be radically

---

15. See, for example, Yoder, *Politics of Jesus*, 112–33; and Yoder, *Discipleship as Political Responsibility*, 49–66.

16. Kerr, *Christ, History, and Apocalyptic*, 134.

dispossessive and missionary if it is to avoid lapsing back into yet another form of ideology. For Kerr, the church-as-*polis* model risks both the "ontologization of the church" and the "instrumentalization of worship."[17] Kerr's solution, then, is to conceive of genuine liturgy, with the help of Michel de Certeau, as a "non-place" whose life consists only as an ongoing "movement of perpetual departure" and thus is not a "stable site of production."[18] Again, the reason Kerr's provocative work is helpful here is that it opens up a space of productive disagreement. While it is clear from what we have seen above that there are profound points where our accounts overlap, particularly with respect to the link between apocalyptic and the particularity of Jesus, there also exist significant divergences. These come to the fore most forcefully in Kerr's appropriation and deployment of doxology as that which is uniquely able to "expose and surpass the intimate connection between functionalist socio-political reasoning and totalizing, ideological schemes of meaning."[19] In Kerr's hands, doxology becomes the mode of God's apocalyptic action that alone is able to "resist the ontological mechanizations of the *analogia entis*."[20] What Kerr's thesis that the church exists only as mission helps us see, then, is that the ongoing redemptive work of God cannot be said to operate solely or even primarily through the institution of the church. In a sense, then, the apocalyptic action of God in the singularity of Jesus has the effect of "blowing the dynamite of the church."[21] Insofar as Kerr's disruptive account of the politics of Christian mission illuminates the sense in which the church cannot be conceived of as the "domicile of the Spirit" or as the construction of a mere *counter-polis* it is certainly a necessary and insightful supplementation of the construction of ecclesiologies that, to varying degrees, domesticate the work of the Spirit and seek to control its operations.

However, Kerr gives us reason to think of his proposal as something more than just a necessary corrective. As we saw in his understanding of metaphysics, it may well be the case that Kerr thinks of ecclesiology itself as ineluctably tending toward a kind of irredeemable "Constantinian" ideology that can therefore not simply be supplemented but rather must be supplanted by something that is impervious to such corrupting tendencies. And, indeed, Kerr's theopolitical vision is articulated less as a rival ecclesiology and more as an apocalyptically inflected diasporic pneumatology that can alone

17. Ibid., 169.
18. Ibid., 179–80.
19. Ibid., 162.
20. Kerr, "Transcendence and Apocalyptic," 144.
21. I borrow this phrase from Baxter, "Blowing the Dynamite," 195–212.

make Christ's lordship over the church and the world visible.[22] Insofar as this is the case, however, Kerr leaves us with a remarkably disembodied Christ and, correlatively, a remarkably disembodied church that only exists, as he suggests, "in the moment of the break with every identifiable social institution and site."[23] In this sense, we are right to wonder whether Kerr's argument that Hauerwas's narrative ecclesiology, which he suggests cleaves even more closely to the church-as-polis model than Yoder's ecclesiology does, is overdetermined by what it is reacting against might also be true of his own account of the singular apocalyptic historicity of Jesus Christ. Indeed, it is difficult to see how Kerr's proposal can be more than reactionary because it is made visible not in any concrete, actually existing, material political body but rather only in the very event of the fracturing of these social bodies, of which the ecclesial body is but one.[24] Kerr seems to be aware of this criticism and in a subsequent essay suggests that "Yoder's vision of the church as a diasporic peoplehood 'fills out' the shape of the politics that Certeau's account of the Christian community as a missionary 'space of encounter' calls for."[25] In this corrective supplementation of his earlier work, Kerr makes use of Yoder's later focus on the prophetic tradition and, particularly, on the exhortation in Jeremiah to "seek the peace of the city where I have sent you . . . because in its peace you will find your peace" (Jer 29:7). For Kerr this has the advantage of being able to positively envision the visibility of the church in a way that exceeds de Certeau's logic while simultaneously avoiding the "kind of fetishization of ecclesiastical sacramentality that insists upon conceiving the Christian community in itself as 'the center of the world and the place of the true.'"[26] Even in this sense, however, Kerr's theopolitical vision prioritizes form and finds the elaboration of any concrete content to be somewhat

22. Throughout his description of liturgy and diaspora Kerr employs the language of pneumatology instead of ecclesiology. See, for example, Kerr's description of the "twofold work of the Spirit," which for him constitutes the "apocalyptic historicity" of Jesus Christ, in Kerr, *Christ, History, and Apocalyptic*, 177.

23. Ibid., 180.

24. In this way, Graham Ward's criticism of de Certeau's notion of tactics goes to the heart of the matter here: "Only as tactics of subversion in an alternative, divine ordering of creation, can tactics *per se* not simply react against the established order but promote a new and foreseeable order." See Ward, *Theology and Contemporary Critical Theory*, 156. Kerr's use of de Certeau is usefully juxtaposed with David Toole's here insofar as Toole's reading of the parables as tactics of resistance highlights their material participation in an alternative ordering of the world. See Toole, *Waiting for Godot in Sarajevo*, 230–41.

25. Kerr, "*Communio Missionis*," 326. Indeed, Kerr concedes that without supplementation "Certeau's heterological account of Christian homelessness, diaspora, and exile might just leave us with a merely reactionary politics" (ibid.).

26. Ibid., 333.

problematic, at least insofar as identifying distinctly Christian forms of life can, so it seems, only be done in contrast to the world and would thereby result in some kind of stable "social datum," which in turn would compromise the apocalyptic singularity of Jesus Christ. In this way, Kerr's form of apocalyptic proceeds in some sympathy with Metz's that, likewise, harbors an innate suspicion of both the totalizing tendencies of metaphysics and the extent to which the institution of the church can suppress the imminent expectation that is the ground of Christian hope.[27] However, the extent to which Kerr's vision is genuinely able to promote a politics that is more than reactionary is nevertheless seriously in doubt because in the end all we are left with is a rather vague suggestion that "the church's sacramental practices are themselves only sacramental *as* practices of mission, as visible practices of that very *love* by which members of the Christian community are bound to one another and to every other *qua* other in Christ."[28] Again, the emphasis for Kerr is decidedly on the shape of Christian mission, which he insists must take the form of perpetual departure. Yet we are left to wonder what this "mission" might actually look like—there is no attempt to discern what it might mean to participate in the new creation that is inaugurated in Christ (2 Cor 5:17)—and in this respect, while Kerr gives us a vision of mission as diaspora, he cannot quite muster the kind of vision of mission as *Nachfolge* that Metz and Yoder articulate in their own ways.[29]

In this respect it is especially telling that Kerr's account only hesitatingly mentions the five key practices—the body politics—that Yoder identifies as concrete visible marks of the believing community.[30] More to the point, however, it is precisely at this point that we can see that the church-

27. For Metz's comments about the church in this respect see, for example, Metz, *Followers of Christ*, 75–83.

28. Kerr, "*Communio Missionis*," 334.

29. At least some of Kerr's worries could be mitigated here with a thicker description of the paradoxical nature of concrete visible institutions and sacramental practices, which can be, on the one hand, ways of abiding in a culture that fetishizes hypermobility and speed and, on the other hand, ways of walking despite appearing quite stationary and stable. For a helpful account of this, see Bauerschmidt, "Walking in the Pilgrim City," 504–17.

30. See Yoder, *Body Politics*. This important work is not cited at all in Kerr's *Christ, History, and Apocalyptic*. In this respect, we can see that for Kerr, the positive advantage that Yoder holds over de Certeau consists not in any elaboration of concrete Christian practice or positive filling out of the shape of Christian witness but in the more formal insight that dispossession just *is* mission: "Missionary dispersion is not the formal byproduct of Christ's original disappearance and perpetual withdrawal; it is rather *constitutive* of the Christian community." See Kerr, "*Communio Missionis*," 335. Even in his later essay, when he finally gets around to mentioning baptism and the Eucharist, Kerr inserts a lengthy footnote that raises the question about whether and to what extent Yoder's account of these practices ends up reducing theology to ethics and/or sociology.

as-*polis* model just isn't the same kind of problem for Yoder as it is for Kerr and that the reason for this has everything to do with Yoder's understanding of the power of nonviolence, which plays absolutely no role whatsoever in Kerr's account. This is the case neither because Yoder explicitly suggests in his earlier work that "the church is properly a political entity, a *polis*" nor because the church-as-*polis* model isn't subject to some of the dangers Kerr rightly worries about.[31] On a more fundamental level, the church-as-*polis* model isn't the same kind of problem for Yoder because he sees, as Kerr does not, that because the power of nonviolence is constitutive of the apocalyptic politics of Jesus and not simply some kind of optional appendage that whatever interruptive function it seeks to exercise with respect to revealing the extent to which existing arrangements of power are corrupt must also be turned back on itself. Put differently, for Yoder theology and its embodiment as a peculiar ecclesial way of life must be the object of such apocalyptic interruption. This is why he emphasizes in his discussion of what it means to see doxologically that it demands "we appropriate . . . those modes of witness which explode the limits that *our own* systems impose on *our* capacity to be illuminated and led."[32] For Yoder, then, part of what the power of nonviolence means is that because all our creaturely modes of vision are subject to some form of blindness, whether willful or not, all our attempts to see must not only be aware of the potential for self-deception but must also actively cultivate a positive capacity for self-criticism or, as he puts it, a readiness for radical reformation. As we saw, this is precisely why Yoder emphasizes both the significance of the open possibility of recantation for the early Anabaptists and the sense in which they held to a positive doctrine of ecclesial fallibility. Thus, Yoder is able to affirm both that "the choice of Jesus . . . risks an option in favor of the restored vision of how things really are" *and* that we must not be "drawn into . . . thinking that we, more than others, see things as they really are."[33] In this way, Yoder's theopolitical vision tarries with the mysterious apocalyptic interplay between unveiling and veiling by remaining in that dangerous and tension-filled space while refusing either to destroy the adversary or to withdraw from the struggle.

For Yoder this is no empty theoretical construction. On the contrary, his suggestion is that we can see the outworking of this kind of theopolitical vision in the forms of life that were embodied by the early Anabaptists. For our purposes, this is especially fortuitous because it also reveals a critical confrontation with Schmitt's understanding of the political. In some form

31. Yoder, *Christian Witness to the State*, 18.
32. Yoder, *Royal Priesthood*, 129.
33. Yoder, *For the Nations*, 212; and *Royal Priesthood*, 203, respectively.

or another, Schmitt's well-known argument that "the specific political distinction to which political actions can be reduced is that between friend and enemy"[34] has been at work in the genealogy of political theology with which we have been concerned, whether as a regulative principle (Schmitt) or as that which must be decisively interrupted (Metz) or as a kind of theo-logic (Milbank). Indeed, as we have seen, Schmitt recognizes that the most significant challenge to this vision of the political is to be found in the words of Jesus, "Love your enemies" (Matt 5:44; Luke 6:27), yet he writes that in this biblical statement "no mention is made of the political enemy. Never in the thousand-year struggle between Christians and Moslems did it occur to a Christian to surrender rather than defend Europe out of love toward the Saracens or Turks."[35] It is precisely on this point that Yoder can again appeal to the witness of the early Anabaptists, who were executed precisely for their refusal to wield the sword against any political enemy of the state. The trial of Michael Sattler, a former Benedictine monk, stands as perhaps the sharpest rebuke of Schmitt's overly confident historical gloss:

> If the Turk comes, he should not be resisted, for it stands written: thou shalt not kill. We should not defend ourselves against the Turks or our other persecutors, but with fervent prayer should implore God that He might be our defense and resistance.[36]

This is no simple indictment of Schmitt's lack of knowledge of Reformation history. Indeed, it is perhaps here most concretely and directly that we can see an interruption of the Hobbesian political ontology of *bellum omnium contra omnes* that underwrites Schmitt's thinking. However, this direct confrontation itself cannot be understood as wholesale refutation of Schmitt, and if we linger slightly longer a paradoxical resonance begins to appear between Schmitt and Yoder. As we have seen, what fascinates Schmitt most are the agonistic moments in which life and death are at stake.[37] While I do not wish to suggest that Yoder straightforwardly follows Schmitt here, there is nevertheless a subversive continuity because he too understands that holding open and inhabiting these tension-filled spaces is politically productive, albeit in a radically different way than Schmitt does. Whereas Schmitt is resigned to displacing the inherent violence between human beings onto an external enemy in an effort to maintain order and, above all, to avoid civil war, Yoder sees the multifarious potential of conflict as capable

---

34. Schmitt, *Concept of the Political*, 26.
35. Ibid., 29.
36. Yoder, *Legacy of Michael Sattler*, 72.
37. See, for example, Schmitt, *Concept of the Political*, 33.

of enriching human existence instead of destroying it. Here again, the extent to which the power of nonviolence is constitutive of Yoder's theopolitical vision is not only evident but also consonant with the kind of theological metaphysics I suggested is implied in his work because, as he says, "there is no enemy to be destroyed; there is an adversary to be reconciled."[38]

Taken together, all of this reveals a new peoplehood, a gathering together of a people committed to practice a peculiar new way of life that rules through suffering servanthood (Matt 20:25–28). With obvious connections to his earlier elaboration of this body politic, Yoder describes it this way:

> When he called his society together Jesus gave its members a new way of life to live. He gave them a new way to deal with offenders—by forgiving them. He gave them a new way to deal with violence—by suffering. He gave them a new way to deal with money—by sharing it. He gave them a new way to deal with problems of leadership—by drawing upon the gift of every member, even the most humble. He gave them a new way to deal with a corrupt society—by building a new order, not smashing the old. He gave them a new pattern of relationships between man and woman, between parent and child, between master and slave, in which was made concrete a radical new vision of what it means to be a human person. He gave them a new attitude toward the state and toward the "enemy nation."[39]

Perhaps somewhat surprisingly, especially given his vehement criticism of Yoder, this way of describing the ecclesial community bears a striking resemblance to Hart's description of the church as nothing less than "a politics, a society, another country, a new pattern of communal being."[40] Despite the fact that Hart's ecclesiological elucidations are much less central to his larger project than they are for Yoder and the fact that Hart tends to be more anxious about the extent to which the "church has no excuse for surrendering the horizon of history to the forces of 'secularity,'"[41] his articulation of how the church is to put into practice the form of life inaugurated by Jesus Christ proceeds down remarkably similar paths to Yoder's. This can be seen in at least two significant ways. First, like Yoder, Hart emphasizes the fallible nature of the church: "The church is a real unfolding of Christ's presence,

---

38. Yoder, *Nonviolence*, 46.

39. Yoder, *For the Nations*, 176. This is one of the clear instances where we can see that even though Yoder recognizes the extent to which fetishization of the church is a distinct problem, he is no less committed to giving an account of the distinctive concrete practices that are marks of the new society that Jesus inaugurates.

40. Hart, *Beauty of the Infinite*, 340.

41. Ibid.

a melismatic extension (so to speak) of the theme he imparts, an *epektasis* toward the fullness of his form; but while the church's every utterance, gift, or response, every act of worship, charity, or art (however poor) may belong to the fullness of that music, a certain accompanying discord—an apostasy from the form of Christ—undeniably burdens each hour."[42] Second, and again in a manner that is evocative of Yoder, Hart emphasizes that "the normal politics of power (or of, to be more precise, the powers) is a politics of chaos and the inhibition thereof; it understands justice in terms of an immediate and hence tautologous reciprocity (in terms, that is, of violence). But the politics of the church can understand justice only according to a disruption of such reciprocity—bearing one another's burdens, forgiving even the debt truly owed, seeking reconciliation rather than due retribution."[43] While I do not wish to over identify Yoder and Hart here—it must be said that although Hart recognizes at least to some extent that the primary Christian path involves a commitment to nonviolence, he nevertheless tends to contrast this with the imperative to do justice, which he favors over the kind of "pacifism" that refuses to struggle in the world of flesh and blood—I do want to suggest that their respective theopolitical visions take their cue from remarkably similar scriptural themes that highlight the sense in which Christian discipleship must take the form of Christ's life.

The strong insistence on the coinherence of form and content indicative of both Yoder's and Hart's theopolitical vision fades much more distantly into the background when we turn to Milbank, however. The sense in which this is the case can be seen if we compare his earlier work, subtitled *Beyond Secular Reason*, with his more recent book *Beyond Secular Order*, which he explicitly offers as a successor volume that deepens his earlier analysis. In his earlier work Milbank forthrightly affirms that for Christianity the "incarnation of the *logos* . . . provides us with the key to all human performance" and, further, that the church "provides a genuine peace by its memory of all the victims, its equal concern for all its citizens and its self-exposed offering of reconciliation to enemies."[44] However, even here we can see that for Milbank "the absolute vision of Christian ontological peace" cannot content itself with an abstract attachment to nonviolence because he admits, following his reading of Augustine, "the need for some measures of coercion . . . because sometimes people can be temporarily blind and will only be prevented from permanent self-

---

42. Ibid., 339.

43. Ibid., 340. Hart's description of the politics of the powers as an inhibition of chaos is also an apt, if far too brief, summary of Schmitt's vision.

44. Milbank, *Theology and Social Theory*, 230 and 392, respectively.

damage when they are forced into some course of action, or prevented from another."[45] In *Beyond Secular Order*, Milbank's earlier work is indeed deepened, for now he presents us not with a reading of Augustine's two cities but rather of Augustine's three cities:

> "The City of this World" is primarily represented by ancient Babylon, which also represents human rule in general. The "City of God" is of course Israel as a foretype of the Church and then the Church itself as a fulfillment and continuation of Israel. But what of Rome? Primarily it is in a literal sense like Babylon and belongs to it also figuratively. Yet Rome is also given a more privileged and specific providential role . . . [Augustine] explicitly declares that God now exercises his governance partially through the mediation of the Roman imperial office, since he has rewarded the just emperor Constantine with the honour of founding a new city in the east, bearing his name, while he has quickly removed the unjust emperor Jovian from his throne.[46]

Significantly, Milbank also affirms that while the secular office was for Augustine significantly "outside the Church" after Constantine it is also "located *within* the Church."[47] It is precisely this intensification to which I want to call attention because in his earlier work coercion is seen, at least to some extent, as a necessary though tragic feature of the earthly city, but by highlighting a further differentiation within the earthly city as he does, coercion and violence can now be fully admitted as forms of divinely authorized rule, albeit ones that must be somehow restrained, compensated for, and ordered toward promotion of the *ecclesia*. Milbank's vision of what he calls christological kingship is thus less and less captivated by the beauty of Jesus Christ and tends rather toward a mediation, as he explicitly confirms, of "Christ as Melchizedek the king-priest."[48] Concomitantly, this is also the reason that Milbank can now lodge an outright denunciation of any form of anti-Constantinianism, which he alleges harbors a "deficient sense of both mission and common humanity."[49] This is the case, for Milbank, because the church "is emphatically not, on a theological conception, a kind of 'extra' religious organisation which some people happen to belong to; it is, rather,

---

45. Ibid., 434 and 418, respectively. Milbank admits that while this kind of coercion is not yet "peaceable," it is nevertheless still capable of being retrospectively "redeemed" and thereby contributes to the final goal of peace.

46. Milbank, *Beyond Secular Order*, 228.

47. Ibid., 229.

48. Ibid.

49. Ibid., 248. Though Milbank does not mention these "anti-Constantinian Christians" by name, it is clear that he has both Yoder and Hauerwas in his sights here.

the *sine qua non* for the existence of human society as such, and so for the existence of humanity as such: *nulla humanitas extra ecclesiam*."[50] Alongside this notion of kingship, which employs ever more sophisticated and historically nuanced methods of theologically justifying a restrained form of violence necessary to promote justice in the earthly city, we can also see here that Milbank self-consciously inhibits any mention of the figure of the martyr because even though, as he says, kings will "eventually cast their crowns at Christ's feet," there is no sense in which doing so commits them to follow the way of life inaugurated by the slain Lamb, who alone is worthy to receive glory and power and honor (Rev 4:10–11).[51] Taken together, all of this logic tends toward a theopolitical vision that is much closer to Schmitt's, and even though Milbank is much clearer that the end to which violence and coercion must be directed is justice and not, as for Schmitt, simply the prevention of chaos, it nevertheless proceeds on the basis of restraining violence, albeit with a kinder, gentler counterviolence, and thereby repeats the katechontic structure of Schmitt's political theology.[52] In this sense, then, it is perhaps less surprising that Milbank makes reference to Schmitt's idea of a new *nomos* of the earth to describe the lineaments of his vision for reconstructing a global Christendom.[53]

If, as we saw in chapter 3, Milbank's reconfiguration of political theology critiques the sense in which Metz's form of apocalyptic negativity remains in a crucial sense too close to Schmitt's and thus cannot in the end escape its violent aporetics, we are now in a position to see the sense in which the theological content that Milbank supplies to supplement Metz's lack of positive vision must itself be subjected to precisely the kind of apocalyptic interruption Metz articulates. In the light of Milbank's theology of ruling, Metz's articulation of the Christian *memoria passionis* stands as a sharp rebuke of its triumphalist tendencies: "Whenever a party, a race, a nation, or a church . . . has misunderstood its identity along the lines of Dostoevsky's Grand Inquisitor . . . the Christian *memoria* must oppose it and unmask [it]

50. Ibid., 240.

51. Ibid., 249. Milbank cites only Revelation 4:10 here and does not make any mention of the slain Lamb.

52. In an essay that brings Milbank and Yoder into constructive conversation, Angus Paddison makes the suggestion that Milbank is insufficiently seized by apocalyptic, at least in part because his mode of theology is unwilling to be interrupted and does not sufficiently take account of biblical apocalyptic. See Paddison, "Reading Yoder against Milbank," 144–63. Although Paddison is not wrong about the extent to which Milbank's vision absorbs all others and pays only scant attention to the biblical text, my suggestion is that this does not mean that he is insufficiently seized by apocalyptic but rather that his form of apocalyptic tends toward a Schmittian rather than a Yoderian inflection.

53. Milbank, *Beyond Secular Order*, 257.

as political idolatry, as a political ideology with totalitarian tendencies, or (to use the language of apocalypticism) with the tendencies of the Beast."[54] As we have seen, it is precisely this kind of self-criticism that Milbank's vision simply cannot countenance, and, indeed, a Schmittian theo-logic is at work shoring up the sense in which any criticism is, in the end, a failure to see deeply enough into the depths of human history.[55] At the risk of simply being accused of such an optical failure, however, it is perhaps Metz's theopolitical vision more than any other that points to blind spots in Milbank's vision. While, as we saw, Hart's theopolitical vision helpfully highlighted the sense in which Milbank's political theology does not (cannot?) give an account of martyrdom, Metz's relentless focus on becoming ever more acutely aware of the suffering of others arguably pushes this even further:

> Considered theologically the Christian memory of suffering is an anticipatory remembering; it holds the anticipation of a specific future for humankind as a future for the suffering, for those without hope, for the oppressed, the disabled, and the useless of this earth . . . What the memory of suffering brings into political life . . . is a new moral imagination with regard to others' suffering, which should bear fruit in an excessive, uncalculated partiality for the weak and the voiceless. This is the way that the Christian *memoria passionis* can become a ferment for that new political life for which we are searching, so that we might have a human future.[56]

For Metz, this relentless refocusing of our vision on the suffering of the outcast, the oppressed, the voiceless, the enemy, takes the form of what he calls a "mysticism of open eyes" that holds out the potential for engendering a "politics of peace."[57] In this sense, Metz's vision reveals that despite Milbank's avowed advocacy of Christian socialism his vision of a "new politics

---

54. Metz, *Faith in History and Society*, 112. To be clear, I do not wish to suggest that Milbank's theopolitical vision can straightforwardly be understood to side with the Grand Inquisitor, as Schmitt's does; however, there is nevertheless still a sense in which Christ is deported, if not all the way to the margins of his genealogy then at least out of its center, despite whatever protests he may wish to make to the contrary. See also Schmitt, *Glossarium*, 243.

55. Milbank positions himself as the true seer who is willing to "run the risk that any claim to illuminate human history at a depth will present conclusions that can seem excessively abstruse or even implausible. Yet it may be this very abstruseness that is the mark of their authenticity" in *Beyond Secular Order*, 2.

56. Metz, *Faith in History and Society*, 112–13.

57. Metz, "God," 38–41.

of trans-organicity" has scant place in it for the wretched of the earth.[58] Moreover, this is also the place at which we can see that the mystical-political structure of Metz's *new* political theology proceeds much more closely with Yoder's, which recognizes that the practice of nonviolence is "a distinctive spirituality . . . [that] presupposes and fosters a distinctive way of seeing oneself and one's neighbor under God."[59]

Against and Beyond Yoder

This process of mutual critique and supplementation could, of course, continue down any number of potential avenues, and the foregoing reflections have only scratched the surface of the potential ecclesiological points of overlap and difference. However, instead of pursuing a comprehensive account of these supplementations, which in any case would be well beyond the scope of this book given the necessary selectivity with which I have engaged each of the main figures at the interpretive heart of the genealogy in the first place, I want to conclude by re-emphasizing the non-epic character of the argument itself. Though, as I have argued, Yoder's understanding of the power of nonviolence holds crucial advantages with respect to subverting Schmitt's theopolitical vision, I have also claimed that it does not hold all of the advantages. We have seen some of the ways that this is the case above, particularly with respect to Hart and Metz; however, perhaps the clearest way to see this is to call attention to Yoder's own blind spots, which also has the happy consequence of pointing up the significant supplementation of Milbank's vision that has hitherto mainly served as the instrument and subject of critique. Indeed, if my suggestion that Yoder's

---

58. See Milbank, *Beyond Secular Order*, 258–69. Indeed, there is a profound sense in which Milbank's vision is forgetful of suffering and a stranger to mourning. How his vision can properly be understood, as he suggests, as a "left reading of Catholic social teaching" without a strong sense of solidarity with the poor and vulnerable simply begs the question. In *Beyond Secular Order*, for example, the poor are mentioned only at one point in the course of a critique of the "bureaucratisation of love" which he suggests led to "a further 'cold' organisation of charitable works, which were increasingly dominated by a top-down sense of simply 'doing something for others', as if we were not all of us, in the end, 'the poor'" (ibid., 258). Alongside this, Milbank suggests that his vision is, to some extent, recognizable primarily by the "more reflective youth of Europe." This latter claim repeats his earlier assertion that the kinds of "re-Catholicizing" trends central to his own vision are, in various ways, already being recognized by an educated elite. See Milbank, "Stale Expressions," especially 121–23.

59. See Yoder, *Nonviolence*, 43. Without mentioning a connection to Yoder, Matthew Ashley suggests that Metz's emphasis on imitating Christ bears a strong resemblance to Anabaptist spirituality in Ashley, *Interruptions*, 181.

understanding of the power of nonviolence is what holds crucial advantages, then it would not be in keeping with the tenor of the genealogy of political theology that I have been attempting to narrate to pretend that with Yoder we have finally arrived at the last, or the best, word. If it is the case, as Yoder argues, that dissonance creates space for renewal, then it is appropriate and perhaps even necessary to "loop back" to Yoder himself to see the sense in which his vision, too, is not fully immune to the Schmittian seductions of political theology.

It is instructive, therefore, to note that Yoder himself is no pure type. To suggest that Yoder's understanding of the apocalyptic politics of Jesus cannot be understood apart from his commitment to nonviolence is not to suggest that he is uniformly consistent in performing this throughout his work.[60] Indeed, there are points at which Yoder frankly and explicitly foregrounds this issue: "I especially do not give scholastic traditions the benefit of the doubt, when one can see that those by whom they were articulated in history were defenders of specific interests distinguishable from the Kingdom of God."[61] For our purposes, this tendency of Yoder to occasionally offer caricatured readings of his interlocutors is visible most clearly in his understanding of Jewish history. Anticipating such a critique, Yoder granted that his reading of Jewish history was "selective" but insisted that he was *not* "co-opting Jews" to enlist them in his cause.[62] These protests notwithstanding, Michael Cartwright suggests, again with unacknowledged debts to Bakhtin, that "polyphony would not be a word that aptly describes Yoder's hermeneutic . . . since his own modes of argument betray a kind of Cartesian 'either-or' logic that requires *the rhetorical displacement and/or the elimination* of that which is opposed."[63] We need not quibble here about whether Cartwright's criticism stands or to what extent Yoder's anticipation

---

60. I am well aware of the fact that the emphases I have highlighted in Yoder's work, particularly a commitment to nonviolence and the cultivation of self-critical practices, are also haunted by his legacy of sexual violence against women. The extent to which his theological vision and his abusive behavior coalesce is again being given serious attention, and although it is beyond the scope of this book to enter into this ongoing debate, it is nevertheless important to recognize this here. For an engagement of this issue from within Yoder's own Mennonite tradition, see, for example, the January 2015 edition of the *Mennonite Quarterly Review*.

61. Yoder, *To Hear the Word*, 60. Although certainly not malicious in intent, Yoder's reading of Aquinas on just war is a good example here. See Yoder, *Christian Attitudes to War*, especially 65–74.

62. Yoder, *Jewish-Christian Schism Revisited*, 115.

63. Cartwright, "Afterword: 'If Abraham is Our Father . . . ,'" 215. In my estimation, Cartwright's criticism of Yoder here is actually closer to describing the kind of Schmittian theo-logic endemic to Milbank's work.

of such a critique mitigates its import; the point is rather that the danger of slipping into monological modes of reflection that silence the other is an ever-present temptation to which Yoder is subject no less than anyone else. In this way, we might suggest, perhaps counterintuitively, that Yoder's mode of engagement occasionally bears some resemblance to the Schmittian theo-logic that I have argued is much more consistently and aggressively deployed in Milbank's vision.[64]

Alongside this, and just as problematic, is the singular trope that most occupied Yoder's vision, namely, his relentless critique of what he referred to as Constantinianism. Yoder's critique is well known and for our purposes is helpfully summed up in his succinct definition: "The term refers to the conception of Christianity that took shape between the Edict of Milan [313] and the *City of God* [427]."[65] To be clear, the reason I wish to call attention to this here is neither that Yoder's critique is not of continuing importance nor simply that it does violence to history—though it often does and is therefore also a form of monological distortion—but rather to highlight what it occludes from Yoder's view.[66] In this sense, Peter Leithart's deliberately polemical *Defending Constantine* should be received as a subversive gift that unsettles Yoder's reading of the historical development of Christianity in the fourth and fifth centuries, which often simply imbibed the narratives undertaken by modern secondary sources. Particularly helpful in this respect is the extent to which Leithart dismantles Yoder's too easy assimilation of Augustine to Constantine and, perhaps even more significantly, the sense in which Constantine himself embodied some of the specific marks of discipleship that Yoder was at pains to emphasize.[67] Likewise, the extent

---

64. This is not to equate Yoder with Milbank here. Indeed, that Yoder explicitly foregrounds this issue and wrestles with it is evidence of a significant difference with Milbank on this point. See Yoder, *Jewish-Christian Schism Revisited*, 112–17.

65. Yoder, *Royal Priesthood*, 153–54. Yoder continues by suggesting that "the nature of this change, which Constantine himself did not invent nor force upon the church, is not a matter of doctrine or of polity; it is the identification of church and world in the mutual approval and support exchanged by Constantine and the bishops. The church is no longer the obedient suffering line of the true prophets; it has a vested interest in the present order of things and uses the cultic means at its disposal to legitimize that order. The church does not preach ethics, judgment, repentance, separation from the world; it dispenses sacraments and holds society together" (ibid.).

66. J. Alexander Sider argues that Yoder's critique of Constantinianism is methodologically Constantinian in Sider, *To See History Doxologically*, especially 97–132. A. James Reimer also helpfully notes that Yoder's critique of Constantiniamism is "one that the church caught in civil religion needs to hear over and over again. But there is an injustice to history . . . that is committed by Yoder and others for whom 'Constantinianism' is a shibboleth for all that is bad" in Reimer, "Mennonites, Christ, and Culture," 295.

67. See Leithart, *Defending Constantine*, 82–85 and 284–87 for Leithart's helpful

to which Yoder's theopolitical vision is excessively captivated by his critique of Constantinianism means that he is unable to appreciate, as Hart does, the vociferous denunciation of the institution of slavery unleashed by Gregory of Nyssa or the sense in which the monastic movement that grew at a remarkable rate after Constantine can be understood as a revolutionary rebellion of the church against its own "success."[68] To highlight these examples, and to recognize that there are many more that could be pointed to, is not to suggest that Yoder's worries about Constantinianism are wrongheaded but rather to point to the sense in which his work leaps from the New Testament and the early church to the Radical Reformation and thereby too easily allows for a reading of everything from the fourth century to the sixteenth as simply a long history of decline and corruption. This is precisely the place that Milbank's vast and nuanced genealogical project becomes an indispensable supplement because of his diagnosis of the sense in which complex changes in late medieval and early modern philosophy can be understood as problematic theological deviations that laid the groundwork for our contemporary theopolitical configurations. As he says, "It is, ironically, certain particular modes of theology which first invent and encourage 'secularisation' and then, because of their unbelievability, invite an agnostic and atheist scepticism which eventually engenders nihilism as a kind of truncated theological *via moderna*."[69] While some of the details of his genealogy invite further criticism—we may question the extent to which, for example, the four problematic assumptions of modern philosophy that Milbank isolates are accurately or helpfully identified as "largely Franciscan-inspired currents"[70]—its capability of discerning these later shifts is no small matter. Particularly when it comes to subverting Schmitt's vision, which likewise recognizes and seizes upon the fact that the modern theory of the state is a secularized theological concept, Milbank's attention to these later developments in theology *and* philosophy is just as important and perhaps even more so than Yoder's more nearly exclusive focus on the

---

dissociation of Augustine from Constantine. In his discussion of slavery on 218–24 Leithart suggests that Constantine opened new avenues for the liberation of slaves and sought to ameliorate their conditions, all of which to some extent embodies just the kinds of practices Yoder highlights in, for example, *Body Politics*, 27.

68. For Hart's reading of Gregory of Nyssa's denunciation of slavery, see Hart, "The 'Whole Humanity,'" 51–69. For Hart's suggestion that the final revolutionary moment in ancient Christianity can be understood as "a renunciation of power even as power was at last granted to the church," see Hart, *Atheist Delusions*, 240–41.

69. Milbank, *Beyond Secular Order*, 3.

70. Ibid. Milbank identifies these four assumptions as "(1) the univocity rather than analogy of being; (2) knowledge of representation rather than identity; (3) the priority of the possible over the actual; and (4) causality as 'concurrence' rather than 'influence.'"

Constantinian problematic. And, indeed, in the end, the reading of Yoder I have offered is itself enabled by such insights in the first place.

Even here, however, despite all of his hesitations about the disastrous effects of Constantinianism, Yoder nevertheless still leaves the door slightly ajar: "Our minds should remain open to the possible rational or biblical arguments of those who might claim that the attainment of a privileged social position by the church in the fourth century called for changes in morals, ecclesiology, and eschatology; thus far it must be admitted that clear and cogent arguments for this have not been brought."[71] This contrasts sharply with Milbank's outright denunciation of any form of anti-Constantinianism and is, again, evidence of a Schmittian theo-logic.[72] Given the extent to which Hart explicitly foregrounds martyrdom as the form Christianity must embrace if it is not to betray its own witness, it is, perhaps, surprising to find Hart in some form of agreement with Milbank on this score in his vociferous denunciation of his non-Constanitnian brethren.[73] I want to conclude by attempting to stay in this tension-filled space and by dwelling on the mysteries of the challenges that arise within it. While Yoder would certainly not demur from Hart's contention that "the path of obedience is anything but easy or clear,"[74] it is precisely at this point that we can see most clearly the tension building:

> there is also small room in theology for that passive collaboration with evil that often only flatters itself with the name of "pacifism." However primary the path of nonviolence is for the Christian, the peace of God's kingdom is exhaustively described in Scripture, and it is the peace of a concrete condition of justice; it is neither the private practice of an "ethical" individual, jealous of his own moral purity, nor the special and quaint regime of a separatist community that stands aloof from (in ill-concealed contempt for) its "Constantinian" brethren. Where the justice of the kingdom is not present, and cannot be made present without any exercise of force, the self-adoring inaction of those who would meet the reality of, say, black smoke billowing from the chimneys of death camps with songs of protest is simply violence by other means, and does not speak of God's kingdom, and does not grant its practitioners the privilege of viewing themselves as more faithful members of Christ's body

---

71. Yoder, *Christian Witness to the State*, 56.
72. Milbank, *Beyond Secular Order*, 248.
73. See Hart, *Beauty of the Infinite*, 341.
74. Ibid.

than those who struggle against evil in the world of flesh and blood where evil works.[75]

This is a truly remarkable passage coming from a theologian who, at the same time, emphasizes that the "politics of the church can understand justice only in terms of a disruption of the reciprocity of violence—by bearing one another's burdens, forgiving even the debt truly owed, seeking reconciliation rather than due retribution."[76] Indeed, it resembles Milbank's theology of justified coercion much more closely and would certainly be easier to understand coming from him. It would be quite straightforward at this point to simply take Hart to task here for a caricatured and crass portrayal of Yoder's pacifism of the messianic community or to suggest that his argument here simply misses its intended target altogether.[77] After all, does Hart not see that, as Yoder says, "leaving evil free to be evil is part of the nature of *agape* itself, as revealed already in creation"?[78] Any simple riposte of this sort, however, would not get us very far because whatever built-up productive tension would thereby be either resolved or side-stepped. What if, instead of assuming that Hart hasn't sufficiently understood Yoder, we entertain the dangerous possibility that he has, in fact, understood what is at stake and is offering his reading not as a kind of last-resort accommodation with the violent proclivities that saturate the world, as is much more the case in Milbank, but rather as a real *evangel*? Romand Coles entertains precisely this troubling possibility when he suggests that a thicker description of many of Yoder's examples of the generative capacities of nonviolence often reveal that the successes we may wish to attribute to nonviolent action may well be of a more mixed constitution. Coles uses the example of the civil rights movement and provocatively suggests that "it is an inconvenient truth that the struggle for the Beloved Community was made possible by *both* the tradition of a politics of Jesus *and* the tradition of 'negroes with guns' willing to use them in self-defense."[79] Hart's evocation of the death camps harkens back also to Metz, and together they pose a stark question, the full force of which must be borne deeply by advocates of nonviolence

75. Ibid.

76. Ibid., 340.

77. I have argued this above but it bears repeating: it is more than a little unfortunate that a theologian who goes to great lengths to defend the doctrine of divine *apatheia* as having nothing whatsoever to do with apathy cannot entertain the possibility that the pacifism he so easily dismisses may have nothing whatsoever to do with a passive complicity with evil.

78. Yoder, *Royal Priesthood*, 151.

79. Coles, "Wild Peace (Not) of John Howard Yoder," 35.

if they are not to "obscenely choose martyrdom for others"[80]: how can an active divine patience be instantiated as good news in the face of black smoke bellowing from the chimneys at Auschwitz? This dangerous question should make us all tremble, yet, as Hölderlin reminds us, "Where there is danger, there grows also what saves."[81] In the end, then, we must struggle to remain in these dangerous contested spaces—spaces of "hope against hope" (Rom 4:18)—where an apocalyptic politics of nonviolence is neither simply relegated to the status of an impossible utopianism nor simply regarded as politically disingenuous and theologically dubious but is rather seen as holding open an infinite potential for reconfiguring our vision in the light of the cross and resurrection of Jesus Christ.[82] While Yoder has certainly not wholly unfairly been perceived as the veritable poster boy for what both Hart and Milbank consider sanctimonious denunciations of Constantinianism, in the light of my reading of Yoder, which explicitly foregrounds his allowance for the possibility of some form of Constantinianism, what I want to suggest is that the power of nonviolence to which Yoder crucially points does not live by the logic of beautiful souls but rather by the logic of cross and resurrection and, in so doing, enables a politics of nonviolence that is more than a gaze that diverts attention from evil. In doing so it does not extricate us from the struggle to remain in those tension-filled and, indeed, dangerous spaces that inevitably follow any attempt to walk in the footsteps of the crucified one (John 15:20) but does, nevertheless, embody a refusal to destroy the adversary in the course of such a struggle. Thus we arrive at a particular nonviolent apocalyptic style, one that tarries with the mysterious interplay between unveiling and veiling and, as such, one that is enabled and empowered to seek out sites of conflict and to enter these not to destroy but

80. Hart, *Beauty of the Infinite*, 341.

81. As quoted in Heidegger, *Poetry, Language, Thought*, 115.

82. While the so-called historic peace churches are often more closely associated with an explicit endorsement of nonviolence, its importance is increasingly being recognized and pursued across the Christian denominational spectrum. Especially notable in this respect is a recent document from the Vatican's International Theological Commission, "Christian Monotheism and its Opposition to Violence," which advocates for a nonviolent humanism on the basis of trinitarian relations, as well as a statement released at the conclusion of a conference sponsored by the Pontifical Council for Justice and Peace entitled "An Appeal to the Catholic Church to Re-commit to the Centrality of Gospel Nonviolence," which advocates abandoning just war theory and for further developing Catholic social teaching on nonviolence in its place. These documents are available online: http://www.vatican.va/roman_curia/congregations/cfaith/cti_documents/rc_cti_20140117_monoteismo-cristiano_en.html, and http://www.paxchristi.net/sites/default/files/documents/appeal-to-catholic-church-to-recommit-to-nonviolence.pdf

to reconcile.[83] As Yoder says, striking a fittingly mysterious note, "the only way to see how this will work will be to see how it will work."[84]

Concluding Remarks

There are many reasons to engage at length the relationship between Schmitt's articulation of political theology and subsequent contemporary reconfigurations of it. It has been one of the goals of the foregoing pages to unsettle the sense in which the discipline of theology itself has largely not seen this engagement as a necessary or helpful one despite the fact that our contemporary sociopolitical context in various ways bears the hallmarks of a distinctly Schmittian disposition toward the political. It should also be clear that the foregoing attempt to seriously wrestle with the Schmittian seductions that continue to bedevil political theology is by no means to suggest that any reconfiguration of political theology that does not explicitly engage Schmitt's work does so at its own peril. Even in the context of the genealogy I have been adumbrating this is not the case because, as I have argued, while only Metz and Milbank mention Schmitt, forms of resistance to Schmitt's violent aporetics can be seen in each of the reconfigurations of political theology that have occupied the foregoing pages, even in Hart and Yoder, who do not engage Schmitt whatsoever. While there is much of value to be gained by exploring Schmitt's work that has hitherto not been sufficiently appreciated within the discipline of theology, I do not wish to suggest that explicit engagement with Schmitt is some kind of unqualified theological good. Nevertheless, I hope that the foregoing has at least to some extent shown why theological engagement with Schmitt is worthwhile. If, as I have been arguing, the failure to seriously wrestle with Schmitt in the theological disciplines continues to have profoundly unsettling effects on subsequent developments of political theology, which are often blind to their own repetitions of his violent aporetics, then the legacy of the effects of Schmitt's work must be seriously reckoned with, and the fact that Milbank's tangential references to Schmitt hint at a more robust engagement with him in future work is good news in this respect.[85]

83. In this sense my genealogy of political theology proceeds in a kindred ambiance with Graham Ward's *Politics of Discipleship*, which likewise aims to recover a form of contestation that is not war. See Ward, *Politics of Discipleship*, 299. For a reading of the sense in which Ward's avowed apophatism bears more than a passing resemblance to Yoder's notion of peace with eschatology, see also Gingerich Hiebert, "The Recovery of Contestation and the Apophatic Body of Christ," 291–97.

84. Yoder, *Priestly Kingdom*, 45.

85. For these hints, which Milbank links with the work of Kant, de Lubac, and Agamben, see Milbank, *Beyond Secular Order*, 149, 203n195, 235n263, and 259–60.

Finally, and to emphasize the non-demonstrative quality of the argument once more, the genealogy that I have been constructing in the foregoing pages is not offered as the only or even the best way to read the transformation of political theology but rather as one particular way to do so that will, hopefully, invite and encourage just the kind of contestation that both refuses to destroy the adversary *and* to withdraw from the struggle that I have emphasized in connection with Yoder's proposal of a nonviolent apocalyptic politics. And, indeed, I foresee that there is much in the foregoing pages with which to disagree. On the one hand, there are eminently relevant voices that I have simply been forced to exclude. Any number could be mentioned here, including Dorothee Sölle, Jürgen Moltmann, and, perhaps most significantly given the overriding theme of violence and apocalyptic, René Girard. On the other hand, there is also much provocation in the ways in which I have reconstructed and positioned the voices that do populate this genealogy. Certainly my reading of Metz will strike a discordant note with those who wish to receive his *new* political theology as decisively at odds with Schmitt's vision. Depending on disposition, my reading of Milbank may have either gone too far or not far enough in linking his reconfiguration of political theology much more closely with Schmitt. Likewise, my attempt to read Hart's theological aesthetics as more amenable to Yoder's understanding of the power of nonviolence may seem positively blind to those who see the violence of Hart's rhetoric rising to a vitriolic level to which even Milbank's pales in comparison. Even my reading of the metaphysical implications of Yoder's apocalyptic politics of Jesus is sure to raise the ire of those, like Kerr, who wish to argue that Yoder pushes us in the direction of a distinctly postmetaphysical theopolitical vision. All of these and perhaps especially the unforeseen disagreements that this book may provoke are all to the good, however, because the development of theology itself is in some sense a prelude to a further unfolding of its own possibilities, implications, and failures, and so, as Balthasar affirms, its meaning "is not irrevocably fixed . . . [and] can always be newly defined and be transformed with the passage of time."[86]

---

86. Balthasar, *Theology of History*, 78.

Bibliography

Adorno, Theodor W. *Negative Dialectics*. Translated by E. B. Ashton. London: Routledge & Kegan Paul, 1973.
Agamben, Giorgio. *Homo Sacer: Sovereign Power and Bare Life*. Translated by Daniel Heller-Roazen. Stanford: Stanford University Press, 1998.
———. "Poiesis and Praxis." In *The Man Without Content*, 68–93. Stanford: Stanford University Press, 1999.
———. *State of Exception*. Translated by Kevin Attell. Chicago: University of Chicago Press, 2005.
Arendt, Hannah. *The Origins of Totalitarianism*. New York: Meridian, 1958.
Ashley, J. Matthew, trans. and ed. *The End of Time? The Provocation of Talking about God*. New York: Paulist, 2004.
———. *Interruptions: Mysticism, Politics, and Theology in the Work of Johann Baptist Metz*. Notre Dame: University of Notre Dame Press, 1998.
Augustine. *The City of God Against the Pagans*. Translated by R. W. Dyson. Cambridge: Cambridge University Press, 1998.
———. *Confessions*. Translated by Henry Chadwick. New York: Oxford University Press, 1991.
———. *On Free Choice of the Will*. Translated by Anna S. Benjamin and L. H. Hackstaff. Englewood Cliffs, NJ: Prentice Hall, 1964.
Badiou, Alain. *Saint Paul: The Foundation of Universalism*. Translated by Ray Brassier. Stanford: Stanford University Press, 2003.
Bakhtin, Mikhail. *Art and Answerability: Early Philosophical Essays*. Edited by Michael Holquist and Vadim Liapunov. Translated by Vadim Liapunov. Austin: University of Texas Press, 1990.
———. *The Dialogic Imagination: Four Essays*. Edited by Michael Holquist. Translated by Caryl Emerson and Michael Holquist. Austin: University of Texas Press, 1981.
———. *Problems of Dostoyevsky's Poetics*. Edited and translated by Caryl Emerson. Minneapolis: University of Minnesota Press, 1984.
———. "Toward a Methodology for the Human Sciences." In *Speech Genres and Other Late Essays*, edited by Caryl Emerson and Michael Holquist, 159–72. Austin: University of Texas Press, 1986.
———. *Toward a Philosophy of the Act*. Edited by Michael Holquist and Vadim Liapunov. Translated by Vadim Liapunov. Austin: University of Texas Press, 1993.

Balthasar, Hans Urs von. *Apokalypse der deutschen Seele: Studien zu einer Lehre von letzen Haltungen*. 3 vols. Freiburg: Johannes Verlag, 1998.

———. *The Glory of the Lord: A Theological Aesthetics*. Translated by Erasmo Leiva-Merikakis. Edited by Joseph Fessio and John Riches. 7 vols. San Francisco: Ignatius Press, 1982–1989.

———. *The Moment of Christian Witness*. Translated by Richard Beckley. San Francisco: Ignatius Press, 1994.

———. *Presence and Thought: An Essay on the Religious Philosophy of Gregory of Nyssa*. Translated by Mark Sebanc. San Francisco: Ignatius Press, 1995.

———. *Theo-Logic: Theological Logical Theory*. Translated by Adrian J. Walker. 3 vols. San Francisco: Ignatius Press, 2000–2005.

———. *The Theology of Henri de Lubac: An Overview*. Translated by Joseph Fessio, Michael M. Waldstein, and Susan Clements. San Francisco: Ignatius Press, 1991.

———. *A Theology of History*. San Francisco: Ignatius Press, 1994.

———. *The Theology of Karl Barth*. Translated by Edward T. Oakes. San Francisco: Ignatius, 1992.

———. *Truth Is Symphonic: Aspects of Christian Pluralism*. Translated by Graham Harrison. San Francisco: Ignatius Press, 1987.

Barth, Karl. "Fate and Idea in Theology." In *The Way of Theology in Karl Barth: Essays and Comments*, edited by H. Martin Rumscheidt, 25–61. Allison Park, PA: Pickwick, 1986.

Bauerschmidt, Frederick Christian. "Michel de Certeau (1925–1986): Introduction." In *The Postmodern God: A Theological Reader*, edited by Graham Ward, 135–42. Oxford: Blackwell, 1997.

———. "Walking in the Pilgrim City." *New Blackfriars* 77 (1996) 504–17.

———. "The Word Made Speculative? John Milbank's Christological Poetics." *Modern Theology* 15 (1999) 417–32.

Baum, Gregory. "The Blondelian Shift." In *Man Becoming: God in Secular Experience*, 1–36. New York: Herder & Herder, 1970.

Baxter, Michael J. "Blowing the Dynamite of the Church: Catholic Radicalism from a Catholic Radicalist Perspective." In *The Church as Counterculture*, edited by Michael L. Budde and Robert W. Brimlow, 195–212. Albany: State University of New York Press, 2000.

Begbie, Jeremy S. *Theology, Music and Time*. Cambridge: Cambridge University Press, 2000.

Bendersky, Joseph W. *Carl Schmitt: Theorist for the Reich*. Princeton: Princeton University Press, 1983.

Benjamin, Walter. "Paralipomena to 'On the Concept of History.'" In *Walter Benjamin: Selected Writings*, vol. 4, *1938–1940*, edited by Howard Eil and Michael W. Jennings. Cambridge: Harvard University Press, 2003.

———. "Theses on the Philosophy of History." In *Illuminations*, edited by Hannah Arendt, 245–55. London: Pimlico, 1999.

Bergen, Jeremy M., and Anthony G. Siegrist, eds. *Power and Practices: Engaging the Work of John Howard Yoder*. Scottdale, PA: Herald, 2009.

Bernardi, Peter J. *Maurice Blondel, Social Catholicism, and Action Française: The Clash of the Church's Role in Society during the Modernist Era*. Washington, DC: Catholic University of America Press, 2009.

Biesecker-Mast, Gerald. *Separation and the Sword in Anabaptist Persuasion: Radical Confessional Rhetoric from Schleitheim to Dordrecht*. Telford, PA: Cascadia, 2006.
Blanchette, Oliva. *Maurice Blondel: A Philosophical Life*. Grand Rapids: Eerdmans, 2010.
Bloch, Ernst. *Atheism in Christianity*. Translated by J. T. Swann. New ed. London: Verso, 2009.
Blond, Phillip, ed. *Post-Secular Philosophy: Between Philosophy and Theology*. London: Routledge, 1998.
Blondel, Maurice. *Action (1893): Essay on a Critique of Life and a Science of Practice*. Translated by Oliva Blanchette. Notre Dame: University of Notre Dame Press, 2003.
———. *The Letter on Apologetics and History and Dogma*. Translated by Alexander Dru and Illtyd Trethowan. London: Harvill, 1964.
Boersma, Hans. *Nouvelle Théologie and Sacramental Ontology: A Return to Mystery*. New York: Oxford University Press, 2009.
Bonhoeffer, Dietrich. *The Cost of Discipleship*. Translated by R. H. Fuller. New York: Touchstone, 1995.
———. *Ethics*. Edited by Clifford J. Green. Translated by Reinhard Krauss, Charles C. West, and Douglas W. Stott. Minneapolis: Fortress, 2009.
Bonino, Serge-Thomas, ed. *Surnaturel: A Controversy at the Heart of Twentieth-Century Thomistic Thought*. Ave Maria, FL: Sapientia, 2009.
Bouillard, Henri. *Blondel and Christianity*. Translated by James M. Somerville. Washington, DC: Corpus Books, 1969.
———. "The Thought of Maurice Blondel: A Synoptic Vision." *International Philosophical Quarterly* 3 (1963) 392–402.
Braght, Thieleman J. van, ed. *Martyrs Mirror: The Story of Seventeen Centuries of Christian Martyrdom, From the Time of Christ to A.D. 1660*. Scottdale, PA: Herald, 2001.
Bredekamp, Horst. "From Walter Benjamin to Carl Schmitt, via Thomas Hobbes." *Critical Inquiry* 25 (1999) 247–66.
Buck-Morss, Susan. *The Origin of Negative Dialectics: Theodor W. Adorno, Walter Benjamin, and the Frankfurt Institute*. New York: Free Press, 1977.
Bultmann, Rudolf. *The New Testament and Mythology and Other Basic Writings*. Selected, edited, and translated by Schubert M. Ogden. Philadelphia: Fortress, 1984.
Bürger, Peter. "Carl Schmitt oder die Fundierung der Politik auf Ästhetik." In *Zerstörung: Rettung der Mythos durch Licht*, edited by Christa Bürger, 170–76. Frankfurt: Suhrkamp, 1986.
Burrell, David. "A Postmodern Aquinas: The Oeuvre of Olivier-Thomas Vernard, O.P." *American Catholic Philosophical Quarterly* 83 (2009) 331–38.
Cartwright, Michael. "Afterword: 'If Abraham is Our Father . . .': The Problem of Christian Supersessionism after Yoder." In *The Jewish-Christian Schism Revisited*, edited by Michael Cartwright and Peter Ochs, 205–40. Grand Rapids: Eerdmans, 2003.
———. *Practices, Politics, and Performance: Toward a Communal Hermeneutic for Christian Ethics*. Eugene, OR: Pickwick, 2006.
Certeau, Michel de. "Is There a Language of Unity?" *Concilium* 1 (1970) 79–93.

Chopp, Rebecca S. *The Praxis of Suffering: An Interpretation of Liberation and Political Theologies*. Maryknoll, NY: Orbis, 1986.

Coates, Ruth. *Christianity in Bakhtin: God and the Exiled Author*. Cambridge: Cambridge University Press, 1998.

Coles, Romand. *Beyond Gated Politics: Reflections for the Possibility of Democracy*. Minneapolis: University of Minnesota Press, 2005.

———. "The Pregnant Reticence of Rowan Williams: Letter of February 27, 2006, and May 2007." In *Christianity, Democracy, and the Radical Ordinary: Conversations between a Radical Democrat and a Christian*, 174–94. Eugene, OR: Cascade, 2008.

———. "The Wild Patience of John Howard Yoder: 'Outsiders' and the 'Otherness of the Church.'" *Modern Theology* 18 (2002) 305–31.

———. "The Wild Peace (Not) of John Howard Yoder: Reflections on Nonviolence—a Brief History." *The Conrad Grebel Review* 29 (2011) 22–41.

Collier, Charles M. "A Nonviolent Augustinianism? History and Politics in the Theologies of Augustine and John Howard Yoder." PhD diss., Duke University, 2008.

Cristi, Renato. *Carl Schmitt and Authoritarian Liberalism: Strong State, Free Economy*. Cardiff: University of Wales Press, 1998.

Cross, Richard. "Duns Scotus and Suárez at the Origins of Modernity." In *Deconstructing Radical Orthodoxy: Postmodern Theology, Rhetoric, and Truth*, edited by Wayne J. Hankey and Douglas Hedley, 65–97. Aldershot, UK: Ashgate, 2005.

———. *Duns Scotus on God*. Aldershot, UK: Ashgate, 2004.

———. "'Where Angels Fear to Tread': Duns Scotus and Radical Orthodoxy." *Antonianum* 76 (2001) 7–41.

Deleuze, Gilles. *Kant's Critical Philosophy: The Doctrine of the Faculties*. Translated by Hugh Tomlinson and Barbara Habberjam. Minneapolis: University of Minnesota Press, 1993.

Derrida, Jacques. *Deconstruction in a Nutshell: A Conversation with Jacques Derrida*. Edited by John D. Caputo. New York: Fordham University Press, 1997.

———. "On a Newly Arisen Apocalyptic Tone in Philosophy." In *Raising the Tone of Philosophy: Late Essays by Immanuel Kant, Transformative Critique by Jacques Derrida*, edited by Peter Fenves, 117–71. Baltimore: Johns Hopkins University Press, 1993.

———. *The Politics of Friendship*. Translated by George Collins. New York: Verso, 2005.

———. *Rogues: Two Essays on Reason*. Translated by Pascale-Anne Brault and Michael Naas. Stanford: Stanford University Press, 2005.

Desmond, William. *Being and the Between*. Albany: State University of New York Press, 1995.

———. "Being Between." *Clio* 20 (1991) 305–31.

———. *Hegel's God: A Counterfeit Double?* Aldershot, UK: Ashgate, 2003.

———. "Neither Servility nor Sovereignty: Between Metaphysics and Politics." In *Theology and the Political: The New Debate*, edited by Creston Davis, John Milbank, and Slavoj Žižek, 153–82. Durham: Duke University Press, 2005.

Dillard, Annie. *Pilgrim at Tinker Creek*. Norwich: Canterbury, 2011.

Donavin, Georgiana, Carol Poster, and Richard Utz, eds. *Medieval Forms of Argument: Disputation and Debate*. Eugene, OR: Wipf and Stock, 2002.

Downey, John K., ed. *Love's Strategy: The Political Theology of Johann Baptist Metz*. Harrisburg, PA: Trinity International Press, 1999.

Dru, Alexander. "From the Action Française to the Second Vatican Council: Blondel's *La Semaine sociale de Bordeaux.*" *Downside Review* 81 (1963) 226–45.

———. "The Importance of Maurice Blondel." *Downside Review* 80 (1962) 118–29.

Dula, Peter, and Chris K. Huebner, eds. *The New Yoder.* Eugene, OR: Cascade, 2010.

Eagleton, Terry. *Sweet Violence: The Idea of the Tragic.* Oxford: Blackwell, 2003.

Evans, G. R. *Augustine on Evil.* Cambridge: Cambridge University Press, 1982.

Fast, Heinold. "The Anabaptists as Trouble Makers." *Mennonite Life* 31 (1976) 10–13.

Feingold, Lawrence. *The Natural Desire to See God according to St. Thomas Aquinas and His Interpreters.* 2nd ed. Ave Maria, FL: Sapientia, 2010.

Fiorenza, Francis P. "Dialectical Theology and Hope, I." *Heythrop Journal* 9 (1968) 143–63.

———. "Dialectical Theology and Hope, II." *Heythrop Journal* 9 (1968) 384–99.

———. "Dialectical Theology and Hope, III." *Heythrop Journal* 10 (1969) 26–42.

Flipper, Joseph S. *Between Apocalypse and Eschaton: History and Eternity in Henri de Lubac.* Minneapolis: Fortress, 2015.

Foucault, Michel. *Discipline and Punish: The Birth of the Prison.* Translated by Alan Sheridan. New York: Vintage, 1995.

———. "Nietzsche, Genealogy, History." In *The Foucault Reader*, edited by Paul Rabinow, 76–100. New York: Pantheon, 1984.

Fritz, Peter Joseph. *Karl Rahner's Theological Aesthetics.* Washington, DC: Catholic University of America Press, 2014.

García-Rivera, Alejandro. *The Community of the Beautiful: A Theological Aesthetics.* Collegeville, MN: Liturgical, 1999.

Garrigou-Lagrange, Reginald. "La nouvelle théologie où va-t-elle?" *Angelicum* 23 (1946) 126–45.

Gingerich Hiebert, Kyle. "The Architectonics of Hope: Apocalyptic Convergences and Constellations of Violence in Carl Schmitt and Johann Baptist Metz." *Telos* 160 (2012) 53–76.

———. "Beauty and Its Violences." *Political Theology* 17 (2016) 316–36.

———. "The Recovery of Contestation and the Apophatic Body of Christ: Engaging Graham Ward's *The Politics of Discipleship.*" *Radical Orthodoxy: Theology, Philosophy, Politics* 2 (2014) 291–97.

Gregg, Richard Bartlett. *The Power of Non-violence.* Rev. ed. London: Routledge, 1936.

Gregory of Nyssa. *Homilies on Ecclesiastes.* Translated by Stuart George Hall and Rachel Moriarty. In *Gregory of Nyssa: Homilies on Ecclesiastes; an English Version with Supporting Studies*, edited by Stuart George Hall, 31–144. Berlin: de Gruyter, 1993.

Grumett, David. "Blondel, Modern Catholic Theology and the Leibnizian Eucharistic Bond." *Modern Theology* 23 (2007) 561–77.

———. "Blondel, the Philosophy of Action and Liberation Theology." *Political Theology* 11 (2010) 507–29.

———. *De Lubac: A Guide for the Perplexed.* London: T. & T. Clark, 2007.

Guenther, Titus F. *Rahner and Metz: Transcendental Theology as Political Theology.* Lanham, MD: University Press of America, 1993.

Gutiérrez, Gustavo. *A Theology of Liberation: History, Politics, and Salvation.* Rev. ed. London: SCM, 2001.

Habermas, Jürgen. *The Divided West.* Edited and translated by Ciaran Cronin. Cambridge: Polity, 2006.

———. *The New Conservatism: Cultural Criticism and the Historians' Debate*. Edited and translated by Shierry Weber Nicholsen. Cambridge: MIT Press, 1989.

Hankey, Wayne J. "One Hundred Years of Neoplatonism in France: A Brief Philosophical History." In *Levinas and the Greek Heritage* [followed by] *One Hundred Years of Neoplatonism in France: A Brief Philosophical History*, 97–248. Leuven: Peeters, 2006.

Hart, David Bentley. "The Angel at the Ford of Jabbok: On the Theology of Robert Jenson." In *In the Aftermath: Provocations and Laments*, 156–69. Grand Rapids: Eerdmans, 2009.

———. "The Anti-Theology of the Body." In *In the Aftermath: Provocations and Laments*, 139–47. Grand Rapids: Eerdmans, 2009.

———. "Article Review: Response from David Bentley Hart to McGuckin and Murphy." *Scottish Journal of Theology* 60 (2007) 95–101.

———. *Atheist Delusions: The Christian Revolution and Its Fashionable Enemies*. New Haven: Yale University Press, 2009.

———. *The Beauty of the Infinite: The Aesthetics of Christian Truth*. Grand Rapids: Eerdmans, 2004.

———. "The Destiny of Christian Metaphysics: Reflections on the Analogia Entis." In *The Analogy of Being: Invention of the Antichrist or the Wisdom of God?*, edited by Thomas Joseph White, 395–410. Grand Rapids: Eerdmans, 2010.

———. *The Doors of the Sea: Where Was God in the Tsunami?* Grand Rapids: Eerdmans, 2005.

———. "Foreword." In *Encounter between Eastern Orthodoxy and Radical Orthodoxy: Transfiguring the World through the Word*, edited by Adrian Pabst and Christoph Schneider, xi–xiv. Farnham, UK: Ashgate, 2009.

———. "Impassibility as Transcendence: On the Infinite Innocence of God." In *Divine Impassibility and the Mystery of Human Suffering*, edited by James F. Keating and Thomas Joseph White, 299–323. Grand Rapids: Eerdmans, 2009.

———. "The Mirror of the Infinite: Gregory of Nyssa on the Vestigia Trinitatis." *Modern Theology* 18 (2002) 541–61.

———. "No Shadow of Turning: On Divine Impassibility." *Pro Ecclesia* 11 (2002) 184–206.

———. "The Offering of Names: Metaphysics, Nihilism, and Analogy." In *Reason and the Reasons of Faith*, edited by Paul J. Griffiths and Reinhard Hütter, 255–91. New York: T. & T. Clark, 2005.

———. "Response to James K. A. Smith, Lois Malcolm and Gerard Loughlin." *New Blackfriars* 88 (2007) 610–23.

———. "Review Essay: Catherine Pickstock, *After Writing*." *Pro Ecclesia* 9 (2000) 367–72.

———. "The 'Whole Humanity': Gregory of Nyssa's Critique of Slavery in Light of His Eschatology." *Scottish Journal of Theology* 54 (2001) 51–69.

Hauerwas, Stanley. "Creation, Contingency, and Truthful Nonviolence: A Milbankian Reflection." In *Wilderness Wanderings: Probing Twentieth-Century Theology and Philosophy*, 188–98. Boulder, CO: Westview, 1997.

———. "The End of Religious Pluralism: A Tribute to David Burrell." In *Democracy and the New Religious Pluralism*, edited by Thomas Banchoff, 283–300. New York: Oxford University Press, 2007.

———. "Introduction: Lingering with Yoder's Wild Work." In *A Mind Patient and Untamed: Assessing John Howard Yoder's Contributions to Theology, Ethics, and Peacemaking*, edited by Ben C. Ollenburger and Gayle Gerber Koontz, 11-19. Telford, PA: Cascadia, 2004.

———. "Some Theological Reflections on Gutierrez's Use of 'Liberation' as a Theological Concept." *Modern Theology* 3 (1986) 67-76.

———. *With the Grain of the Universe: The Church's Witness and Natural Theology.* Grand Rapids: Brazos, 2001.

Hauerwas, Stanley, and Chris K. Huebner. "History, Theory, and Anabaptism: A Conversation on Theology after John Howard Yoder." In *The Wisdom of the Cross: Essays in Honor of John Howard Yoder*, edited by Stanley Hauerwas et al., 391-408. Grand Rapids: Eerdmans, 1999.

Hauerwas, Stanley, and John Milbank. "Christian Peace: A Conversation between Stanley Hauerwas and John Milbank." In *Must Christianity Be Violent? Reflections on History, Practice, and Theology*, edited by Kenneth R. Chase and Alan Jacobs, 207-23. Grand Rapids: Brazos, 2003.

Hedley, Douglas. "Radical Orthodoxy and Apocalyptic Difference: Cambridge Platonism, and Milbank's Romantic Christian Cabbala." In *Deconstructing Radical Orthodoxy: Postmodern Theology, Rhetoric, and Truth*, edited by Wayne J. Hankey and Douglas Hedley, 99-115. Aldershot, UK: Ashgate, 2005.

Hegel, G. W. F. *Early Theological Writings.* Translated by T. M. Knox. Philadelphia: University of Pennsylvania Press, 1975.

———. *Elements of the Philosophy of Right.* Translated by H. B. Nisbet. Edited by Allen W. Wood. New York: Cambridge University Press, 1991.

———. *Hegel's Philosophy of Mind.* Translated by William Wallace. Oxford: Clarendon, 1971.

———. *Lectures on the Philosophy of World History.* Translated by Robert F. Brown and Peter C. Hodgson. Vol. 1, *Manuscripts of the Introduction and the Lectures of 1822-33.* Oxford: Oxford University Press, 2011.

———. *Phenomenology of Spirit.* Translated by A. V. Miller. New York: Oxford University Press, 1977.

———. *Political Writings.* Edited by Laurence Dickey and H. B. Nisbet. Translated by H. B. Nisbet. New York: Cambridge University Press, 1999.

Heidegger, Martin. *Being and Time.* Translated by John Macquarrie and Edward Robinson. Malden, MA: Blackwell, 2000.

———. *Identity and Difference.* Translated by Joan Stambaugh. Chicago: University of Chicago Press, 2002.

———. *Poetry, Language, Thought.* Translated by Albert Hofstadter. New York: Harper, 2001.

Henrici, Peter. *Hegel und Blondel: Eine Untersuchung uber Form und Sinn der Dialektik in der "Phänomenologie des Geistes" und der ersten "Action".* Pullach bei München: Berchmanskolleg, 1958.

Hobbes, Thomas. *Leviathan.* Edited by Richard Tuck. New York: Cambridge University Press, 1996.

Hoelzl, Michael. "Before the Anti-Christ Is Revealed: On the Katechontic Structure of Messianic Time." In *The Politcs to Come: Power, Modernity and the Messianic*, edited by Arthur Bradley and Paul Fletcher, 98-110. London: Continuum, 2010.

Hoff, Johannes. *The Analogical Turn: Rethinking Modernity with Nicholas of Cusa.* Grand Rapids: Eerdmans, 2013.

Hopkins, Jasper. "Nicholas of Cusa (1401-1464): First Modern Philosopher?" *Midwest Studies in Philosophy* 26 (2002) 13-29.

Horkheimer, Max, and Theodor W. Adorno. *Dialectic of Enlightenment: Philosophical Fragments.* Edited by Gunzelin Schmid Noerr. Translated by Edmund Jephcott. Stanford: Stanford University Press, 2002.

Huebner, Chris K. *A Precarious Peace: Yoderian Explorations on Theology, Knowledge, and Identity.* Scottdale, PA: Herald, 2006.

Hütter, Reinhard. "*Desiderium Naturale Visionis Dei—Est autem duplex hominis beatitudo sive felicitas*: Some Observations about Lawrence Feingold's and John Milbank's Recent Interventions in the Debate over the Natural Desire to See God." *Nova et Vetera* 5 (2007) 81-132.

Hyman, Gavin. *The Predicament of Postmodern Theology: Radical Orthodoxy or Nihilist Textualism?* Louisville: Westminster John Knox, 2001.

Jantzen, Grace M. *Violence to Eternity.* Edited by Jeremy Carrette and Morny Joy. London: Routledge, 2009.

Jay, Martin. *The Dialectical Imagination: A History of the Frankfurt School and the Institute of Social Research, 1923-1950.* Boston: Little, Brown, 1973.

———. *Downcast Eyes: The Denigration of Vision in Twentieth-Century French Thought.* Berkeley: University of California Press, 1993.

Jenson, Robert W. "*Ipse Pater Non Est Impassibilis*." In *Divine Impassibility and the Mystery of Human Suffering*, edited by James F. Keating and Thomas Joseph White, 117-26. Grand Rapids: Eerdmans, 2009.

———. "Review Essay: David Bentley Hart, *The Beauty of the Infinite*." *Pro Ecclesia* 14 (2005) 235-37.

———. *Systematic Theology.* Vol. 1, *The Triune God*. New York: Oxford University Press, 1997.

Kant, Immanuel. *Critique of the Power of Judgment.* Edited by Paul Guyer. Translated by Paul Guyer and Eric Matthews. New York: Cambridge University Press, 2000.

———. *Religion Within the Bounds of Mere Reason.* In *Religion and Rational Theology*, translated and edited by Allen W. Wood and George di Giovanni, 57-213. Cambridge: Cambridge University Press, 1996.

Kaufmann, Walter, ed. *The Portable Nietzsche.* New York: Penguin 1981.

Kerr, Fergus. "A Catholic Response to the Programme of Radical Orthodoxy." In *Radical Orthodoxy? A Catholic Enquiry*, edited by Laurence Paul Hemming, 46-59. Aldershot, UK: Ashgate, 2000.

———. "Why Medievalists Should Talk to Theologians." *New Blackfriars* 80 (1999) 369-75.

Kerr, Nathan R. *Christ, History, and Apocalyptic: The Politics of Christian Mission.* London: SCM, 2008.

———. "*Communio Missionis*: Certeau, Yoder, and the Missionary Space of the Church." In *The New Yoder*, edited by Peter Dula and Chris K. Huebner, 317-35. Eugene, OR: Cascade, 2010.

———. "Transcendence and Apocalyptic: A Reply to Barber." *Political Theology* 10 (2009) 143-52.

Kierkegaard, Søren. *Fear and Trembling; Repetition.* Edited and translated by Howard Hong and Edna Hong. Princeton: Princeton University Press, 1983.

Kołakowski, Leszek. "Georges Sorel: A Jansenist Marxist." In vol. 2 of *Main Currents of Marxism: Its Origins, Growth, and Dissolution*, translated by P. S. Falla, 151–74. Oxford: Oxford University Press, 1981.

Kristeva, Julia. "Word, Dialogue and Novel." In *The Kristeva Reader*, edited by Toril Moi, 34–61. New York: Columbia University Press, 1986.

Kervégan, Jean-François. *Hegel, Carl Schmitt: Le politique entre spéculation et positivité*. Paris: Presses universitaires de France, 1992.

Laclau, Ernesto, and Chantal Mouffe. *Hegemony and Socialist Strategy: Toward a Radical Democratic Politics*. 2nd ed. London: Verso, 2001.

Ladner, Gerhart B. "The Philosophical Anthropology of Saint Gregory of Nyssa." *Dumbarton Oaks Papers* 12 (1958) 59–94.

Lakeland, Paul. *The Politics of Salvation: The Hegelian Idea of the State*. Albany: State University of New York Press, 1984.

Lamb, Matthew. *Solidarity with Victims: Toward a Theology of Social Transformation*. New York: Crossroad, 1982.

———. "The Theory-Praxis Relationship in Contemporary Christian Theologies." *Proceedings of the Catholic Theological Society of America* 31 (1976) 149–78.

Laruelle, François. *Philosophies of Difference: A Critical Introduction to Non-Philosophy*. Translated by Rocco Gangle. London: Continuum, 2010.

Lash, Nicholas. "Where Does Holy Teaching Leave Philosophy? Questions on Milbank's *Aquinas*." *Modern Theology* 15 (1999) 433–44.

Leibniz, G. W. *New Essays on Human Understanding*. Translated and edited by Peter Remnant and Jonathan Bennett. Cambridge: Cambridge University Press, 1996.

Leithart, Peter J. *Defending Constantine: The Twilight of an Empire and the Dawn of Christendom*. Downers Grove, IL: InterVarsity, 2010.

Levering, Matthew. *Scripture and Metaphysics: Aquinas and the Renewal of Trinitarian Theology*. Oxford: Blackwell, 2004.

Lock, Charles. "Carnival and Incarnation: Bakhtin and Orthodox Theology." *Journal of Literature and Theology* 5 (1991) 68–82.

Long, D. Stephen. *Speaking of God: Theology, Language, and Truth*. Grand Rapids: Eerdmans, 2009.

López, Antonio. *Spirit's Gift: The Metaphysical Insight of Claude Bruaire*. Washington, DC: Catholic University of America Press, 2006.

Losonczi, Péter. "Humanization, Eschatology, Theodicy: Metz, Schmitt, and the 'Hidden Nexus.'" *Political Theology* 16 (2015) 116–29.

Loughlin, Gerard. "Rhetoric and Rhapsody: A Response to David Bentley Hart." *New Blackfriars* 88 (2007) 600–609.

Löwith, Karl. "The Occasional Decisionism of Carl Schmitt." In *Martin Heidegger and European Nihilism*, edited by Richard Wolin and translated by Gary Steiner, 137–69. New York: Columbia University Press, 1995.

Lubac, Henri de. *At the Service of the Church: Henri de Lubac Reflects on the Circumstances That Occasioned His Writings*. Translated by Anne Elizabeth Englund. San Francisco: Ignatius, 1993.

———. *Augustinianism and Modern Theology*. Translated by Lancelot Sheppard. New York: Herder & Herder, 2000.

———. *A Brief Catechesis on Nature and Grace*. Translated by Richard Arnandez. San Francisco: Ignatius, 1984.

———. *Catholicism: Christ and the Common Destiny of Man*. Translated by Lancelot C. Sheppard and Elizabeth Englund. San Francisco: Ignatius, 1988.

———. *Christian Resistance to Anti-Semitism: Memories from 1940–1944*. Translated by Elizabeth Englund. San Francisco: Ignatius, 1990.

———. *Corpus Mysticum: The Eucharist and the Church in the Middle Ages*. Translated by Gemma Simmonds. Edited by Laurence Paul Hemming and Susan Frank Parsons. London: SCM, 2006.

———. *The Drama of Atheist Humanism*. Translated by Edith M. Riley, Anne Englund Nash, and Mark Sebanc. San Francisco: Ignatius, 1995.

———. *The Mystery of the Supernatural*. Translated by Rosemary Sheed. New York: Herder & Herder, 1998.

———. *Paradoxes of Faith*. Translated by Paul Simon and Sadie Kreilkamp. San Francisco: Ignatius, 1987.

———. *Theology in History*. Translated by Anne Englund Nash. San Francisco: Ignatius, 1996.

Lukács, Georg. *The Theory of the Novel: A Historico-Philosophical Essay on the Forms of Great Epic Literature*. Translated by Anna Bostock. Cambridge: MIT Press, 1971.

Manemann, Jürgen. "Abandoned by God? Reflections on the Margins of Theology." In *Missing God? Cultural Amnesia and Political Theology*, edited by John K. Downey, Jürgen Manemaan, and Steven T. Ostovich, 19–35. Berlin: LIT Verlag, 2006.

Manent, Pierre. *An Intellectual History of Liberalism*. Translated by Rebecca Balinski. Princeton: Princeton University Press, 1994.

Martens, Paul. *The Heterodox Yoder*. Eugene, OR: Cascade, 2012.

Martinez, Gaspar. *Confronting the Mystery of God: Political, Liberation, and Public Theologies*. New York: Continuum, 2001.

Marx, Karl. "The German Ideology." In *Karl Marx: Selected Writings*, edited by David McLellan, 175–208. 2nd ed. New York: Oxford University Press, 2000.

———. "On the Jewish Question." In *Karl Marx: Selected Writings*, edited by David McLellan, 46–70. 2nd ed. New York: Oxford University Press, 2000.

———. "Towards a Critique of Hegel's Philosophy of Right: Introduction." In *Karl Marx: Selected Writings*, edited by David McLellan, 71–82. 2nd ed. New York: Oxford University Press, 2000.

McCormack, Bruce L. "Karl Barth's Historicized Christology: Just How Chalcedonian Is It?" In *Orthodox and Modern: Studies in the Theology of Karl Barth*, 201–34. Grand Rapids: Baker Academic, 2008.

McNeill, J. J. *The Blondelian Synthesis: A Study of the Influence of German Philosophical Sources on the Formation of Blondel's Method and Thought*. Leiden: E. J. Brill, 1966.

Mehring, Reinhard. *Carl Schmitt: A Biography*. Translated by Daniel Steuer. Malden, MA: Polity, 2014.

Meier, Heinrich. *Carl Schmitt and Leo Strauss: The Hidden Dialogue*. Translated by J. Harvey Lomax. Chicago: University of Chicago Press, 1995.

———. *The Lesson of Carl Schmitt: Four Chapters on the Distinction between Political Theology and Political Philosophy*. Translated by Marcus Brainard. Chicago: University of Chicago Press, 1998.

Metz, Johannes Baptist. "Anamnestic Reason: A Theologian's Remarks on the Crisis in the *Geisteswissenschaften*." In *Cultural-Political Interventions in the Unfinished Project of Enlightenment*, edited by Axel Honneth et al., 189–94. Cambridge: MIT Press, 1992.

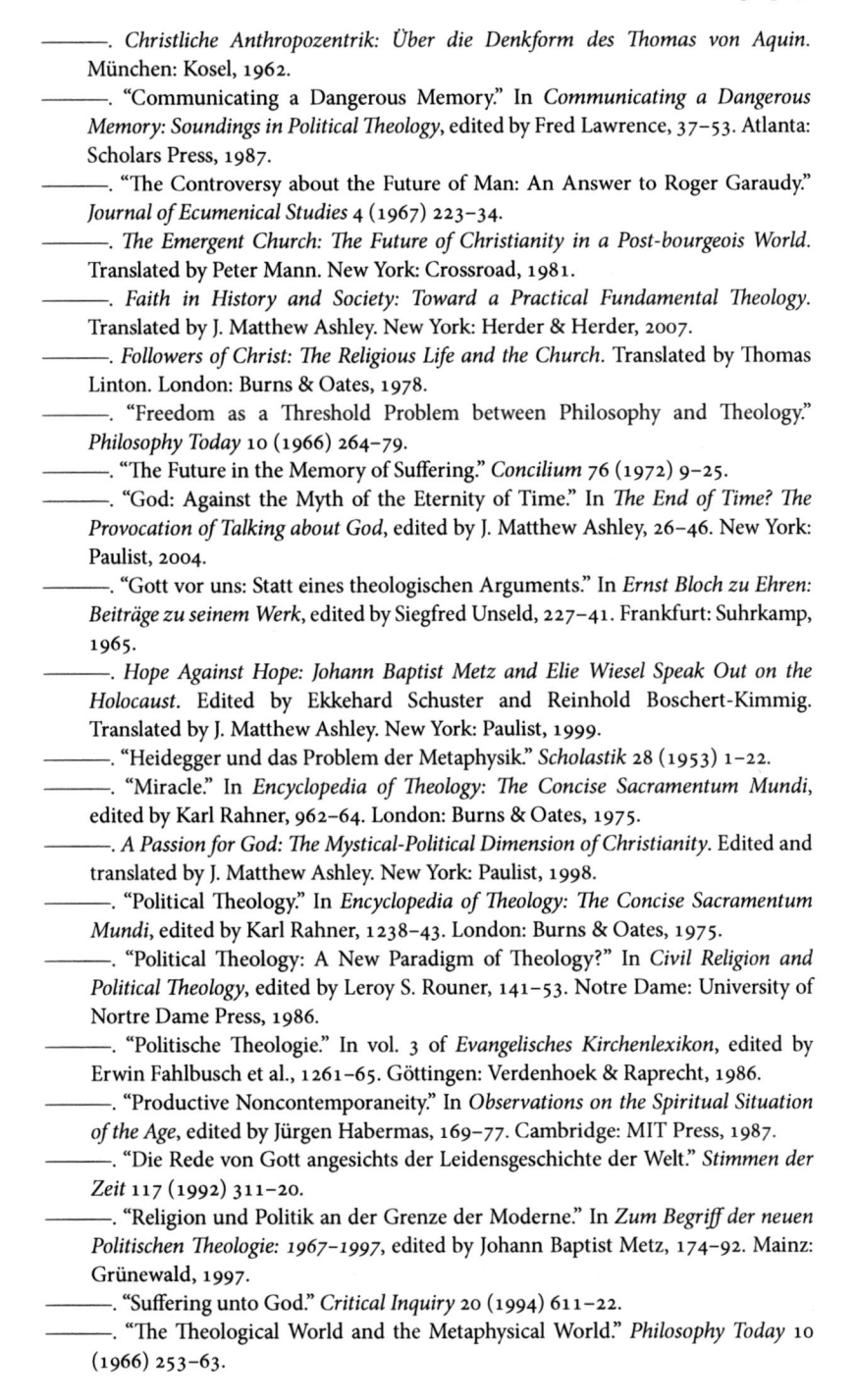

———. *Christliche Anthropozentrik: Über die Denkform des Thomas von Aquin.* München: Kosel, 1962.

———. "Communicating a Dangerous Memory." In *Communicating a Dangerous Memory: Soundings in Political Theology*, edited by Fred Lawrence, 37–53. Atlanta: Scholars Press, 1987.

———. "The Controversy about the Future of Man: An Answer to Roger Garaudy." *Journal of Ecumenical Studies* 4 (1967) 223–34.

———. *The Emergent Church: The Future of Christianity in a Post-bourgeois World.* Translated by Peter Mann. New York: Crossroad, 1981.

———. *Faith in History and Society: Toward a Practical Fundamental Theology.* Translated by J. Matthew Ashley. New York: Herder & Herder, 2007.

———. *Followers of Christ: The Religious Life and the Church.* Translated by Thomas Linton. London: Burns & Oates, 1978.

———. "Freedom as a Threshold Problem between Philosophy and Theology." *Philosophy Today* 10 (1966) 264–79.

———. "The Future in the Memory of Suffering." *Concilium* 76 (1972) 9–25.

———. "God: Against the Myth of the Eternity of Time." In *The End of Time? The Provocation of Talking about God*, edited by J. Matthew Ashley, 26–46. New York: Paulist, 2004.

———. "Gott vor uns: Statt eines theologischen Arguments." In *Ernst Bloch zu Ehren: Beiträge zu seinem Werk*, edited by Siegfred Unseld, 227–41. Frankfurt: Suhrkamp, 1965.

———. *Hope Against Hope: Johann Baptist Metz and Elie Wiesel Speak Out on the Holocaust.* Edited by Ekkehard Schuster and Reinhold Boschert-Kimmig. Translated by J. Matthew Ashley. New York: Paulist, 1999.

———. "Heidegger und das Problem der Metaphysik." *Scholastik* 28 (1953) 1–22.

———. "Miracle." In *Encyclopedia of Theology: The Concise Sacramentum Mundi*, edited by Karl Rahner, 962–64. London: Burns & Oates, 1975.

———. *A Passion for God: The Mystical-Political Dimension of Christianity.* Edited and translated by J. Matthew Ashley. New York: Paulist, 1998.

———. "Political Theology." In *Encyclopedia of Theology: The Concise Sacramentum Mundi*, edited by Karl Rahner, 1238–43. London: Burns & Oates, 1975.

———. "Political Theology: A New Paradigm of Theology?" In *Civil Religion and Political Theology*, edited by Leroy S. Rouner, 141–53. Notre Dame: University of Nortre Dame Press, 1986.

———. "Politische Theologie." In vol. 3 of *Evangelisches Kirchenlexikon*, edited by Erwin Fahlbusch et al., 1261–65. Göttingen: Verdenhoek & Raprecht, 1986.

———. "Productive Noncontemporaneity." In *Observations on the Spiritual Situation of the Age*, edited by Jürgen Habermas, 169–77. Cambridge: MIT Press, 1987.

———. "Die Rede von Gott angesichts der Leidensgeschichte der Welt." *Stimmen der Zeit* 117 (1992) 311–20.

———. "Religion und Politik an der Grenze der Moderne." In *Zum Begriff der neuen Politischen Theologie: 1967-1997*, edited by Johann Baptist Metz, 174–92. Mainz: Grünewald, 1997.

———. "Suffering unto God." *Critical Inquiry* 20 (1994) 611–22.

———. "The Theological World and the Metaphysical World." *Philosophy Today* 10 (1966) 253–63.

———. *Theology of the World*. Translated by William Glen-Dopel. New York: Herder and Herder, 1969.
———. "Unbelief as a Theological Problem." *Concilium* 6 (1965) 59–77.
———. *Zum Begriff der neuen Politischen Theologie: 1967–1997*. Edited by Johann Baptist Metz. Mainz: Grünewald, 1997.
———. "Zum 'katholischen Prinzip' der Repräsentation." In *Zum Begriff der neuen Politischen Theologie: 1967–1997*, edited by Johann Baptist Metz, 192–96. Mainz: Grünewald, 1997.
Metz, Johannes Baptist, and Jürgen Moltmann. *Faith and the Future: Essays on Theology, Solidarity, and Modernity*. Maryknoll, NY: Orbis, 1995.
Michalson, Gordon E., Jr. "Re-reading the Post-Kantian Tradition with Milbank." *Journal of Religious Ethics* 32 (2004) 357–83.
Milbank, Alison. *Chesterton and Tolkien as Theologians: The Fantasy of the Real*. London: T. & T. Clark, 2007.
Milbank, John. "Atonement: Christ the Exception." In *Being Reconciled: Ontology and Pardon*, 94–104. London: Routledge, 2003.
———. "Beauty and the Soul." In *Theological Perspectives on God and Beauty*, 1–34. Harrisburg, PA: Trinity Press International, 2003.
———. "'Between Purgation and Illumination': A Critique of the Theology of Right." In *Christ, Ethics, and Tragedy: Essays in Honour of Donald MacKinnon*, edited by Kenneth Surin, 161–96. Cambridge: Cambridge University Press, 1989.
———. *Beyond Secular Order: The Representation of Being and the Representation of the People*. Malden, MA: Wiley Blackwell, 2013.
———. "Can a Gift Be Given? Prolegomena to a Future Trinitarian Metaphysic." *Modern Theology* 11 (1995) 119–61.
———. "A Christological Poetics." In *The Word Made Strange: Theology, Language, Culture*, 123–44. Malden, MA: Blackwell, 1997.
———. "The Double Glory, or Paradox versus Dialectics: On Not Quite Agreeing with Slavoj Žižek." In *The Monstrosity of Christ: Paradox or Dialectic?*, edited by Creston Davis, 110–233. Cambridge: MIT Press, 2009.
———. "Ecclesiology: The Last of the Last." In *Being Reconciled: Ontology and Pardon*, 105–37. London: Routledge, 2003.
———. "Evil: Darkness and Silence." In *Being Reconciled: Ontology and Pardon*, 1–25. London: Routledge, 2003.
———. "Faith, Reason, and Imagination: The Study of Theology and Philosophy in the Twenty-First Century." In *The Future of Love: Essays in Political Theology*, 316–34. Eugene, OR: Cascade, 2009.
———. "Fictioning Things: Gift and Narrative." *Religion and Literature* 37 (2005) 1–37.
———. "The Future of Love: A Reading of Benedict XVI's Encyclical *Deus Caritas Est*." In *The Future of Love: Essays in Political Theology*, 364–70. Eugene, OR: Cascade, 2009.
———. *The Future of Love: Essays in Political Theology*. Eugene, OR: Cascade, 2009.
———. "The Gift and the Mirror: On the Philosophy of Love." In *Counter-Experiences: Reading Jean-Luc Marion*, edited by Kevin Hart, 253–317. Notre Dame: University of Notre Dame Press, 2007.
———. "The Gift of Ruling: Secularization and Political Authority." *New Blackfriars* 85 (2004) 212–38.

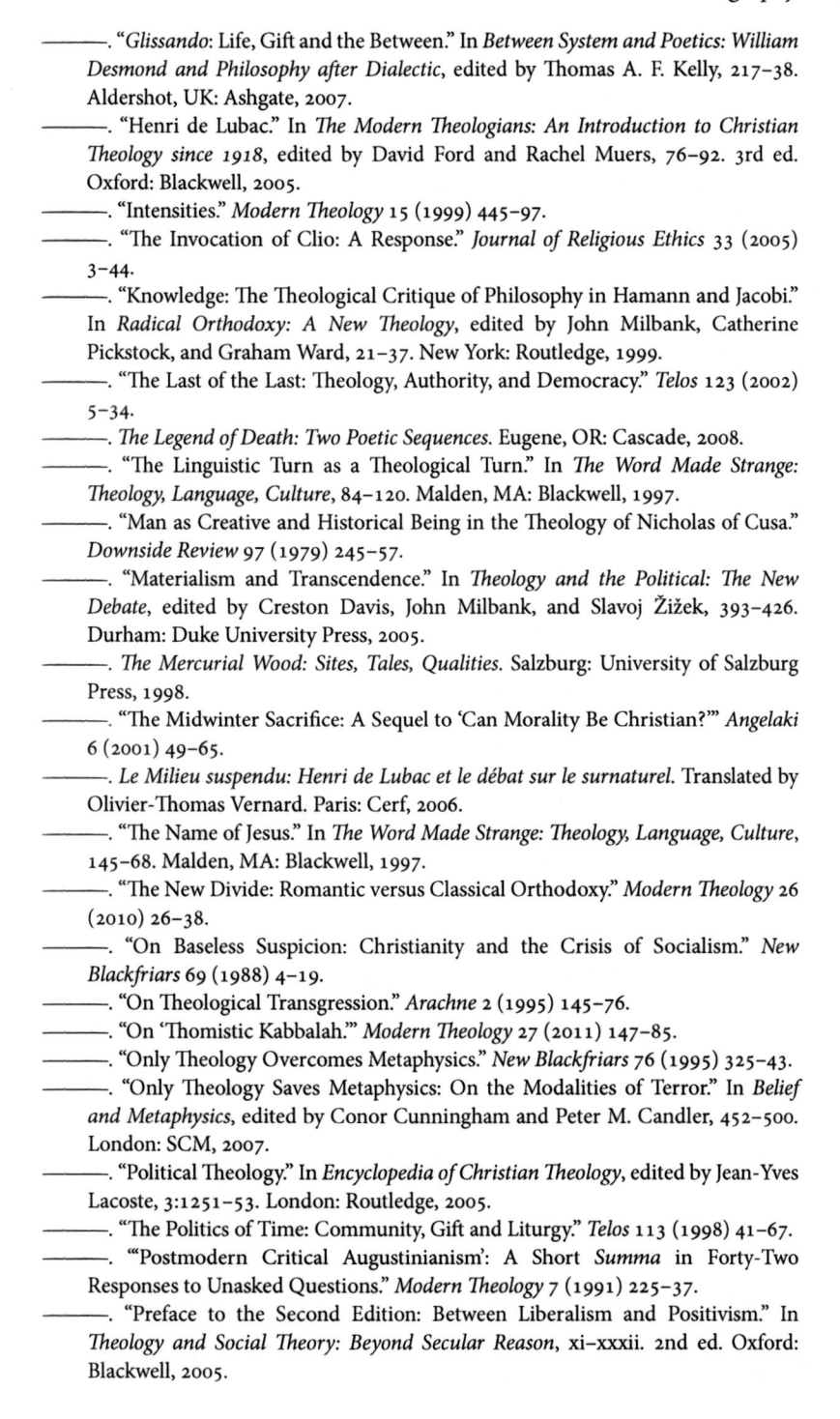

———. "*Glissando*: Life, Gift and the Between." In *Between System and Poetics: William Desmond and Philosophy after Dialectic*, edited by Thomas A. F. Kelly, 217–38. Aldershot, UK: Ashgate, 2007.

———. "Henri de Lubac." In *The Modern Theologians: An Introduction to Christian Theology since 1918*, edited by David Ford and Rachel Muers, 76–92. 3rd ed. Oxford: Blackwell, 2005.

———. "Intensities." *Modern Theology* 15 (1999) 445–97.

———. "The Invocation of Clio: A Response." *Journal of Religious Ethics* 33 (2005) 3–44.

———. "Knowledge: The Theological Critique of Philosophy in Hamann and Jacobi." In *Radical Orthodoxy: A New Theology*, edited by John Milbank, Catherine Pickstock, and Graham Ward, 21–37. New York: Routledge, 1999.

———. "The Last of the Last: Theology, Authority, and Democracy." *Telos* 123 (2002) 5–34.

———. *The Legend of Death: Two Poetic Sequences*. Eugene, OR: Cascade, 2008.

———. "The Linguistic Turn as a Theological Turn." In *The Word Made Strange: Theology, Language, Culture*, 84–120. Malden, MA: Blackwell, 1997.

———. "Man as Creative and Historical Being in the Theology of Nicholas of Cusa." *Downside Review* 97 (1979) 245–57.

———. "Materialism and Transcendence." In *Theology and the Political: The New Debate*, edited by Creston Davis, John Milbank, and Slavoj Žižek, 393–426. Durham: Duke University Press, 2005.

———. *The Mercurial Wood: Sites, Tales, Qualities*. Salzburg: University of Salzburg Press, 1998.

———. "The Midwinter Sacrifice: A Sequel to 'Can Morality Be Christian?'" *Angelaki* 6 (2001) 49–65.

———. *Le Milieu suspendu: Henri de Lubac et le débat sur le surnaturel*. Translated by Olivier-Thomas Vernard. Paris: Cerf, 2006.

———. "The Name of Jesus." In *The Word Made Strange: Theology, Language, Culture*, 145–68. Malden, MA: Blackwell, 1997.

———. "The New Divide: Romantic versus Classical Orthodoxy." *Modern Theology* 26 (2010) 26–38.

———. "On Baseless Suspicion: Christianity and the Crisis of Socialism." *New Blackfriars* 69 (1988) 4–19.

———. "On Theological Transgression." *Arachne* 2 (1995) 145–76.

———. "On 'Thomistic Kabbalah.'" *Modern Theology* 27 (2011) 147–85.

———. "Only Theology Overcomes Metaphysics." *New Blackfriars* 76 (1995) 325–43.

———. "Only Theology Saves Metaphysics: On the Modalities of Terror." In *Belief and Metaphysics*, edited by Conor Cunningham and Peter M. Candler, 452–500. London: SCM, 2007.

———. "Political Theology." In *Encyclopedia of Christian Theology*, edited by Jean-Yves Lacoste, 3:1251–53. London: Routledge, 2005.

———. "The Politics of Time: Community, Gift and Liturgy." *Telos* 113 (1998) 41–67.

———. "'Postmodern Critical Augustinianism': A Short *Summa* in Forty-Two Responses to Unasked Questions." *Modern Theology* 7 (1991) 225–37.

———. "Preface to the Second Edition: Between Liberalism and Positivism." In *Theology and Social Theory: Beyond Secular Reason*, xi–xxxii. 2nd ed. Oxford: Blackwell, 2005.

———. *The Religious Dimension in the Thought of Giambattista Vico, 1668–1744*. Vol. 2, *Language, Law and History*. Lewiston, NY: E. Mellen, 1992.

———. "Socialism of the Gift, Socialism by Grace." *New Blackfriars* 77 (1996) 532–48.

———. "Sophiology and Theurgy: The New Theological Horizon." In *Encounter between Eastern Orthodoxy and Radical Orthodoxy: Transfiguring the World through the Word*, edited by Adrian Pabst and Christoph Schneider, 45–85. Farnham, UK: Ashgate, 2009.

———. "The Soul of Reciprocity Part One: Reciprocity Refused." *Modern Theology* 17 (2001) 335–91.

———. "The Soul of Reciprocity Part Two: Reciprocity Granted." *Modern Theology* 17 (2001) 485–507.

———. "Stale Expressions: The Management-Shaped Church." *Studies in Christian Ethics* 21 (2008) 117–28.

———. "Stories of Sacrifice." *Modern Theology* 12 (1996) 27–56.

———. "The Sublime in Kierkegaard." *The Heythrop Journal* 37 (1996) 298–321.

———. "Sublimity: The Modern Transcendent." In *Religion, Modernity, and Postmodernity*, edited by Paul Heelas, 258–84. Malden, MA: Blackwell, 1998.

———. *The Suspended Middle: Henri de Lubac and the Debate Concerning the Supernatural*. Grand Rapids: Eerdmans, 2005.

———. *The Suspended Middle: Henri de Lubac and the Renewed Split in Modern Catholic Theology*. 2nd ed. Grand Rapids: Eerdmans, 2014.

———. *Theology and Social Theory: Beyond Secular Reason*. Malden, MA: Blackwell, 1990.

———. "Theology without Substance: Christianity, Signs, Origins Part One." *Literature & Theology* 2 (1988) 1–17.

———. "Theology without Substance: Christianity, Signs, Origins Part Two." *Literature & Theology* 2 (1988) 131–52.

———. "The Thomistic Telescope: Truth and Identity." *American Catholic Philosophical Quarterly* 80 (2006) 193–226.

———. "Violence: Double Passivity." In *Being Reconciled: Ontology and Pardon*, 26–43. London: Routledge, 2003.

———. *The Word Made Strange: Theology, Language, Culture*. Malden, MA: Blackwell, 1997.

Milbank, John, and Catherine Pickstock. *Truth in Aquinas*. London: Routledge, 2001.

Moltmann, Jürgen. "Christian Theology and Political Religion." In *Civil Religion and Political Theology*, edited by Leroy S. Rouner, 41–58. Notre Dame: University of Notre Dame Press, 1986.

———. *The Crucified God: The Cross of Christ as the Foundation and Criticism of Christian Theology*. Translated by R. A. Wilson and John Bowden. London: SCM, 2001.

———. *Theology of Hope*. Translated by James W. Leitch. London: SCM, 2002.

———. *The Trinity and the Kingdom of God: The Doctrine of God*. Translated by Margaret Kohl. London: SCM, 1981.

Morrill, Bruce T. *Anamnesis as Dangerous Memory: Political and Liturgical Theology in Dialogue*. Collegeville, MN: Liturgical Press, 2000.

Morson, Gary Saul, and Caryl Emerson. *Mikhail Bakhtin: Creation of a Prosaics*. Stanford: Stanford University Press, 1990.

Mouffe, Chantal, ed. *The Challenge of Carl Schmitt*. London: Verso, 1999.

———. "Introduction: Schmitt's Challenge." In *The Challenge of Carl Schmitt*, edited by Chantal Mouffe, 1–6. London: Verso, 1999.

Nation, Mark Thiessen. *John Howard Yoder: Mennonite Patience, Evangelical Witness, Catholic Convictions*. Grand Rapids: Eerdmans, 2006.

Nicholas of Cusa. *On Learned Ignorace*. In *Selected Spiritual Writings*, translated by H. Lawrence Bond, 85–206. New York: Paulist, 1997.

———. *On the Vision of God*. In *Selected Spiritual Writings*, translated by H. Lawrence Bond, 233–90. New York: Paulist, 1997.

Nichols, Aidan. *Scattering the Seed: A Guide through Balthasar's Early Writings on Philosophy and the Arts*. Washington, DC: Catholic University of America Press, 2006.

———. "Thomism and the Nouvelle Théologie." *The Thomist* 64 (2000) 1–19.

Niebuhr, H. Richard. *Christ and Culture*. New York: Harper, 1951.

Niebuhr, Reinhold. "Love and Justice and the Pacifist Issue." In *Love and Justice: Selections from the Shorter Writings of Reinhold Niebuhr*, edited by D. B. Robertson, 241–301. Philadelphia: Westminster, 1957.

———. "Why the Christian Church Is Not Pacifist." In *Christianity and Power Politics*, 1–25. New York: Scribner, 1952.

Northcott, Michael S. *A Political Theology of Climate Change*. Grand Rapids: Eerdmans, 2014.

Oakes, Edward T. "The Paradox of Nature and Grace: On John Milbank's *The Suspended Middle: Henri de Lubac and the Debate Concerning the Supernatural*." *Nova et Vetera* 4 (2006) 667–95.

O'Regan, Cyril. *The Anatomy of Misremembering: Von Balthasar's Response to Philosophical Modernity*. Vol. 1, *Hegel*. New York: Herder & Herder, 2014.

———. *The Heterodox Hegel*. Albany: State University of New York Press, 1994.

———. *Theology and the Spaces of Apocalyptic*. Milwaukee: Marquette University Press, 2009.

———. "Žižek and Milbank and the Hegelian Death of God." *Modern Theology* 26 (2010) 278–86.

Paddison, Angus. "Reading Yoder against Milbank: A Yoderian Critique of Radical Orthodoxy." In *The Poverty of Radical Orthodoxy*, edited by Lisa Isherwood and Marko Zlomislić, 144–63. Eugene, OR: Pickwick, 2014.

Palaver, Wolfgang. "Carl Schmitt's 'Apocalyptic' Resistance against Global Civil War." In *Politics and Apocalypse*, edited by Robert Hamerton-Kelly, 69–94. East Lansing: Michigan State University Press, 2007.

———. "A Girardian Reading of Schmitt's Political Theology." *Telos* 93 (1992) 43–68.

Peterson, Erik. "Monotheism as a Political Problem: A Contribution to the History of Political Theology in the Roman Empire." In *Theological Tractates*, edited and translated by Michael J. Hollerich, 68–105. Stanford: Stanford University Press, 2011.

Phillips, Elizabeth. *Political Theology: A Guide for the Perplexed*. New York: T. & T. Clark, 2012.

Pickstock, Catherine. *After Writing: On the Liturgical Consummation of Philosophy*. Malden, MA: Blackwell, 1998.

———. "Duns Scotus: His Historical and Contemporary Significance." *Modern Theology* 21 (2005) 543–74.

———. "Imitating God: The Truth of Things according to Thomas Aquinas." *New Blackfriars* 81 (2000) 308–26.

———. "Liturgy and Modernity." *Telos* 113 (1998) 19–40.

Pinker, Steven. *The Better Angels of Our Nature: A History of Violence and Humanity.* London: Penguin, 2011.

Pseudo-Dionysius. *Pseudo-Dionysius: The Complete Works.* Translated by Colm Luibheid. New York: Paulist, 1987.

Quash, Ben. "'Between the Brutally Given, and the Brutally, Banally Free': Von Balthasar's Theology of Drama in Dialogue with Hegel." *Modern Theology* 13 (1997) 293–318.

———. *Theology and the Drama of History.* Cambridge: Cambridge University Press, 2005.

Rahner, Karl. "Antwort." *Orientierung* 14 (1950) 141–45.

———. "Concerning the Relationship between Nature and Grace." In vol. 1 of *Theological Investigations,* 297–317. London: Darton, Longman & Todd, 1961.

———. "Eschatology." In *Encyclopedia of Theology: The Concise Sacramentum Mundi,* edited by Karl Rahner, 434–39. London: Burns & Oates, 1975.

———. *Foundations of Christian Faith: An Introduction to the Idea of Christianity.* Translated by William V. Dych. London: Darton, Longman and Todd, 1978.

———. "The Hermeneutics of Eschatological Assertions." In vol. 4 of *Theological Investigations,* 323–46. New York: Crossroad, 1982.

———. "Introduction." In *Apologetics and the Eclipse of Mystery: Mystagogy according to Karl Rahner,* ix–xii. Notre Dame: University of Notre Dame Press, 1980.

———. "Nature and Grace." In vol. 1 of *Theological Investigations,* 165–88. London: Darton, Longman & Todd, 1961.

———. *The Trinity.* Translated by Joseph Donceel. London: Burns & Oates, 1970.

Rasmusson, Arne. "Historicizing the Historicist: Ernst Troeltsch and Recent Mennonite Theology." In *The Wisdom of the Cross: Essays in Honor of John Howard Yoder,* edited by Stanley Hauerwas et al., 213–48. Grand Rapids: Eerdmans, 1999.

Reimer, A. James. "Mennontes, Christ, and Culture: The Yoder Legacy." In *Mennonites and Classical Theology: Dogmatic Foundations for Christian Ethics,* 288–99. Kitchener, ON: Pandora, 2001.

Ricoeur, Paul. *Essays on Biblical Interpretation.* Translated by Lewis S. Mudge. Philadelphia: Fortress, 1980.

Rose, Gillian. *The Broken Middle: Out of Our Ancient Society.* Oxford: Blackwell, 1992.

———. "From Speculative to Dialectical Thinking—Hegel and Adorno." In *Judaism and Modernity: Philosophical Essays,* 53–63. Oxford: Blackwell, 1993.

Rousseau, Jean-Jacques. *The Basic Political Writings.* Translated and edited by Donald A. Cress. Indianapolis: Hackett, 1987.

Rowland, Christohper. *The Open Heaven: A Study of Apocalyptic in Judaism and Early Christianity.* London: SPCK, 1982.

Rowland, Tracey. *Culture and the Thomist Tradition: After Vatican II.* London: Routledge, 2003.

Ruskin, John. *The Works of John Ruskin.* Library ed. Edited by E. T. Cook and Alexander Wedderburn. Vol. 16. London: George Allen, 1905.

Scarry, Elaine. *On Beauty and Being Just.* Princeton: Princeton University Press, 1999.

Schlitt, Dale M. *Hegel's Trinitarian Claim: A Critical Reflection.* Leiden: Brill, 1984.

Schmitt, Carl. "Die andere Hegel-Linie: Hans Freyer zum 70. Geburtstag." *Christ und Welt* 10 (July 25, 1957) 2.

———. *The Concept of the Political*. Translated by George Schwab. Chicago: University of Chicago Press, 1996.

———. *The Crisis of Parliamentary Democracy*. Translated by Ellen Kennedy. Cambridge: MIT Press, 1988.

———. *Dictatorship: From the Beginning of the Modern Concept of Sovereignty to the Proletarian Class Struggle*. Translated by Michael Hoelzl and Graham Ward. Cambridge: Polity, 2014.

———. "Eröffnung der wissenschaftlichen Vorträge durch den Reichsgruppenwalter Prof. Dr. Carl Schmitt." In *Die deutsche Rechtswissenschaft im Kampf gegen den jüdischen Geist*, 14–17. Berlin: Deutscher Rechtsverlag, 1936.

———. "Ethic of State and Pluralistic State." In *The Challenge of Carl Schmitt*, edited by Chantal Mouffe, 195–208. London: Verso, 1999.

———. "Der Führer schützt das Recht: zur Reichstagsrede Adolf Hitlers vom 13. Juli 1934." In *Positionen und Begriffe im Kampf mit Weimar-Genf-Versailles 1923–1939*. Berlin: Duncker & Humblot, 1994.

———. *Glossarium: Aufzeichnungen der Jahre 1947–1951*. Berlin: Duncker & Humblot, 1991.

———. *The Leviathan in the State Theory of Thomas Hobbes: Meaning and Failure of a Political Symbol*. Translated by George Schwab and Erna Hilfstein. Chicago: University of Chicago Press, 2008.

———. *The Nomos of the Earth in the International Law of the Jus Publicum Europaeum*. Translated by G. L. Ulmen. New York: Telos, 2003.

———. *Political Romanticism*. Translated by Guy Oakes. Cambridge: MIT Press, 1991.

———. *Political Theology: Four Chapters on the Concept of Sovereignty*. Translated by George Schwab. Chicago: University of Chicago Press, 1985.

———. *Political Theology II: The Myth of the Closure of Any Political Theology*. Translated by Michael Hoelzl and Graham Ward. Cambridge: Polity, 2008.

———. *Roman Catholicism and Political Form*. Translated by G. L. Ulmen. Westport, CT: Greenwood, 1996.

———. "Theory of the Partisan: Intermediate Commentary on the Concept of the Political." *Telos* 127 (2004) 11–78.

Schmutz, Jacob. "La doctrine médiévale des causes et la théologie de la nature pure (XIIIe-XVIIe siècles)." *Revue Thomiste* 101 (2001) 217–64.

———. "Escaping the Aristotelian Bond: The Critique of Metaphysics in Twentieth-Century French Philosophy." *Dionysius* 17 (1999) 169–200.

Schüssler Fiorenza, Elisabeth. *The Book of Revelation: Justice and Judgment*. 2nd ed. Minneapolis: Fortress, 1998.

Senden, Marius von. *Space and Sight: The Perception of Space and Shape in the Congenitally Blind Before and After Operation*. Translated by Peter Heath. London: Methuen, 1960.

Shanks, Andrew. *Hegel's Political Theology*. New York: Cambridge University Press, 1991.

Sider, J. Alexander. *To See History Doxologically: History and Holiness in John Howard Yoder's Ecclesiology*. Grand Rapids: Eerdmans, 2011.

Siebert, Rudolf J. "From Conservative to Critical Political Theology." In *The Influence of the Frankfurt School on Contemporary Theology: Critical Theory and the Future of Religion*, edited by A. James Reimer, 147–219. Lewiston, NY: E. Mellen, 1992.

Simon, Derek. "The New Political Theology of Johann Baptist Metz: Confronting Schmitt's Decisionist Political Theology of Exclusion." *Horizons* 30 (2003) 227–54.

Sorel, Georges. *Reflections on Violence*. Translated by Jeremy Jennings. Cambridge: Cambridge University Press, 1999.

Soskice, Janet Martin. "Naming God: A Study in Faith and Reason." In *Reason and the Reasons of Faith*, edited by Paul J. Griffiths and Reinhard Hütter, 241–54. New York: T. & T. Clark, 2005.

Souletie, Jean-Louis. "Le statut contemporain du théologico-politique: Une permanence petersonienne de J. B. Metz à J. Milbank?" *Laval théologique et philosophique* 63 (2007) 205–23.

Spinoza, Benedict de. "Ethics." In *A Spinoza Reader: The Ethics and Other Works*, edited by Edwin Curley. Princeton: Princeton University Press, 1994.

———. *Theological-Political Treatise*. Edited by Jonathan Israel. Translated by Michael Silverthorne and Jonathan Israel. Cambridge: Cambridge University Press, 2007.

Stanley, Timothy. *Protestant Metaphysics after Karl Barth and Martin Heidegger*. Eugene, OR: Cascade, 2010.

Stout, Jeffrey. *Ethics after Babel: The Languages of Morals and Their Discontents*. Boston: Beacon, 1988.

Sturzo, Luigi. *The True Life: Sociology of the Supernatural*. Translated by Barbara Barclay Carter. Washington, DC: Catholic University of America Press, 1947.

Taubes, Jacob. "Carl Schmitt—ein Apokalyptiker der Gegenrevolution." In *Ad Carl Schmitt: Gegenstrebige Fügung*, 7–30. Berlin: Merve, 1987.

———. *The Political Theology of Paul*. Translated by Dana Hollander. Stanford: Stanford University Press, 2004.

Taylor, Charles. *Hegel*. Cambridge: Cambridge University Press, 1975.

Teschke, Benno. "Decisions and Indecisions: Political and Intellectual Receptions of Carl Schmitt." *New Left Review* 67 (2011) 63–95.

Tolstoy, Leo. "Three Deaths." In *The Death of Ivan Ilyich and Other Stories*, edited by Anthony Briggs, 71–87. New York: Penguin, 2008.

Toole, David. *Waiting for Godot in Sarajevo: Theological Reflections on Nihilism, Tragedy, and Apocalypse*. Boulder, CO: Westview, 1998.

Tresmontant, Claude. "Is There a Biblical Metaphysic?" *Theology Today* 15 (1959) 454–69.

Troeltsch, Ernst. *The Social Teaching of the Christian Churches*. Translated by Olive Wyon. 2 vols. London: George Allen & Unwin, 1931.

Vernard, Olivier-Thomas. *Thomas d'Aquin poète théologien*. 3 vols. Geneva: Ad Solem, 2002–2009.

Vincent, K. Steven. "Interpreting Georges Sorel: Defender of Virtue or Apostle of Violence?" *History of European Ideas* 12 (1990) 239–57.

Virilio, Paul, and Sylvère Lotringer. *Pure War*. Translated by Mark Polizotti; postscript translated by Brian O'Keefe. New York: Semiotext(e), 1997.

Ward, Graham. "The Beauty of God." In *Theological Perspectives on God and Beauty*, 35–65. Harrisburg, PA: Trinity International Press, 2003.

———. *The Politics of Discipleship: Becoming Postmaterial Citizens*. Grand Rapids: Baker Academic, 2009.

———. "Steiner and Eagleton: The Practice of Hope and the Idea of the Tragic." *Literature & Theology* 19 (2005) 100–111.

———. *Theology and Contemporary Critical Theory*. 2nd ed. London: Macmillan, 2000.

Weber, Max. "Science as a Vocation." In *From Max Weber: Essays in Sociology*, edited by H. H. Gerth and C. Wright Mills, 129–58. London: Routledge & Kegan Paul, 1948.

Williams, Rowan. "Balthasar, Rahner and the Apprehension of Being." In *Wrestling With Angels: Conversations in Modern Theology*, edited by Mike Higton, 86–105. Grand Rapids: Eerdmans, 2007.

———. "Politics and the Soul: A Reading of the *City of God*." *Milltown Studies* 19/20 (1987) 55–72.

———, ed. *Sergii Bulgakov: Towards a Russian Political Theology*. Edinburgh: T. & T. Clark, 1999.

Winfield, Richard Dien. "Rethinking Politics: Carl Schmitt vs. Hegel." *The Owl of Minerva* 22 (1991) 209–25.

Wolin, Richard. "Carl Schmitt, Political Existentialism, and the Total State." *Theory and Society* 19 (1990) 389–416.

Wood, Susan K. "The Nature-Grace Problematic within Henri de Lubac's Christological Paradox." *Communio* 19 (1992) 389–403.

———. *Spiritual Exegesis and the Church in the Theology of Henri de Lubac*. Edinburgh: T. & T. Clark, 1998.

Xhaufflaire, Marcel. *Feuerbach et la théologie de la sécularisation*. Paris: Cerf, 1970.

———. *La "théólogie politique": Introduction à la théólogie politique de J. B. Metz*. Paris: Cerf, 1972.

Yoder, John Howard. *Anabaptism and Reformation in Switzerland: An Historical and Theological Analysis of the Dialogues between Anabaptists and Reformers*. Translated by David Carl Stassen and C. Arnold Snyder. Edited by C. Arnold Snyder. Kitchener, ON: Pandora, 2004.

———. "The Anabaptist Shape of Liberation." In *Why I Am a Mennonite: Essays on Mennonite Identity*, edited by Harry Loewen, 338–48. Scottdale, PA: Herald, 1988.

———. "'Anabaptists and the Sword' Revisited: Systematic Historiography and Undogmatic Nonresistants." *Zeitschrift für Kirchengeschichte* 85 (1974) 126–39.

———. "Armaments and Eschatology." *Studies in Christian Ethics* 1 (1988) 43–61.

———. "Biblical Roots of Liberation Theology." *Grail* 1 (1985) 55–74.

———. *Christian Attitudes to War, Peace, and Revolution*. Edited by Theodore J. Koontz and Andy Alexis-Baker. Grand Rapids: Brazos, 2009.

———. *The Christian Witness to the State*. Newton, KS: Faith and Life, 1964.

———. "Cult and Culture in and after Eden: On Generating Alternative Paradigms." In *Human Values and the Environment: Conference Proceedings Report 140*, 56–62. Madison: University of Wisconsin Academy of Sciences, Arts, and Letters, 1992.

———. *Discipleship as Political Responsibility*. Translated by Timothy J. Geddert. Scottdale, PA: Herald, 2003.

———. "Ethics and Eschatology." *Ex Auditu* 6 (1990) 119–28.

———. *For the Nations: Essays Public and Evangelical*. Grand Rapids: Eerdmans, 1994.

———. *He Came Preaching Peace*. Scottdale, PA: Herald, 2004.

———. "How H. Richard Niebuhr Reasoned: A Critique of *Christ and Culture*." In *Authentic Transformation: A New Vision of Christ and Culture*, edited by Glen Stassen, D. M. Yeager, and John Howard Yoder, 31–90. Nashville: Abingdon, 1996.

———. "Jesus and Power." *The Ecumenical Review* 25 (1973) 447–54.

———. *The Jewish-Christian Schism Revisited*. Edited by Michael Cartwright and Peter Ochs. Grand Rapids: Eerdmans, 2003.

———, ed. *The Legacy of Michael Sattler*. Scottdale, PA: Herald, 1973.

———. "Meaning after Babble: With Jeffrey Stout beyond Relativism." *Journal of Religious Ethics* 24 (1996) 125–39.

———. *Nevertheless: The Varieties and Shortcomings of Religious Pacifism*. Rev. ed. Scottdale, PA: Herald, 1992.

———. *Nonviolence—a Brief History: The Warsaw Lectures*. Edited by Paul Martens, Matthew Porter, and Myles Werntz. Waco: Baylor University Press, 2010.

———. "Orientation in Midstream: A Response to the Responses." In *Freedom and Discipleship: Liberation Theology in Anabaptist Perspective*, edited by Daniel S. Schipani, 159–68. Maryknoll, NY: Orbis, 1989.

———. *The Original Revolution: Essays on Christian Pacifism*. Scottdale, PA: Herald, 2003.

———. "'Patience' as Method in Moral Reasoning: Is an Ethic of Discipleship 'Absolute'?" In *The Wisdom of the Cross: Essays in Honor of John Howard Yoder*, edited by Stanley Hauerwas et al., 24–44. Grand Rapids: Eerdmans, 1999.

———. "Political Theology: Revolutionary Violence, Status Quo or . . . ?" Unpublished collation of two lectures given in Dublin and Belfast, 1975.

———. *The Politics of Jesus: Vicit Agnus Noster*. 2nd ed. Grand Rapids: Eerdmans, 1998.

———. "The 'Power' of 'Nonviolence.'" Unpublished essay, 1994.

———. Preface to *Theology: Christology and Theological Method*. Grand Rapids: Brazos, 2002.

———. *The Priestly Kingdom: Social Ethics as Gospel*. Notre Dame: University of Notre Dame Press, 1984.

———. "Reinhold Niebuhr and Christian Pacifism." *Mennonite Quarterly Review* 29 (1955) 101–17.

———. "Reinhold Niebuhr's 'Realist' Critique." In *Christian Attitudes to War, Peace, and Revolution*, edited by Theodore J. Koontz and Andy Alexis-Baker, 285–98. Grand Rapids: Brazos, 2009.

———. *Revolutionary Christianity: The 1966 South American Lectures*. Edited by Paul Martens et al. Eugene, OR: Cascade, 2011.

———. *The Royal Priesthood: Essays Ecclesiological and Ecumenical*. Edited by Michael Cartwright. Grand Rapids: Eerdmans, 1994.

———. *To Hear the Word*. Eugene, OR: Wipf & Stock, 2001.

———. "To Serve Our God and to Rule the World." In *The Royal Priesthood: Essays Ecclesiological and Ecumenical*, edited by Michael G. Cartwright, 128–40. Grand Rapids: Eerdmans, 1994.

———. "Walk and Word: The Alternatives to Methodologism." In *Theology without Foundations: Religious Practice and the Future of Theological Truth*, edited by Stanley Hauerwas, Nancey Murphy, and Mark Nation, 77–90. Nashville: Abingdon, 1994.

———. *The War of the Lamb: The Ethics of Nonviolence and Peacemaking*. Edited by Glen Stassen, Mark Thiessen Nation, and Matt Hamsher. Grand Rapids: Brazos, 2009.

———. "The Wider Setting of 'Liberation Theology.'" *Review of Politics* 52 (1990) 285–96.

———. "Withdrawal and Diaspora: The Two Faces of Liberation." In *Freedom and Discipleship: Liberation Theology in Anabaptist Perspective*, edited by Daniel S. Schipani, 76–84. Maryknoll, NY: Orbis, 1989.
Žižek, Slavoj. "The Atheist Wager." *Political Theology* 11 (2010) 136–40.
———. "Carl Schmitt in the Age of Post-Politics." In *The Challenge of Carl Schmitt*, edited by Chantal Mouffe, 18–37. London: Verso, 1999.
———. "Dialectical Clarity versus the Misty Conceit of Paradox." In *The Monstrosity of Christ: Paradox or Dialectic?*, edited by Creston Davis, 234–306. Cambridge: MIT Press, 2009.
———. *Living in the End Times*. London: Verso, 2010.
———. "Resistance Is Surrender." *London Review of Books*, November 15, 2007. https://www.lrb.co.uk/v29/n22/slavoj-zizek/resistance-is-surrender.
———. *The Ticklish Subject: The Absent Centre of Political Ontology*. London: Verso, 1999.

Author Index

Adorno, Theodor W., 8, 29, 33, 34n89, 44, 80n97
Agamben, Giorgio, xiv, 2, 13n6, 17n18, 89n130, 90n135, 117n7, 180n85
Altizer, Thomas, xiv
Aquinas, Thomas, 60, 61n20, 62, 75, 77n88, 82, 92n139, 96n161, 116, 174n61
Arendt, Hannah, 2n8, 46n141, 76
Ashley, J. Matthew, 14n8, 44n132, 47n146, 173n59
Augustine, 60, 95, 96n160, 98n168, 116, 169, 170, 175, 176n67

Bacon, Francis, 49
Badiou, Alain, xiv, 117n7
Bakhtin, Mikhail, 5, 11, 128–35, 157, 174
Balthasar, Hans Urs von, xiv, 10, 55–56, 65–68, 72, 76n87, 85, 86, 89–93, 95, 100, 101n180, 102, 111n214, 112, 113n213, 120, 123, 125–27, 150, 160–61, 181
Barth, Karl, xii, 72n66, 116, 138, 143–47, 149
Bauerschmidt, Frederick Christian, 12n2, 90, 165n29
Baum, Gregory, 68n49
Baxter, Michael J., 165n21
Begbie, Jeremy S., 87n123
Bendersky, Joseph W., 14n10
Benedict XVI, Pope, 86

Benjamin, Walter, xiv, 8, 14, 29, 34n89, 36–39, 44, 47n144, 53n160, 102, 110n213, 150n134
Bergen, Jeremy M., 120n17
Bernardi, Peter J., 71n63
Biesecker-Mast, Gerald, 133n70
Blanchette, Oliva, 68n49, 69n59, 72n67
Bloch, Ernst, 8, 29, 39–41, 44, 49, 102
Blondel, Maurice, 56, 64–65, 67–74, 76–77, 79, 87, 142n100
Boersma, Hans, 61n22
Boff, Leonardo, 73n69
Bonaventure, 92n140, 102, 120n15
Bonhoeffer, Dietrich, 27n63, 35n92, 73, 140
Bonino, Serge-Thomas, 78n89
Bouillard, Henri, 68n49and51, 69
Brecht, Bertolt, 41
Bredekamp, Horst, 37n102
Bruaire, Claude, 78
Buck-Morss, Susan, 34n89
Bulgakov, Sergei, xiv, 90n136, 102
Bultmann, Rudolf, 122n23
Bürger, Peter, 158n5
Burrell, David, 92n139

Cajetan, Thomas, 76
Cartwright, Michael, 129n56, 174
Cassirer, Ernst, 80n98
Certeau, Michel de, 12, 80n98, 163–65
Chardin, Pierre Teilhard de, 73n69
Chopp, Rebecca S., 40n118
Coates, Ruth, 129n55

Author Index

Coles, Romand, 120n17, 128n47, 129–30, 178
Collier, Charles M., 138
Congar, Yves, 73n71
Copleston, Frederick, 80n98
Cristi, Renato, 15n14
Cross, Richard, 61n20

Day, Dorothy, 126n39, 136
Deleuze, Gilles, 99n171, 105n194, 106n197
Derrida, Jacques, 13n6, 47–49, 105n194, 106n197, 121–22
Descartes, René, 80n98,
Desmond, William, 2n4, 79, 81n99, 136–37
Dillard, Annie, 5
Donoso Cortés, Juan, 7, 16, 18–19, 24, 44, 58n12
Dostoyevsky, Fyodor, 11, 40, 105, 107, 130–34, 171
Downey, John K., 14n9, 30n75
Dru, Alexander, 68n49 and 51, 71n63
Dula, Peter, 120n17

Eagleton, Terry, 113
Evans, G. R., 96n160
Eusebius of Caesarea, 43n135

Fast, Heinold, 134n72
Feingold, Lawrence, 73n70, 81–83, 106n198
Figgis, John Neville, 49
Fiorenza, Francis P., 39n112, 40
Flipper, Joseph S., 56n7
Foucault, Michel, 5–7, 22n44, 80n98, 105n194
Frankfurt School, 8, 29, 31–34, 44, 49, 55
Fritz, Peter Joseph, 30n74

Gadamer, Hans-Georg, 80n98
Gandhi, Mohandas, 119n14, 122, 136
García-Rivera, Alejandro, 100n177
Garrigou-Lagrange, Reginald, 56n7, 82
Gingerich Hiebert, Kyle, xi–xv, 13n5, 180n83
Girard, René, xiv, 19n29, 27n63, 181
Grebel, Conrad, 133n71

Gregg, Richard Bartlett, 121n14
Gregory of Nyssa, 102, 108, 110n210 and 212, 111n214, 176
Grumett, David, 70n59, 73n69, 74n73
Guenther, Titus F., 30n72
Gutiérrez, Gustavo, 62n25, 73n69

Habermas, Jürgen, 17, 24, 154
Hankey, Wayne J., 77n88, 94n150
Harink, Douglas, xiv
Hart, David Bentley, xi, xiii, 9–10, 56–59, 96n159, 98n168, 101–16, 119, 122n25, 136–37, 154, 156–57, 159–61, 168–69, 172–73, 176–81
Hauerwas, Stanley, xii, 54, 60, 62n25, 63, 98n169, 116n2, 121n19, 138, 143, 145–46, 164, 170n49
Hedley, Douglas, 67n44
Hegel, G. W. F., vii, xii, xv, 1–2, 8, 10, 12, 13n3, 18, 24–25, 27, 32n82, 40n115, 44–45, 55–56, 68–69, 72n67, 79–81, 85, 87–88, 94, 99, 101–3, 106–7, 109–116, 130n59, 143–44, 157
Heidegger, Martin, xiii, 31n76, 34, 38n106, 41, 43n131, 61n20, 77n88, 96, 102, 105–7, 109n207, 147, 154n1, 179n81
Henrici, Peter, 68n51
Hitler, Adolf, 7
Hobbes, Thomas, 7, 16, 21–26, 34n89, 40n114, 44n135, 49, 102, 155, 167
Hoelzl, Michael, xvii, 81n100
Hoff, Johannes, 56n7, 80n98
Hölderlin, Friedrich, 179
Hopkins, Jasper, 80n98
Horkheimer, Max, 8, 29, 33–34
Huebner, Chris K., 120n17, 121n19, 132n65, 136n80
Hütter, Reinhard, 82
Hyman, Gavin, 80n99, 94

Jantzen, Grace, 100n174
Jaspers, Karl, 116
Jay, Martin, 5n17, 33n84
Jenson, Robert W., 96n161, 106–8
John Paul II, Pope, 138n86

Author Index

John XXIII, Pope, 31

Kant, Immanuel, 17–18, 61n20, 62, 65, 92n139, 94n151, 96, 99n171, 106n197, 109n207, 116, 154, 180n85
Kaufmann, Walter, 4n15
Keller, Catherine, xiv
Kelsen, Hans, 17
Kerr, Fergus, 68, 105n196
Kerr, Nathan, xii–xiv, 11, 143–52, 157, 162–66, 181
Kervégan, Jean-François, 2n3
Kierkegaard, Søren, 17, 79–80, 85–86, 109n207
King, Martin Luther, Jr., 119n14, 136
Kojève, Alexandre, 13, 106n200
Kołakowski, Leszek, 94n148
Kristeva, Julia, 129n53

Laclau, Ernesto, 48n148, 133n70
Ladner, Gerhart B., 111n214
Lakeland, Paul, 13n3
Lamb, Matthew, 34n90, 38n107
Laruelle, François, 78
Lash, Nicholas, 60n17
Leibniz, G. W., 18, 19n27, 70n59, 70n59
Leithart, Peter, 125n38, 175
Levering, Matthew, 151n139
Levinas, Emmanuel, 106n197
Lock, Charles, 129n54
Lombard, Peter, 116
López, Antonio, 78n92
Losonczi, Péter, 13n5
Loughlin, Gerard, 102n186
Löwith, Karl, 49
Lubac, Henri de, 56, 58n19, 64–68, 70–71, 73–79, 81–86, 91, 100, 180n85
Lukács, Georg, 34n91

Machiavelli, Niccolò, 24
Maistre, Joseph de, 7, 16, 18–19, 24, 44, 58n12, 67n44, 102
Maneman, Jürgen, 14n11
Manent, Pierre, 22n43
Mantz, Felix, 133n71
Martens, Paul, 150n136
Martinez, Gaspar, 30n72, 50

Martyn, Louis, xiv
Marx, Karl, 13, 31, 33, 35n94, 37, 39–40, 44, 49, 55, 62–66, 73n69, 89n130, 94n148
Maurras, Charles, 71
Maximus the Confessor, 96n159, 102
McCormack, Bruce L., 146n118
McNeill, J. J., 68n51
Mehring, Reinhard, 14n10
Meier, Heinrich, 13n6, 15n14, 16n14, 23n45, 27
Metz, Johannes Baptist, xi–xiii, 3, 8–9, 13–15, 28–55, 57–59, 61–63, 73n69, 81, 86, 87n121and123, 88–90, 93, 101–03, 109–12, 116n1, 117, 119, 153–56, 158–59, 161, 165, 167, 171–73, 178, 180–81
Michalson, Gordon E., 94
Míguez-Bonino, José, 117n9
Milbank, Alison, 100n176
Milbank, John, xi–xiv, 9–10, 56–106, 111, 113–14, 116, 119, 122n24, 136, 145n114, 154, 156–57, 159, 161–62, 167, 169–73, 175–81
Moltmann, Jürgen, 3, 8, 28, 29n68, 34, 35n92, 39n112, 40n116, 41n121, 44n133, 54, 88n126, 101n182, 106–7, 181
Montcheuil, Yves de, 73n69
Morrill, Bruce T., 38n107
Mouffe, Chantal, 13n6, 15, 48n148, 133n70
Müller, Adam, 20n32
Mussolini, Benito, 71

Nation, Mark Thiessen, 116n2
Nicholas of Cusa, vi, 56n7, 80n98
Nichols, Aidan, 55n1, 61n22
Niebuhr, H. Richard, 118n10
Niebuhr, Reinhold, 50, 113, 114n224, 124n33
Nietzsche, Friedrich, xii–xiii, xv, 4, 7n22, 102, 105, 112n216, 125
Northcott, Michael S., 2n4, 16n15

O'Donovan, Oliver, xiv
O'Regan, Cyril, 2n4, 53n160, 56n5, 6 and 7, 81, 106n200, 157

Author Index

Oakes, Edward T., 77n87

Paddison, Angus, 171n52
Palaver, Wolfgang, 19n29, 25, 27n63
Peterson, Erik, 14, 51, 62n22
Phillips, Elizabeth, 2n6, 16n15
Pickstock, Catherine, 61n20, 92n142, 95n158, 96n161
Pinker, Steven, 4n14
Plato, 23, 77n88
Przywara, Erich, 104n191, 116n4
Pseudo-Dionysius, 95

Quash, Ben, 56n5

Rahner, Karl, 8, 29–31, 34, 42n126, 55, 62–66, 70n58, 76, 84, 106, 109n207, 112n218
Rasmusson, Arne, 138
Rawls, John, 100n177
Reimer, A. James, 175n66
Ricoeur, Paul, 87, 88n124
Rose, Gillian, 58n13, 80n97
Rousseau, Jean-Jacques, 19
Rowland, Christopher, 121n22
Rowland, Tracey, 31, 74
Ruskin, John, 3–4, 59n15

Scarry, Elaine, 100n177
Schelling, F. W. J., 96
Schlitt, Dale M., 106n200
Schmitt, Carl, xi–xv, 1–3, 7–11, 13–29, 32, 33n88, 34n89, 35n92, 37n102, 40n114, 44–55, 56n6, 57–8, 60–3, 67, 80–2, 84n114, 86n116, 89, 90n135, 92n142, 93–5, 101–02, 112n218, 117, 119, 138n83, 143, 153–59, 161, 166–67, 169n43, 171–76, 180–81
Schmutz, Jacob, 77, 94n150
Schüssler Fiorenza, Elisabeth, 121n22
Scotus, John Duns, 61, 80n98, 105
Segundo, Juan Luis, 73n69
Senden, Marius von, 5
Shanks, Andrew, 2n4, 13n3, 45n136
Sider, J. Alexander, 175n66

Siebert, Rudolph J., 45n137
Simon, Derek, 13n5, 46–48
Sobrino, Jon, 54
Sölle, Dorothee, 3, 8, 181
Sorel, Georges, 33n88, 93–95, 100
Soskice, Janet Martin, 96n159
Souletie, Jean-Louis, 61n21
Spinoza, Benedict de, 23n45, 34n89, 44n135, 72n67
Stanley, Timothy, 146n118
Stout, Jeffrey, 135n78
Sturzo, Luigi, 71
Suárez, Francisco, 29, 61n20, 75n77, 77n88

Taubes, Jacob, 26–28, 46n141
Taylor, Charles, 99n173
Teschke, Benno, 7n24
Tolstoy, Leo, 131, 135
Toole, David, 138, 151n140, 164n24
Tresmontant, Claude, 142n100
Troeltsch, Ernst, xii, 118n10, 143–46

Vernard, Olivier-Thomas, 91
Vico, Giambattista, 87
Vincent, K. Steven, 94n148
Virilio, Paul, 97n165

Ward, Graham, xvii, 93n146, 95n157, 113n223, 164n24, 180n83
Weber, Max, 18, 33n87
Williams, Rowan, 55n4, 98n168, 102, 129
Winfield, Richard Dien, 44n135
Wolin, Richard, 14n10
Wood, Susan K., 75–76

Xhauffaire, Marcel, 34n91

Yoder, John Howard, xii–xiv, 5, 10–11, 98n169, 114n224, 115–30, 132–43, 145–52, 154, 157, 159–62, 164–71, 173–81

Žižek, Slavoj, xiv, 25–26, 52n159, 80–81, 117n7, 118n10
Zwingli, Huldrych, 132, 133n71

Subject Index

aesthetics, xi, 10, 30n74, 66, 99n171, 160–61
   and relation to apocalyptic, xi, 7, 16, 26, 28, 43–44, 53–54, 58, 89, 155, 158
   in Hart, 10, 57, 98n168, 101, 103–04, 156, 181
   in Metz, 43–44
   in Milbank, 91–92, 159
   in Schmitt, 16, 20n32, 26, 28, 158
   in Yoder, 160
   of violence, xi, 7, 16, 24, 26, 28, 43, 44, 53–54, 58, 89, 155
Anabaptism, 11, 116, 121n19, 132–33
Anabaptist(s), 128, 132–34, 166–67
analogia entis (analogy of being), 104n191, 147n123, 163
anamnesis, 36–38, 52. *See also* memory
anthropology, 50, 62
   theological, 8–9, 19, 22, 25, 49–50, 62, 64, 66, 111n214, 155
Antichrist, 37, 81n100, 147n123
anti-Judaism, 2, 23n45, 46
anti-Semitism, 3, 46, 76n73
apocalyptic, xi, xiii–xiv, 4–7, 9–10, 15, 27–28, 30, 42, 47–48, 55–57, 81, 85, 88, 121, 130, 134, 137, 143–46, 148n127, 149–50, 155–60, 171
   and relation to aesthetics, xi, 9, 30n74, 57, 86, 90, 93, 157–58
   and relation to (non)violence, xiv, 4–6, 10, 16, 26, 28, 44, 49–54, 57–58, 89, 103, 118, 121, 134–35, 155–57, 159, 166, 171–72, 174, 179–81
   biblical, 42, 121–22, 124–25, 171n52
   in Hart, 57, 101, 111–13
   in Metz, 29–30, 39–44, 50–54, 111
   in Milbank, 56, 59, 63, 66, 76–83, 86, 88, 93–94, 98, 100, 171–72
   in Schmitt, 7, 16, 25n54, 26–28, 50–54, 82n104
   in Yoder, xii, 11, 118–28, 134–41, 143, 151–52, 162–66, 174, 181
architectonics, 5–7
ars moriendi (art of dying), 43, 113n222
Aufhebung (sublation), 101, 112
Augustinianism, xii, 56, 62n22, 83, 138
Auschwitz, 4, 14, 39, 52, 101n182, 154n1, 155, 179

Bakhtin, Mikhail (Bakhtinian), 129–30, 132–34, 135n78
Balthasar, Hans Urs von (Balthasarian), 160, 181
   and aesthetics, 55–56. 160–61
   and Yoder, 123, 125, 127, 150
   as apocalyptic, 56n6 and 7
   in Hart, 102, 111n214, 112
   in Milbank, 65–67, 72, 77n87, 86, 89–93, 95, 100
   on patience, 125–27
   on theological style, 10, 120, 160
beautiful soul (Hegel's logic of), 10, 99, 103, 114, 157, 179

Subject Index

beauty, vi, 9–10, 55, 57, 81n99, 86–87, 91n138, 92–93, 95, 96n161, 102n184, 108, 156, 158–60, 161n14, 168n40, 170
   and relation to (non)violence, 10, 99n171, 100–101, 160
   and relation to reason, 95
Bible (Scripture), 39, 41n123, 89n129, 122
   Exodus, Book of, 40
   John, Gospel of, 38, 148, 179
   Paul, 110n212, 117, 124, 134, 151n140, 165
   Revelation, book of, vi, xiv, 32, 121, 123–24
   synoptic Gospels, 23, 42, 109, 121, 124, 167–68
biblical, xi–xiv, 11, 39–40, 117n9, 121–22, 124–25, 129, 142, 167, 177
Blondel, Maurice (Blondelian), 71, 73
   in Milbank, 64–65, 67–73, 76, 79, 87

Catholicism, xiv, 7, 9, 17, 47, 55, 61, 71n63, 73n69
Christ, 8, 10–11, 31–32, 40, 43–44, 55, 57, 81, 87, 89, 100–101, 103–5, 108, 111–13, 120n15, 123–24, 128, 136, 139–45, 156–57, 159–62, 164–65, 168, 170–71, 173n59, 179
   body of, 85n114, 88, 90, 162, 180n83 (*see also* ecclesiology)
   death of, xiii, 5, 11, 32, 87, 124, 140, 145, 150
   resurrection of, xiii, 11, 104, 109–10, 124, 138, 140, 145, 150
Christology, 144–45, 147, 149
   in Hart, 103–5, 108–114, 168–69, 177
   in Metz, 32n82, 49, 53n160, 63, 173n59
   in Milbank, 85–91, 170–71, 172n54
   in Schmitt, 167
   in Yoder, 123–25, 128, 139–42, 150–51
church, xiv, 14n11, 15n14, 18, 21–22, 27, 29, 31, 36, 40n116, 42–43, 48, 57, 71, 73–76, 84, 88–90, 103, 111, 113, 120, 128n47, 130n57, 134–35, 148, 160, 162–71, 175–79. *See also* ecclesiology
coercion, 104, 111, 113, 156, 169–71, 178. *See also* persuasion
complexio oppositorum (complex of opposites), 18, 80. *See also* paradox
conflict, 22, 26, 45, 72, 85, 112, 126, 134
   hospitality to, 10–11, 108, 118, 135–36, 141, 143, 157, 167, 179
Constantinian(ism), 114, 125n38, 144, 146, 163, 175–77, 179
   anti-, 170, 177
   non-, 138n86
   pre-, 129n57
counterrevolution(aries), 7, 16, 18–21, 26–27, 44, 58n12, 155
creation, 39–40, 65, 104n191, 109, 112, 127, 140–42, 148n128 and 129, 164n24, 165, 178
critical theory, 30, 32, 164n24. *See also* Frankfurt School

death, vi, 5, 22, 32, 38–39, 43n131, 59, 69, 81, 87–88, 106n198, 112–14, 124, 131, 158, 167, 178. *See also ars moriendi*)
   of Jesus Christ, xiii, 11, 87, 140, 145, 150
decision(ism), 7, 46, 48–50, 58, 82n105, 128, 156
   in Metz, 35n92, 45
   in Milbank, 67, 80–82, 86n116, 94–95
   in Schmitt, 9, 17–20, 22–23, 25–26, 155, 158
democracy, 15, 18, 33n88, 45–48
dialectic(al), 30, 34, 37, 39, 45n136, 62, 68n51, 72n67, 76, 87n123, 97, 104, 109–10, 114, 130n59. *See also* negative dialectics
   and relationship to paradox, 78–80
   of emacipation, 35–36
   of enlightenment, 33, 34n91, 49
dialogic/dialogically, 11, 130–34
diaspora, 164–65

Subject Index 211

discipleship (*Nachfolge*), 34, 35n92, 36, 42–3, 51, 53, 95n157, 151, 158, 162, 165, 169, 175
doxology, 11, 128, 134–36, 140, 147n125, 157, 163

ecclesiology, 11, 62, 63n26, 71, 95n157, 118n10, 143, 145, 146n119, 161–64, 177. *See also* church
enemy, xi, 8, 37, 50, 61, 102, 137n83, 141, 155–56, 158, 168, 172
    and relation to friend, 7, 16, 23–28, 45, 67, 85, 167
Enlightenment, 4, 19, 30, 33, 34n89, 36, 63
eschatology, 30, 40–43, 109–11, 122–23, 128, 138, 177, 180n83. *See also* apocalyptic
ethics, 62, 65–66, 122, 124, 125n38, 135n78, 140, 165n30, 175n65
Eucharist, 38n107, 70n59, 150n134, 165n30
exception. *See* state of exception
existential(ism), 14n10, 25, 33–34, 41, 55, 64

faith, 15n14, 25, 27–28, 35n92, 36, 86, 108, 134
fallibility, 50, 126n39, 134–35, 166. *See also* infallibility
Frankfurt School, 8, 29, 31–32, 33n84, 34n91, 44, 49, 55. *See also* critical theory
freedom, 19, 33, 35–38, 42–43, 45, 62–63

genealogy, xii, 6, 7n22, 10–11, 22, 34n89, 59, 102–3, 114–16, 118, 121, 129, 135–36, 146, 149, 150n134, 154, 155, 157–58, 160–62, 167, 173–74, 176, 180–81
Girard, René (Girardian), xiv, 19n29, 27n63, 181
grace, 5, 66, 70, 79, 87
    and relation to nature, 58n14, 64–65, 67, 74–77, 83–84, 100–101, 151

Hart, David Bentley,
Beauty of the Infinite, 57, 92n140, 101–14, 137, 159, 168, 177, 179
Hegel, G. W. F., vii, xii, xv, 1, 10, 12, 24, 27, 55, 72n67, 79, 85, 115, 130n59, 143–44, 157
    in Hart, 102–3, 106–7, 109n207, 110–14
    in Metz, 32n82, 40n114, 44, 45n136
    in Milbank, 68–69, 87, 99, 101
    in Schmitt, 2, 43n135
    in Yoder, 116n1
Hegelian(ism), 8, 13n3, 18, 25, 44–45, 56, 79–80, 85, 88, 99, 101–2, 106–7, 110–12, 116n1
Heidegger, Martin (Heideggerian), xiii, 147, 154n1
    in Hart, 102, 105, 107n202
    in Metz, 31n76, 34, 38n106, 41, 43n131, 109n207
    in Milbank, 61n20, 77n88, 96
history, xii, 6, 11, 14–15, 28, 31–42, 44–45, 56, 59, 63, 81, 87, 94, 98n168, 105n194, 107, 109, 111, 113, 123–28, 132–33, 140, 142–45, 147–49, 154, 167–68, 172, 174–76
    end of, 121,
    interruption of, 88, 110, 158
Hobbes, Thomas (Hobbsian), 34n89, 102, 167
    in Schmitt, 7, 16, 21–26, 44n135, 49, 155
hope, 5–7, 48, 55, 143
    in Hart, 104, 109, 113
    in Metz, 37–39, 41–42, 51, 53, 155, 165, 172, 179
    in Milbank, 89, 100
    in Schmitt, 8, 19, 26, 50, 53
    in Yoder, 11, 122, 126–28, 140

idealism, 29, 98n169, 109n207, 110
idolatry, 41, 172
ideology (ideologies, ideological), 3, 8, 14, 28, 36, 43, 45n136, 136, 143–7, 149, 157, 163, 172
    totalitarian, 36, 41, 49, 172

Subject Index

impassibility, divine, 32n82, 96n159, 101n182, 106n197
incarnation, 31–32, 49, 79, 81, 86–87, 90n136, 148, 151, 161n14, 169. See also Christology
infallibility, 19. See also fallibility
infinite, 57, 105n196, 108–9, 179
injustice, 88, 175n66. See also justice
integralism, 64–67, 71n63, 76, 84
interruption, 9–10, 30, 36, 43–44, 49, 58, 87n121, 88, 103, 109–13, 119, 141, 156, 166–67, 171. See also history, interruption of

jurist(ic), 1–2, 7, 17, 21, 27, 46n141
jurisprudence, 2, 14n9, 19n27, 20–21, 48, 58n14. See also law
justice, 46, 62, 100n177, 112, 114, 120, 124n33, 137–38, 161, 169, 171, 177–78. See also injustice

Kant, Immanuel (Kantian/Kantianism), 17–18, 61n20, 62, 65, 91, 94n151, 96, 99n171, 106n197, 109n207, 116, 154, 180n85
katechon (katechontic), xi, xiv, 27, 50, 81, 171
kenosis, 65, 140
Kerr, Nathan, xiv, 11, 157, 181
   Christ, History, and Apocalyptic, xii, 143–52, 162–66
Kierkegaard, Søren (Kierkegaardian), 109n207
   in Milbank, 79–80, 85–86
   in Schmitt, 17

language, 59, 79, 93, 135, 149, 151n140
law/lawless/lawlessness, 1, 3, 17, 26–27, 46, 142, 150–51
   suspension of the, 20, 53
Leibniz, G. W. (Leibnizian), 18, 19n27, 70n59
liberation, 35, 37, 41, 62n25, 135, 176n67
   theology of, 64–65, 72–73, 117
life, 1, 11, 13, 17–18, 20, 23, 37, 42, 69, 71, 74, 80, 86, 88–90, 93, 111, 113, 124, 127, 130, 132, 134, 138, 140, 142, 144, 147–48, 150, 156, 158n5, 162–63, 165–69, 171–72
liturgy, 163–64
Logos, 90, 146
love, 38n107, 57, 70, 100n174, 101, 102n184, 112, 120n15, 124, 127, 159–60, 165, 173n58
   of enemies, 23, 140, 167
Lubac, Henri de, 100
   in Milbank, 56, 58n14, 64–68, 70–71, 73–79, 81–84, 91

martyrdom, 10, 94, 98, 103, 108, 112–13, 156–57, 159, 171–72, 177, 179
Marx, Karl (Marxism), 13, 31, 33, 37, 39–40, 44, 49, 55, 64–66, 73n69, 89n130
   Christian, 62–63
mediation, 65, 70, 76, 79n97, 170
memory, xiii, 7, 30n75, 36–39, 44–46, 88, 169, 172
   dangerous, 49, 51, 58n13
   See also *anamnesis*
metaphysics, 11, 21–22, 136–38, 144–48, 150–51, 161, 165
   in Hart, 57n10, 106n197, 109, 157, 165
   in Kerr, 148n127, 157, 162–65
   in Metz, 41, 168
   in Milbank, 56, 62, 65–68, 70, 77
   in Schmitt, 25, 51
   in Yoder, 11, 136, 138–39, 141–43, 150–51, 160, 168
Metz, Johannes Baptist (Metzian), 9, 58, 156
   Faith in History and Society, 30, 34n90, 35–39, 42–43, 49, 88n126, 172
   Theology of the World, 3, 14, 28, 29n69, 31–32, 34n91, 35n92, 36, 41, 49, 88n126
Milbank, John,
   Theology and Social Theory, 56, 58, 60, 62, 64–68, 70–73, 84n111, 87–89, 105, 159, 169n44
   Beyond Secular Order, 58–60, 70n58, 77n89, 84n114, 159, 169–72, 173n58, 176–77, 180

Subject Index 213

modernity, 7–9, 12–13, 30–33, 39n110, 44, 49, 55, 57–58, 61, 77n88, 102, 105, 119
monophysitism, 90
mysticism, 159n6, 172
myth/mythology, 33–34, 39–40, 45, 49, 63, 93–95, 100, 109n207

negative dialectics, 34n89, 76, 79. *See also* dialectic
Neoplatonism, 77, 94. *See also* Platonism
Nietzschean, xii, 105, 125
nihilism, 4, 57, 67, 80n99, 105, 176
nonviolence, 10–11, 98n169, 114, 119, 121, 124, 126n39, 127, 130, 134–36, 138–41, 157, 160, 166, 168–69, 174, 177–79, 181.
  as spirituality, 128, 173
  See also violence; peace

ontology (ontological), xii, 8, 10, 39n110, 43, 49, 57, 61, 65, 67–8, 70, 73n72, 75, 77–78, 81, 103–8, 147n125, 159, 163, 167, 169
ontotheology, 61n20, 77n88, 107n202, 147. *See also* metaphysics
optics, 3–6, 57, 65, 81n99, 93, 108–13, 122n25, 156

pacifism, 24, 50, 98n169, 113–14, 124n33, 127n45, 128, 137, 169, 177–78. *See also* nonviolence
paradox, 17n18, 28, 51, 52n159, 165n29, 167
  in Anabaptism, 133
  in de Lubac, 70n59, 75, 78–79
  in Milbank, 9, 65–66, 76–81, 83, 85–87, 94, 156
  in Schmitt, 17, 20, 80
  See also *complexio oppositorum*
pathos, 4, 67n44, 82n105, 97, 147, 157
patience, 11, 125–28, 134–36, 140, 157, 179
peace, xii, 4, 10, 22, 25n57, 26, 49–50, 55–57, 58n13, 63, 68n48, 80n98, 85–86, 95–100, 103–5, 112–14, 119, 136, 157, 164, 169, 170n45, 172, 177, 179n82, 180n83. *See also* nonviolence
persuasion, 55, 57–58, 86, 93, 95, 103–4, 112, 133n70. *See also* coercion
phenomenology, 10, 31n76, 34, 65, 68–70, 72, 96–99, 101, 156
Platonism, 109n207, 110. *See also* Neoplatonism
pneumatology, 163–64
poetic(s), 11, 57, 76, 85–92, 94, 123, 128, 134–36, 157
poiesis, 11, 72, 76, 86–87, 89n130, 90, 156
political romanticism, 20n32, 158
positivism, 17, 71

Rahner, Karl (Rahnerian), 55, 84, 106, 109n207, 112n218
  in Metz, 8, 29–31, 34, 42n126,
  in Milbank, 62–66, 70n58, 76
reason, 10, 22, 36–38, 63, 81n99, 85–88, 90n132, 93–95, 151n139, 163
  anamnestic, 47, 49, 51
  instrumental, 33–34
reconciliation, 10, 35, 46, 112, 118, 157, 169, 178
Reformation, 2, 21–22, 130n58, 167
  radical, 98n168, 134, 166, 176
religion, 1–2, 8, 13n3, 29, 36, 40, 46, 60n19, 161, 175n66
Resurrection, 81, 104, 110, 124, 126–28, 138
  of Christ, xiii, 11, 109, 140, 145, 150, 179
revelation, 72, 123–24, 140, 161

Schmitt, Carl (Schmittian), xi–xiii, 3, 9–10, 25n57, 46–47, 58, 60–63, 66–67, 71, 73n70, 81–82, 84–85, 92, 98n169, 103, 105n194, 153–54, 156, 171n52, 172, 174–75, 177, 180
  Concept of the Political, 16, 19n29, 23–26, 45, 67n44, 158n5, 167
  Political Theology, 2, 7, 16–20, 22n44, 49
  Political Theology II, 2, 13–14, 21–22, 28, 44n135, 51n158

Subject Index

Schmitt, Carl (Schmittian) *(continued)*
   Roman Catholicism and Political Form, 7, 16n14, 17–18, 33n88, 47, 80n98
   State Theory of Thomas Hobbes, 21–22, 25, 49
Scotism, 61n20, 84, 105. *See also* univocity
secular/secularity/secularization/secularized, xii, 1, 16, 22n43, 30–32, 34n91, 49n153, 59–60, 65n36, 66, 73n72, 74, 105n194, 168, 170, 176
slavery, 109n207, 110, 112, 176
socialism, 62, 63n26, 64, 66, 172
sovereign(ty), xii, 16–20, 25, 49–50, 55, 126, 130, 142–43
spirituality, 128, 136, 173
state, xi, 1–2, 7, 16–22, 24–27, 45, 49, 155, 167–68, 176
suffering, 8, 11, 28, 30n75, 32, 37, 39, 43–47, 49–51, 53, 112, 120n15, 124–25, 127, 139–40, 155, 158–60, 168, 172, 173n58, 175n65
supernatural, 64–67, 69–77, 83–84, 90n136, 100–101

theo-logic,
   in Hart, 10, 103, 105–6
   in Milbank, 9, 60–63, 66–67, 71, 73n70, 81, 84–85, 92, 98n169, 105n195, 156, 172, 175, 177
   in Yoder, 126, 150, 174n63
Third Reich, xiii, 2, 7–8, 14, 28, 46n141, 158
Thomism, 29, 55, 61, 71, 74, 83, 109n207, 138, 142n100
time, vii, 37, 40–44, 96, 109, 111–13, 125, 148n125, 150n134
transcendental(ism), 19, 29–30, 33–34, 36, 55, 62, 64–66, 76, 77n88, 109n207
transcendentals (e.g., being, the one, the true, the good, the beautiful), 55, 81n99, 92n139, 93–96, 101n181, 105n196

Trinity/trinitarian, 34, 35n92, 55–57, 66–67, 70, 96n161, 101n182, 106–7, 138, 179n82

univocity, 61n20, 105, 176n70. *See also* Scotism

veiling/unveiling, 6, 123, 142, 166, 179
violence/violent, xi–xiii, 6, 8–11, 17, 19, 22, 24–26, 34, 41, 43–44, 46, 48–51, 56–57, 80n98, 85, 87n123, 89, 93–94, 96–105, 111, 114, 119, 121–24, 126n39, 127, 134n73, 135–37, 140–41, 153–59, 167–71, 174n60, 175, 177–78, 180–81
   aesthetics of, xi, 7, 16, 24, 26, 28, 43, 44, 53–54, 58, 89, 155
   and relation to apocalyptic, xiv, 4–6, 10, 16, 26, 28, 44, 49–54, 57–58, 89, 103, 118, 121, 134–35, 155–57, 159, 166, 171–72, 174, 179–81
   See also nonviolence
vision, 2, 4–7, 10–11, 15–16, 31, 48, 50, 52–55, 56n7, 57, 59–60, 65–67, 75, 81–82, 85, 89, 91n138, 92, 94–95, 97, 101, 103–5, 108–13, 119–24, 128, 134–35, 139–42, 144, 145n117, 152, 154–76, 179, 181. *See also* optics

war, 15, 25–26, 51, 52n159, 57, 97, 176n61, 179n82, 180n83
   civil, 8, 23–24, 27–28, 50, 82n105, 155, 167
witness, 43, 103, 113, 138, 157, 160, 165n30, 166–67, 177

Yoder, John Howard (Yoderian), xiv, 138, 171n52,
   Christian Witness to the State, 120, 166, 177
   For the Nations, 116n1, 117n11, 118n11, 120n15, 128, 139, 140–41, 147n125, 166n33, 168n39
   Nonviolence, 116n1, 121n18, 126n39, 128, 135, 141, 168, 173

Politics of Jesus, 116–17, 120–28,
 140, 142n100, 148n127 and 129,
 149, 150n137, 151n139, 160,
 162n15
Priestly Kingdom, 5, 116n1, 119, 125,
 134–35, 180
War of the Lamb, 116n1, 121n18,
 124, 127n44, 134, 141